Imports of Manufactures
from
Less Developed Countries

NATIONAL BUREAU OF ECONOMIC RESEARCH
Studies in International Economic Relations

HAL B. LARY

Imports of Manufactures
from
Less Developed Countries

NATIONAL BUREAU OF ECONOMIC RESEARCH

NEW YORK 1968

Distributed by COLUMBIA UNIVERSITY PRESS

NEW YORK AND LONDON

RELATION OF THE DIRECTORS TO THE
WORK AND PUBLICATIONS OF THE
NATIONAL BUREAU OF ECONOMIC RESEARCH

1. The object of the National Bureau of Economic Research is to ascertain and to present to the public important economic facts and their interpretation in a scientific and impartial manner. The Board of Directors is charged with the responsibility of ensuring that the work of the National Bureau is carried on in strict conformity with this object.

2. To this end the Board of Directors shall appoint one or more Directors of Research.

3. The Director or Directors of Research shall submit to the members of the Board, or to its Executive Committee, for their formal adoption, all specific proposals concerning researches to be instituted.

4. No report shall be published until the Director or Directors of Research shall have submitted to the Board a summary drawing attention to the character of the data and their utilization in the report, the nature and treatment of the problems involved, the main conclusions, and such other information as in their opinion would serve to determine the suitability of the report for publication in accordance with the principles of the National Bureau.

5. A copy of any manuscript proposed for publication shall also be submitted to each member of the Board. For each manuscript to be so submitted a special committee shall be appointed by the President, or at his designation by the Executive Director, consisting of three Directors selected as nearly as may be one from each general division of the Board. The names of the special manuscript committee shall be stated to each Director when the summary and report described in paragraph (4) are sent to him. It shall be the duty of each member of the committee to read the manuscript. If each member of the special committee signifies his approval within thirty days, the manuscript may be published. If each member of the special committee has not signified his approval within thirty days of the transmittal of the report and manuscript, the Director of Research shall then notify each member of the Board, requesting approval or disapproval of publication, and thirty additional days shall be granted for this purpose. The manuscript shall then not be published unless at least a majority of the entire Board and a two-thirds majority of those members of the Board who shall have voted on the proposal within the time fixed for the receipt of votes on the publication proposed shall have approved.

6. No manuscript may be published, though approved by each member of the special committee, until forty-five days have elapsed from the transmittal of the summary and report. The interval is allowed for the receipt of any memorandum of dissent or reservation, together with a brief statement of his reasons, that any member may wish to express; and such memorandum of dissent or reservation shall be published with the manuscript if he so desires. Publication does not, however, imply that each member of the Board has read the manuscript, or that either members of the Board in general, or of the special committee, have passed upon its validity in every detail.

7. A copy of this resolution shall, unless otherwise determined by the Board, be printed in each copy of every National Bureau book.

(Resolution adopted October 25, 1926,
as revised February 6, 1933, and February 24, 1941)

CONTENTS

TABLES

CHARTS

PREFACE

This study stems from my participation in one of the consultative groups preceding the United Nations Conference on Trade and Development in 1964 and, more specifically, from Geoffrey H. Moore's suggestion that I explore further some of the impressions which I then formed with regard to exports of manufactures by less developed countries. The task has lasted longer than either of us foresaw, largely because it has taken on a dual nature, being not only an analysis of trends in the trade but also an empirical investigation, across industries and countries, of factor intensities in manufacturing.

The work on factor intensities may be the more interesting, and no doubt the more debatable, part of the study with respect to its implications for economic theory and also with respect to the tools of analysis employed. The use of value added by manufacture per employee as a guide to relative inputs of labor and capital permits a unified treatment of both physical and human capital and exploits a rich body of data from the various national censuses of manufacture, the potentialities of which for research on this topic have, to the best of my knowledge, largely passed unnoticed.

The analysis of past trends and other features of the trade leads, I believe, to more hopeful conclusions than most other studies regarding the potentialities of exports of manufactures by less developed to developed countries. In accord with the National Bureau's research objectives, the study seeks to illuminate but not to espouse policies. It will be evident, I trust, that the basic conditions for the successful growth of the trade include a receptive and cooperative attitude on the part of the importing countries and "outward-looking" policies on the part of the less developed countries—that is, a readiness on both sides to share in the international division of labor among countries at varying levels of economic development. If these conditions are not met, only meager results could be expected from various policy prescriptions now in the limelight, notably the extension of tariff preferences by developed countries to less developed countries or the formation among the latter of regional common markets.

It is hoped that this study will be useful to the United States and other countries in evaluating their past performance as importers and exporters and in developing policies conducive to the future growth of a segment of world trade which, though still small, is of considerable importance to the economic prospects of the larger and poorer part of the world's population.

Various members of the National Bureau's staff have been most helpful in reviewing drafts of the study and in advising on specific questions. They include in particular members of the staff reading committee for the project—Victor R. Fuchs, Robert E. Lipsey, and Ilse Mintz—and also Irving B. Kravis and H. G. Georgiadis. My thanks for valuable criticism and suggestions are also due to Joseph A. Beirne, Gottfried Haberler, Boris Shishkin, and Willard L. Thorp of the National Bureau's Board of Directors. Among those who assisted in the project, Peter Lao and Ludmila Monkevic demonstrated skill and perseverance in extracting and coordinating production and trade data from disparate sources. Stephen Pappayliou and Nadeschda Bohsack assisted in this work during part of the time. Merle Yahr joined the project at a late stage, but still in time to make a much appreciated contribution in evaluating the statistical results and in improving the analysis. Irving Leveson, in connection with his participation in the National Bureau's study of the service industries, prepared the correlations of "expected" and actual earnings in Chapter 2.

Among those outside the National Bureau to whom thanks are due for comments and suggestions, I should particularly mention Maxwell R. Conklin, Chief of the Industry Division, Bureau of the Census, and Edward A. Robinson and Willis K. Jordan, members of that Division, though they may consider that my response to some of their criticisms of Chapters 2 and 3 has been defensive rather than positive. The same general absolution from responsibility for the final results needs to be made in recording my thanks to various other readers of an early draft of the report, including Robert E. Asher, Brookings Institution; Don Daly, Economic Council of Canada; William Diebold, Jr., Council on Foreign Relations; Francesco Forte, University of Turin; Finn Gundelach, General Agreement on Tariffs and Trade; Gary Hufbauer, University of New Mexico; Jacob J. Kaplan, Consultant; Hirotaka Kato, Kanagawa University; Julius L. Katz, U.S. Department of State; Charles P. Kindleberger, M.I.T.; Ian M. D. Little, OECD; Gardner Patterson,

General Agreement on Tariffs and Trade; Walter S. Salant, Brookings Institution; David J. Steinberg, Committee for a National Trade Policy; Robert W. Stevens, Indiana University; Raymond Vernon, Harvard University; and Helen Waehrer, New York University.

We were fortunate in entering into an arrangement with the Statistical Office of the United Nations for processing the import statistics of the developed countries in form suitable for our research needs. I want to thank Patrick J. Loftus, Director of that office, and Sidney Cashton and Bipin L. Amrute, members of his staff, for delivering the data according to our specifications.

I am grateful to James F. McRee, Jr., for preparing the text for publication; H. Irving Forman for his usual skill in drawing the charts; and Mildred E. Courtney for her help in preparing the manuscript and in keeping track of work in progress.

Finally, I wish to acknowledge with thanks the financial support which the Rockefeller Foundation and the Ford Foundation have provided for the National Bureau's program of international studies, of which this project forms a part.

August 1967   HAL B. LARY

1

THE PROBLEM AND
A SUMMARY OF FINDINGS

Introduction

Some Initial Assumptions

It seems to be generally agreed that newly developing countries will need to achieve a rapid and sustained rise in export earnings to cover their growing imports of capital goods and other essentials and to service their foreign borrowings. Failure to attain such an increase, or to receive ever larger foreign aid, would impose a foreign exchange constraint on their growth, even though the major transformation required is in their internal economic and social structures and in their capacity to save and invest.

Looked at from this point of view, the figures in Table 1 are not reassuring with respect to the export performance of the less developed countries.[1] Over the period 1950 to 1965 these countries, exclusive of the major oil producers among them, increased the current dollar value of their exports to the developed countries by 4.2 per cent annually on the average.[2] Their exports to each other, again omitting the major oil producers, were only slightly larger in 1965 than in 1950. Over the same period the dollar value of trade among the developed countries rose at an average annual rate of about 9.4 per cent, or perhaps a percentage point less if figured at constant prices. Total exports of

---

[1] Throughout this study the composition of the less developed countries corresponds to that of "Economic Class II" in the foreign trade statistics of the United Nations: all of the Western Hemisphere except the United States and Canada; all of Africa except the Union of South Africa; the Middle East except Turkey; the rest of Asia and the Far East except Japan, Mainland China, and North Korea; and Oceania except Australia and New Zealand.

[2] Figured at constant prices, the increase over the period as a whole would average about the same, since export prices of the less developed countries rose rapidly during the Korean War in the early 1950's and declined thereafter to about the 1950 level.

TABLE 1

Exports of Developed and Less Developed Countries, 1950 and 1965

	Value ($ billion, current prices)		Compound Annual Rate of Growth, 1950–65 (per cent)
	1950	1965	
World exports, total	53.5	156.3	7.4
Exports of developed countries, total	35.9	122.5	8.5
To each other	25.0	95.5	9.4
To less developed countries	10.9	27.0	6.2
Exports of less developed countries, total	17.6	33.8	4.5
To developed countries	12.4	26.2	5.2
To each other	5.2	7.6	2.5
Exports of less developed countries, excluding major petroleum producers,[a] total	14.1	23.7	3.6
To developed countries	10.0	18.5	4.2
To each other	4.1	5.2	1.7

Source: Various statistical publications of the United Nations.
   Note: All figures exclude exports to and exports of Eastern Europe, the USSR, and Mainland China. Figures may not add to totals shown because of rounding.
   [a]Countries excluded are Algeria, Iran, Kuwait, Libya, Netherlands Antilles, Saudi Arabia, Trinidad and Tobago, and Venezuela.

developed countries to the destinations covered by Table 1 were about two and a half times those of the non-oil-producing less developed countries in 1950 and were five times as great in 1965.

   The need for a faster increase in exports of the less developed countries will not be elaborated here, since it has been studied at length by the United Nations and others. One may question alternative projections of the likely "foreign exchange gap," or the validity of the gap approach.[3] But there seems to be little room for doubt that, unless economic aid to the less developed countries is increased far above present levels, their exports will need to rise faster than heretofore as one of the conditions for their economic development.

The contrasting performance of exports of developed and less developed countries reflects, in addition to factors on the supply side, the faster growth of world demand for manufactures than for most of the primary products which make up the bulk of the exports of the less developed countries. Reasons for the relative lag in trade in primary products include economies in their use, the continuing development of synthetic substitutes, and the growing complexity and sophistication of final products, all of which tend to reduce the input of raw materials per unit of output.[4]

Some less developed countries exceptionally well endowed with natural resources may be able to meet their growing foreign exchange needs through sales of primary products in crude or processed form. The oil-exporting countries form a small and privileged group in this regard. Broadly viewed, however, there is little reason to suppose that the influences tending to retard the growth of trade in primary products have run their course. If this is a correct judgment, a solution commensurate with the growth needs of the less developed countries will presumably entail a rapid increase in their exports of manufactures to the affluent markets of the advanced countries.

Focus of the Study: Labor-Intensive Manufactures

This study seeks to identify the kinds of manufactures best suited to the growth of exports and to examine the pattern and prospects of

[3] A summary review of the estimates and their rationale is given by Sydney Weintraub in *The Foreign-Exchange Gap of the Developing Countries,* Essays in International Finance No. 48, Princeton, 1965. I. M. D. Little and J. M. Clifford raise serious questions about the usefulness of the gap approach in *International Aid,* London, 1965 (see especially Chapter VI). Isaiah Frank observes that exports of the less developed countries increased faster in the first half of the 1960's than in the preceding five years, thanks to accelerated economic growth in ,the developed countries, but notes that the ability of the less developed countries to import did not increase correspondingly because of greatly increased payments for debt service, shipping, and other invisibles ("New Perspectives on Trade and Development," *Foreign Affairs,* April 1967, pp. 520–540).

[4] A detailed analysis of the trade outlook for less developed countries is given by Alfred Maizels in *Industrial Growth and World Trade,* Cambridge, Eng., 1963. He concludes (page 409) that both the shift in the pattern of demand and technological developments in the industrial countries are likely to continue to react adversely on the exports of the primary producing countries, and that no alleviation is likely to come from changes in the terms of trade.

trade in these items. By definition, the less developed countries have little accumulated capital or technical skill. Any comparative advantage which they may hold or attain in manufacturing for export, apart from strongly resource-based industries, is therefore likely to be in industries which are intensive in the use of relatively unskilled labor and sparing in the use of both physical and human capital. It will be seen in this study that industries rank much the same on this basis from country to country, even from the richest to the poorest—a circumstance which helps to identify those in which low-wage countries may best compete.

Such a course encounters obvious problems and resistances on the side of the developed countries. But it also offers them the possibility of shifting scarce manpower from traditional lines of production to other industries where labor can be more productively combined with their capital resources.

Such a course may also be unwelcome to some of the less developed countries, implying concentration on relatively simple types of manufacturing and perhaps excessive exposure to the risks of international trade. These disadvantages are scarcely greater, however, than those entailed in their present heavy reliance on exports of primary products. And, if the analysis given here points in the right direction, a willingness to focus initially on labor-intensive lines of manufacturing may be a necessary condition for evolving toward the production of goods with, as Fei and Ranis say, "an increasing skill and ingenuity component over time." [5]

It may be further objected that, apart from qualifications such as that just given, the approach taken here makes no specific allowance for the possibility that comparative advantage may shift as development proceeds, thanks to internal and external economies of scale and other dynamic influences associated with growth. How much weight should be attached to this possibility in the present context is difficult to say, particularly since so little is available by way of empirical evidence or even illustrative case histories bearing on the dynamics-of-growth argument.[6]

---

[5] John C. H. Fei and Gustav Ranis, *Development of the Labor Surplus Economy*, Homewood, Ill., 1964, p. 303.

[6] Viewed with regard to the possibilities of increasing exports, it is not clear a priori that the argument could justify a strategy of emphasizing capital-intensive industries in the early stages of industrial development, since the more developed countries not only have access to capital on more favorable terms but also the great advantage of economies of scale already realized. Initially, therefore, and until their capital resources and market size are increased, the gains from trade by the less developed countries in importing capital-intensive manufactures are likely to be particularly large in relation to the volume of trade. See Paul A.

One factual observation deriving from the data examined in Chapter 4 of this study is that, if the argument is deemed to be relevant to, or consistent with, the need to increase export earnings of the less developed countries, there is little indication that any of these countries have so far become competitive in the more capital-intensive lines of manufacturing (except, of course, those based on the exploitation of natural resources). Usually, however, dynamic considerations have not been related to problems of export promotion but have been invoked rather to favor a strategy of import substitution and may be subject to the same need of cautious reappraisal as that seen below.[7]

Still another possible objection to the present approach is that, even within a comparative cost framework, the emphasis may be too much on labor intensity to the neglect of other conditions affecting the ability of less developed countries to sell manufactures in the markets of the more advanced countries. Some industries are more strongly market-oriented than others, and ease of communications between producer and customer may bear importantly on their location.[8] Among consumer goods, market orientation seems likely to be more important in furniture than in plywood or wood containers, for instance, and in high-style fashions than in textile flat goods or work clothes. The production of some producer goods, such as fabricated metals and instruments, tends to be located near the industries which use these goods as inputs into their own production. Even in such cases, the increasing speed of international communications and growing experience in procuring abroad may open up new possibilities of siting production where costs are lowest. This is illustrated by the evolution of the garment industry in Hong Kong toward high-fashion goods and also by the encouragement given by American companies to the production of electronic and other components in low-wage countries.

Samuelson, *Stability and Growth in the American Economy,* Stockholm, 1963, p. 48, and also Gottfried Haberler, "Integration and Growth of the World Economy in Historical Perspective," *American Economic Review,* March 1964, pp. 1–22.

[7] At the end of his article on "Comparative Advantage and Development Policy" (*American Economic Review,* March 1961, pp. 18–48), Hollis B. Chenery concludes that "To most economists, a survey of the procedures actually followed in designing development policy would probably suggest that balance is overemphasized and that the potential gains from trade are often neglected."

[8] For a discussion of this and other influences on industrial location, see Raymond Vernon, *Metropolis 1985,* Cambridge, 1960, pp. 38–85, and also a paper, "Problems and Prospects in the Export of Manufactured Goods from the Less-Developed Countries," contributed by Vernon to the meeting of UNCTAD in 1964 (*Proceedings of the United Nations Conference on Trade and Development,* Vol. IV, *Trade in Manufactures, 1964,* pp. 200–210).

The "Overspill" View of Exports

The usual approach to the problem of increasing exports of manufactures by the less developed countries has been along the lines of what Winston Churchill once called the "overspill" view of exports in Britain. That is, concentrate first on developing the home market, and this will create the conditions needed for an efficient and rising export trade. Theoretical support for this view has been elaborated by the Swedish economist Staffan B. Linder, who takes strong issue with the factor-proportions explanation of trade, except in primary products. For the rest, he advances as a "basic proposition" that the "range of exportable products is determined by internal demand." That is to say, "it is a necessary, but not a sufficient, condition that a product be consumed (or invested) in the home country for this product to be a potential export product." [9]

W. W. Rostow has put the point in the following way, with more specific reference to the problems of the less developed countries: "What I am asserting, then, is that the expansion of the domestic market which is required to produce a modernization of rural life and an ample market for domestic industry is also the proper base for the development of diversified exports." [10]

A similar conception seems to infuse programs of financial assistance to the less developed countries. The International Bank's loans and feasibility studies have mainly focused on the "infrastructure" and the home markets of the less developed countries and have rarely served more directly to develop their exports of manufactures. Our AID programs have also been chiefly concerned with strengthening the internal conditions for development, though some of the studies of investment opportunities which it has helped to finance point toward export possibilities. The Export-Import Bank has well merited the first half of its name by granting credits to finance sales of capital equipment and other goods to the less developed countries. But little of its financing has been aimed at stimulating imports from them.

The power and transportation facilities, machinery, and technology made available through these loans and grants do, of course, help to build up the economies of the less developed countries and may ultimately serve to diversify and strengthen their exports. Moreover, these

[9] *An Essay on Trade and Transformation,* Uppsala, 1961, p. 87.
[10] W. W. Rostow, "Economic Development in Asia," *Department of State Bulletin,* May 31, 1965, p. 850.

public agencies no doubt consider, with some reason, that investment opportunities offering attractive export prospects are particularly suited to private initiative and financing and do not require public development aid.

In a perceptive commentary on these and related policies, Harry Johnson may go too far in saying that "the notion became firmly established—especially in the United States—that development is an autarchic process." [11] Nevertheless, it does seem fair to observe that the advanced countries have accepted restrictive import policies by the less developed countries as a necessary accompaniment of industrial development, and have so far made little adjustment in their own policies to facilitate the growth of imports of manufactures from the less developed countries.

Under these conditions, it is remarkable that this trade, at least in some products, has grown as fast as it has in recent years. The growth has, however, been very unevenly distributed by exporting as well as by importing countries—a fact that underlies the trade demands put forward with increasing vigor by the less developed countries during and since the United Nations Conference on Trade and Development (UNCTAD) in 1964. The need to find better ways of expanding their exports is evident. The means proposed to this end—on either side—are more debatable, sometimes seeming primarily designed to shift responsibility for action to other countries while avoiding commitments that might entail awkward adjustments on one's own part.

Limitations of Market Size in the Less Developed Countries

Proliferation of Small Countries

However persuasive the argument may seem, it rather begs the question to say, with Rostow, that "The most effective base for the export of manufactures is a large domestic market." According to one estimate,[12] only five of the less developed countries have national incomes (converted to dollars at prevailing rates of exchange) larger than Con-

---

[11] Harry G. Johnson, "United States Policy and the Problems of Developing Countries," *Journal of Business,* October 1965, p. 339.

[12] Donald B. Keesing, "Outward-Looking Policies and Economic Development," *Economic Journal,* June, 1967. Keesing actually refers to six countries, including Spain, but Spain (along with the rest of Southern Europe) is not counted among the less developed (or developing) countries in United Nations practice, which is followed here.

necticut. These are India, Pakistan, Brazil, Mexico, and Argentina, to which perhaps Indonesia (with poor statistics but a population of 100 million) should be added. Though the beginnings of industry go back rather far in some of these countries, none of them has yet done sufficiently well in exporting manufactures to vindicate the "overspill" view.[13]

The six countries just mentioned account for more than half of the total population of the less developed countries, but that still leaves a host of people and problems outside as well as inside. Close to 100 of the less developed countries have a population smaller than 15 million, and in two-thirds of them it is less than 5 million.[14] On the whole very poor, they are smaller still in size of market compared with most developed countries. More such countries are being born as Malta, Gambia, the Mauritius Islands, and the few other remaining European possessions move toward and achieve independence. This proliferation of small and minuscule nations is largely a product of the swift unraveling of colonialism after World War II, though in Central America it goes far back into the last century.

The dilemma facing these small countries is evident upon comparing two quotations from Charles Kindleberger.[15] On the one hand, he expresses a view like Linder's that "A further important modification of the law of comparative advantage based on abundant labor is that exports can be developed only in those products for which there is a significant home market." On the other hand, he says elsewhere: "The smaller the economy in geographic area, the more skewed [i.e., specialized in resources and production] it is likely to be and the more it must trade outside its borders." Together, the two statements imply that (apart from products of such natural resources as they may have) small and poor countries will be able to develop only an extremely narrow range of goods for export. These would be a few mass-consumption products for which even the smaller less developed countries may provide "significant home markets" in relation to the levels of output needed for efficient production.

---

[13] Mexico might be considered an exception, yet during recent years the Mexican government has found it desirable to take a number of measures to limit sharply the protection of domestic industry and to try to make it more competitive internationally. See *International Commerce*, U.S. Department of Commerce, June 6, 1966, pp. 14–17.

[14] *Proceedings of the United Nations Conference on Trade and Development*, Vol. II, *Policy Statements*, 1964, p. 15.

[15] Charles P. Kindleberger, *Foreign Trade and the National Economy*, New Haven, 1962, pp. 32 and 58.

Uncertain Prospects for Regional Integration

In principle, one way of meeting this dilemma is by integration of these splinter economies into larger and more viable regional groupings following, at a great distance, the example of the European Common Market. There are excellent reasons favoring this course and commending it to outside support—even apart from any hope which harried officials in developed countries may hold of being thereby relieved in some measure of the problem of increasing imports from the less developed countries.

So far, efforts to combine into larger regional entities have brought little specific result. In some areas, the trend is rather the other way, as indicated by the strains and disruptions experienced in the West Indies, Malaysia, East Africa, and Nigeria. Little progress is evident in the Maghreb, which was supposed to embrace the Arab states of North Africa. The most promising of these regional endeavors, the Central American Common Market, illustrates the limitations more than the potentialities of such arrangements. It brings together a fairly homogeneous group of countries, compared with most others, and even so adds up to only 12 million people with a combined purchasing power less than that of any one of a number of European and American cities. Now a far larger, more difficult, and more distant objective has been set with the commitment by the heads of the Latin American states in April 1967 at Punta del Este, "Beginning in 1970, to establish progressively the Latin American Common Market, which should be substantially in operation within a period of no more than fifteen years." [16] The length of the period set for achievement of the objective attests to the difficulties to be overcome.

In some regions political and social frictions may well be the major obstacle to regional integration. The economic difficulties include disparities in the levels of development attained by different countries of the same region, since laggard countries tend to fear competition by their more advanced neighbors. Even more awkward problems may be presented by disparities among countries in the levels and structures of production costs and prices. Barriers of the latter nature are, in turn, largely the result of the exaggerated pursuit of "import substitution" as a means of promoting industrial development.

[16] From the "Declaration of the Presidents of America," *Department of State Bulletin,* May 8, 1967, pp. 712–721.

Costs of Excessive Import Substitution

A developing country has some room for choice in orienting its new industries toward replacing imports rather than expanding exports. Initially, the emphasis is likely to be on the former course, since imports attest to a market already in being at home and susceptible of being reserved against foreign competition.[17] Most and perhaps all developed countries have followed this course in the early stages of their growth and, indeed, still cling to protection even though with little basis any more for invoking the "infant industry" argument. Within limits, this course is consistent with the "overspill" view of exports, since, if the industries chosen for protection are well suited to a country's potentials, substitution for imports in its home market may set the stage for competition in export markets later on.

These limits, however, can be quickly exceeded. A less developed country's imports typically embrace a far greater variety of goods than its exports. The difference is all the more striking if one considers not merely final goods but also the materials, parts, and capital equipment entering into their production. Import substitution may therefore soon spread a country's resources too thin over numerous small and inefficient enterprises, and extend to types of production ill suited to its conditions, with the unfortunate result of raising costs even in industries in which it should otherwise be able to compete. A further consequence is to deny the economy the stimulus to efficiency and innovation which exposure to competition in domestic and foreign markets can provide.

In other words, "backward and forward linkages" with other industries [18] may prove to be a burden rather than a blessing if the industries selected for promotion are not well suited to a country's capabilities and size. This may happen even in the largest of the less developed countries, as is suggested by India's difficulties in providing the range and quality of parts and other inputs needed to produce diesel engines for trucks and by the cost and insufficiency of domestic synthetic fibers and artificial rubber used in the production of tires.[19] Similarly, a

[17] As Albert O. Hirschman put it, "imports still provide the safest, most incontrovertible proof that the market is there" (*The Strategy of Economic Development,* New Haven, 1958, p. 212).

[18] *Ibid.,* pp. 98ff.

[19] Jack Baranson, "Transfer of Technical Knowledge by International Corporations to Developing Economies," *American Economic Review,* May 1966, pp. 259–267, and Wilfred Malenbaum, "Comparative Costs and Economic Development: The Experience of India," *American Economic Review,* May 1964, p. 396.

United Nations review of protectionism and industrial development in Latin America is illustrated by examples from Argentina showing the unfavorable effects of high-cost sulphur and sulphuric acid on the production of chemicals and of high-cost caustic soda on the manufacture of soap.[20] Considerable caution would therefore seem to be warranted with respect to the various internal and external economies which have frequently been invoked in favor of capital-intensive industries at early stages of economic development.

The frustrations of import substitution were the subject of an urgent warning by Raúl Prebisch in his advance message, as Secretary General, to the United Nations Conference on Trade and Development.[21] Based largely on his close observation of the Latin American countries, he found that the "easy phase" of import substitution had about reached its limit in the countries which had followed that course, and that it could not go farther without considerable waste. He also found that high tariffs to protect narrow national markets had "encouraged the establishment of small uneconomical plants, weakened the incentive to introduce modern techniques, and slowed down the rise in productivity."

"Thus," Prebisch continued, "a real vicious circle has been created as regards exports of manufactured goods. These exports encounter great difficulties because internal costs are high, and internal costs are high because, among other reasons, the exports which would enlarge the markets are lacking. Had it been possible to develop industrial exports, the process of industrialization would have been more economical, for it would have made possible the international division of labour in manufacturing."

Responsibility for exaggerated import substitution does not fall only on the governments of the less developed countries and their advisers. Two world wars and the Great Depression in between were reason enough for many countries to try to produce at home what, in those circumstances, they were no longer able to buy abroad. But the least to be said in criticism of the less developed countries is that so far they have shown little tendency to reverse course and expose their small monopolies to outside competition.

[20] Santiago Macario, "Protectionism and Industrialization in Latin America," *Economic Bulletin for Latin America*, United Nations, March 1964, p. 79. The same issue contains a relevant article on "The Growth and Decline of Import Substitution in Brazil."

[21] *Proceedings of the United Nations Conference on Trade and Development*, Vol. II, *Policy Statements*, p. 14.

Regional or International Integration

Under the conditions described, negotiations for regional integration by various groups of less developed countries are likely to mean hard bargaining for mutual support, and reciprocal sacrifice, of high-cost industries.[22] With each participant concerned lest it lose more than it gains, the difficulties of arriving at agreement and successful implementation are apparent.

Considered in this light, it may be significant that the one regional grouping which has been showing signs of progress toward integration —the Central American Common Market—is one whose member states had previously remained relatively open to the outside world and consequently did not differ widely from each other in their cost and price structures. Nor, it must be added, did the members differ much in the relatively low state of their industrial development. There may be, in fact, some risk that the progress now being registered in their manufacturing output and in their trade with each other could prove to be another example of what Prebisch called the "easy phase" of import substitution. The outcome is likely to depend on how successful they are in diversifying and expanding their exports to other countries at the same time as they increase their trade within the area.

Political conditions permitting, other countries with relatively simple and open economies may be able to form local economic unions on the Central American model. That experience also suggests the paradoxical thought that countries where import substitution has gone much further, such as most of the other Latin American countries, may be able to move toward regional integration only by first reintegrating with the world economy and bringing their cost and price structures more in line with those outside.[23] A different, and perhaps more realistic, strat-

---

[22] In a sympathetic review of the slow progress and special difficulties of integration among the less developed countries, Gunnar Myrdal states, "This means that a simple 'common market' is not enough; it must be completed by formal agreements, reached after negotiation, concerning what industries should be located in what countries. When thought through with all its consequences, this implies the need for a joint common planning" (paper, "The Efforts Toward Integration in Rich and Poor Countries," delivered in Mexico City on October 3, 1966). Myrdal notes, however, that the difficulties of achieving this objective are "formidable," and Sydney Dell, in *A Latin American Common Market?* (New York, 1966), while also stressing the necessity of common planning, says, "Of course, it may be unrealistic to talk of regional planning in Latin America at a time when even national planning cannot be said to have a very firm foundation in most countries of the region" (p. 212).

[23] In that event, the objectives of integration would presumably be largely political.

egy is evidently reflected in the renewed effort toward economic union undertaken at Punta del Este; namely, as Joseph Grunwald has expressed it, that integration is a "means of lifting the Latin American countries to a level of economic maturity where, without the aid of inefficient protection, they will eventually be able to compete as equal partners with the developed nations." [24] The expectation underlying this strategy, as expounded by Grunwald, is that integration would expand market perspectives, allow a more rational allocation of resources, permit economies of scale, spur competition, and stimulate private investment. Also, a "protected region-wide market" would provide the catalyst needed to break down economic, political, and social rigidities and restore economic viability.

This may be a correct appraisal of the Latin American problem and the most promising way of accelerating growth in the region. It seems unlikely, however, that this approach will significantly alleviate the need for a rapid increase in exports to other areas, particularly in view of the extended period—1970 to 1985—over which the common market is to be achieved. In the worst case, regional integration could hinder such an increase in exports if it were to mean the spread of cost-raising import substitution to countries in the region which, otherwise, would set their policies toward becoming more competitive in world markets.

Summary of the Study

To recapitulate, this study accepts as its point of departure that if the less developed countries are to earn foreign exchange in amounts commensurate with their needs, they will have to achieve a rapid increase in their exports of manufactures to the developed countries. This is where the world's buying power is concentrated, as long as levels of economic development remain so far apart, and it is also where the less developed countries will have to obtain most of the capital equipment and much of the materials and even some of the food needed by their growing economies and population.

[24] "Some Reflections on Latin American Industrialization Policy," paper presented at the conference on Key Problems of Economic Policy in Latin America, University of Chicago, November 9, 1966 (mimeographed, p. 40). W. W. Rostow expressed much the same thought in a lecture at the University of Leeds, England, on February 23, 1967; that is, that the Latin American countries "must go through a transitional stage of regional protectionism before they can emerge with competitive efficiency on the world scene" (*Department of State Bulletin,* March 27, 1967, p. 498).

Value Added as a Guide to Factor Intensity

The next question, to which Chapter 2 is devoted, is to try to identify the kinds of manufactures in which the less developed countries are most likely to hold or to be able to achieve a comparative advantage in international trade. According to the factor-proportions theorem and leaving aside strongly resource-based industries, these would be products requiring large inputs of relatively unskilled labor compared with both human capital, or skills, and physical capital. Rejecting certain criticisms of this theorem, the chapter examines the rationale of taking value added by manufacture per employee (roughly, value of output minus value of materials used divided by employment) as a guide to interindustry differences in capital intensity. By this criterion, the higher the value added per employee, the more capital-intensive the industry, and the lower the value added per employee, the more labor-intensive it is.

Though affected by various market imperfections, value added per employee has significant advantages as a measure of factor intensity in manufacturing. One is that this measure may be taken to reflect the flows of services into the manufacturing process from both human capital and physical capital, and permits their treatment on a common basis. Another advantage is that value added per employee is available in considerable industrial detail for the United States and a number of other countries from their censuses of manufactures. The use of this measure contrasts with the usual reliance on more infrequent statistics of stocks of physical capital as a measure of capital intensity, sometimes supplemented by verbal qualifications with regard to skill requirements.

To test the validity of this approach, value added per employee is then broken down into its wage-and-salary component and the rest, and significant relations are found across industries between the first component and other measures of skill and between the second and stocks of physical capital. It appears that value added per employee is a reasonably good, though not infallible, guide to the capital intensity of different industries.

By this criterion, the labor-intensive industries include such major industry groups in the census of manufactures as textiles, clothing, lumber and wood products, furniture, leather and leather products, and the broad group of miscellaneous manufactures. They would also include many important components of other groups, such as motorcycles and bicycles, cutlery and various other metal products, chinaware and pottery, ceramic tiles, glass containers, paperboard containers, pleasure craft and other small boats, and various kinds of printed matter and printing services.

All of these items are counted as labor-intensive on the basis of the direct factor inputs into manufacturing, ignoring the factor intensity of material inputs on the assumption that the latter are ubiquitous or readily transportable. The final section of Chapter 2 suggests that a few other items more closely tied to the origin of the material inputs—chiefly certain canned or preserved foods—may also be counted as labor-intensive on the basis that, in these cases, the material inputs themselves as well as the processing of the materials are labor-intensive.

A Common World Pattern

Chapter 3 explores the question whether or not the interindustry pattern of factor intensity found for the United States would be valid for other countries as well, particularly for countries in which skills and physical capital are relatively scarce and unskilled labor abundant. Theoretical arguments, along with some limited empirical evidence, have been given elsewhere for supposing that industries would differ significantly in their propensities to substitute labor for capital, and that they would therefore rank differently from country to country in factor intensity. The question is of crucial significance to the factor-proportions theorem, which could not provide reliable guidance to comparative advantage and specialization in international trade if the notion of "factor-intensity reversals" were borne out.

Despite problems of comparability, the analysis of value added per employee in the United States and other countries, developed in Chapter 3 at various levels of industrial aggregation, gives little evidence of factor-intensity reversals. The comparisons tend rather to support the strong-factor-intensity hypothesis underlying the factor-proportions theorem and, more specifically, the relevance of the U.S. pattern of factor intensities to other countries at very different levels of economic development and with very different factor-price ratios. The selection of labor-intensive manufactures based on value added per employee in the United States stands up well on the basis of similar data for other countries, including detailed comparisons with the United Kingdom, Japan, and India.

The concluding section of Chapter 3 is devoted to cotton textiles in the light of various statements to the effect that this industry is becoming "highly capital-intensive"—a change virtually completed in the United States and Japan, according to an OECD committee report, but still slowly proceeding in Europe. This view is sometimes invoked as a reason why, pending completion of the transformation and to assist in it, imports of cotton textiles from the less developed countries should continue to be curbed. The analysis given here indicates that, though capital expenditures in the industry increased significantly during the first half of the 1960's, it still ranks as strongly labor-intensive by comparison with other industries according to the criterion of value added per employee. It seems unlikely that the less developed countries are about to lose their comparative advantage in cotton textiles.

Characteristics of the Trade

A detailed selection of labor-intensive manufactures is made at the beginning of Chapter 4 on the basis of the criteria developed in the two preceding chapters. Then, after compressing the trade figures into four main groups, the import values of those foreign countries which include freight and insurance (c.i.f.) are adjusted down to an f.o.b. basis to render the data both more comparable with United States imports and more meaningful as a measure of payments to less developed countries.

Analysis of the imports of labor-intensive manufactures by developed from less developed countries brings out the following main features:

1. The trade is relatively small, accounting in 1965 for less than 10 per cent of total imports by developed from less developed countries. The share of imports from less developed countries in total imports of labor-intensive manufactures by developed countries was also small— about 13½ per cent (excluding certain items near the margin between labor-intensive and capital-intensive, which are much less important in imports from less developed countries than in imports from other sources).

2. The trade is highly concentrated by origin, destination, and product. Hong Kong alone supplied 28 per cent of the 1965 total, and all together the less developed countries of the Far East supplied two-thirds. The United States took almost 42 per cent of the imports and, together with the United Kingdom and West Germany, 72 per cent. Textiles and clothing, exclusive of products of jute and other coarse fibers, made up almost one-third of the total, or 45 per cent if the coarse-fiber items are included.

3. The trade has grown very rapidly in recent years. In 1965 the total was 4.3 times the 1953 level, an increase averaging about 13 per cent per annum, unadjusted for price increases, or perhaps one or two percentage points less if so adjusted. This is much faster than seems to have been generally expected only a few years ago. Recently, the increase

has been much faster in miscellaneous light consumer manufactures than in the other three groups (textiles, food products, and processed materials).

Reasons are given in the final section of Chapter 4 for thinking that there may be a continued rapid growth in the trade. An important condition, however, is that the structure of wages in less developed countries not be such as to nullify their comparative advantage in labor-intensive products. This qualification seems to apply to a number of the less developed countries and may explain why some of the more advanced among them have not done well as exporters of labor-intensive manufactures while still unable to compete in other manufactures. Otherwise, the ability of the less developed countries to export labor-intensive manufactures should continue to strengthen as they gain experience and as incomes rise in the developed countries.

Policy Choices and Results

How fast imports of manufactures from the less developed countries increase depends not only on the strengthening of their competitive position and the growth of demand in the importing countries but also on the extent to which the latters' commercial policies inhibit these forces. Chapter 5 reviews two main types of interference with the flow of trade. One is direct controls exemplified in the "Long-Term Cotton Textile Arrangement." The other is the structure of tariffs, rates generally rising with the stage of manufacture so that the effective level of protection of finished products is typically higher than the nominal level. This is scarcely less true of the United States than of other countries, but the effect, judged by the composition of trade, nevertheless seems to be much less restrictive here than in western Continental Europe and Japan.

The final section of Chapter 5 concerns the debate over commercial policy in the developed countries and, in particular, the demand of the less developed countries for tariff preferences. It is suggested that the outcome is likely to be a mixed bag at best, with both positive and negative features in enlarging market opportunities for less developed countries. Under these conditions, it would be important to make sure that the policies followed by the developed countries, however they may differ from each other, are at least consistent with the results aimed at and, therefore, to express the results anticipated in explicit quantitative terms with regard to the level and growth of imports of manufactures from the less developed countries.

2

FACTOR INTENSITIES
IN THE UNITED STATES

The Factor-Proportions Theorem

If it is agreed that the less developed countries need to generate a large and growing volume of exports of manufactures to developed countries, the next question is what products best lend themselves to this purpose. The "factor-proportions" theorem identified with Heckscher and Ohlin provides a persuasive, but much disputed, answer to this question.[1] According to that theorem, countries may be expected to have a comparative advantage in goods requiring relatively large inputs of the particular factors of production—whether labor, capital, or natural resources—with which they are most liberally endowed and, correspondingly, a comparative disadvantage in the production of goods embodying their scarce factors. A given country would therefore export goods of the first type and import goods of the second type, on the assumption that there are no hindrances to the flow of trade. In the context of the present study this would mean that, apart from industries based on such natural resources as they might have, the less developed countries would tend to specialize in labor-intensive goods and to import capital-intensive goods. More developed countries with greater capital resources and a highly skilled labor force would show the opposite pattern, at least in their trade with less developed countries.

Plausible though it sounds, the factor-proportions theorem has been severely criticized. Some of the points made against it—notably its

[1] Eli Heckscher's contribution, originally published in the Swedish journal *Ekonomisk Tidskrift* in 1919, appeared in English thirty years later under the title "The Effect of Foreign Trade on the Distribution of Income" (in *Readings in the Theory of International Trade*, Philadelphia, 1949, pp, 272–300). Midway between, in 1935, Bertil Ohlin's major work was published, *Interregional and International Trade* (Cambridge, Mass.), in which he paid particular tribute to Heckscher as well as to other economists of the Stockholm group.

shortcomings as an explanation of the complexities of trade in advanced manufactures—are probably more relevant to trade among the developed countries than to their trade with less developed countries. More generally disturbing is certain empirical evidence which seems to run counter to what the theorem would lead one to expect. Most famous of all is the Leontief paradox—i.e., his finding that the United States, though obviously using more capital per worker than other countries, exports labor-intensive goods and imports capital-intensive goods.[2] This upside-down result is frequently cited in support of alternative approaches to the explanation of trade and is regarded by some, though not by Leontief himself, as demolishing the Heckscher-Ohlin approach.

In the real world, tariffs, subsidies, quotas, and the like do interfere with the flow of trade and are one reason, along with others, for questioning the significance of any of the tests of the factor-proportions theorem which have been attempted.[3] The present analysis does not aim at providing such a test. The methods employed and results found do, however, bear on the validity of the theorem in two important respects:

First, the variable here used as a guide to factor intensities in different industries—i.e., value added per employee in manufacturing—permits an integrated treatment of the flows of services rendered by capital and labor in manufacturing. This contrasts with most previous studies in which the contribution of capital is measured as a stock rather than as a flow of services, and that of labor merely by total man-hours or man-years without regard to differences in skills.

Second, the international comparisons made on this basis support the assumption, crucial to the factor-proportions theorem, that the ranking of industries by factor intensities is much the same from country to country, even from the most developed to the least developed. That is to say, the phenomenon of "factor-intensity reversals" seems to be much less common, at least in manufacturing, than some other empirical studies would suggest.

[2] Leontief judged the factor intensity of U.S. imports by the capital/labor ratios found for U.S. import-competing production, but he interpreted his results more broadly. See, for instance, his remarks on page 343 of his original article (W. Leontief, "Domestic Production and Foreign Trade: The American Capital Position Re-examined," *Proceedings of the American Philosophical Society*, September 1953).

[3] To what extent do Leontief's findings reflect the influence of factor proportions at home and abroad on the composition of U.S. trade, or to what extent do they reflect, much less paradoxically, the effects of U.S. commercial policy? The latter influence is strongly stressed by W. P. Travis in *The Theory of Trade and Protection*, Cambridge, Mass., 1964.

These points form the subject matter of Chapters 2 and 3. They lead, at the beginning of Chapter 4, to a detailed identification of labor-intensive industries in which, presumably, the less developed countries might expect to find their comparative advantage in international trade.

Value Added per Employee as a Guide to Factor Intensity in Manufacturing

Economists have long recognized that differences in the quality of labor largely reflect differences in the amount of training and other forms of investment in people, but it is only in recent years, particularly through the work of Schultz and Becker,[4] that the concept of human capital has begun to be incorporated into the general framework of economic analysis. Most empirical work on factor intensities in different industries and countries has consequently been in terms of the stock of physical capital per worker and has failed to take account, except qualitatively, of the contribution attributable to different levels of skill.[5]

A similar, and perhaps not unrelated, failure can be seen in the actual direction of investment activity in the less developed countries. Thus, Schultz, noting the emphasis on physical capital in loans by the World Bank and the Export-Import Bank, as well as in private investment, comments: "This one-sided effort is under way in spite of the fact that the knowledge and skills required to take on and use efficiently the superior techniques of production, the most valuable resource that we could make available to them, is in very short supply in these under-developed countries. Some growth of course can be had from the increase in more conventional capital even though the labor that is available is lacking both in skill and knowledge. But the rate of growth will be seriously limited. It simply is not possible to have the fruits of a

---

[4] These contributions include T. W. Schultz, "Investment in Human Capital," *American Economic Review,* March 1961, and Gary S. Becker, *Human Capital,* New York, National Bureau of Economic Research, 1964. More recently, Peter B. Kenen has presented an integrated treatment of both human and physical capital in a theoretical model of international trade in "Nature, Capital and Trade," *Journal of Political Economy,* October 1965. Kenen concludes his article with a brief empirical application to factor proportions in U.S. foreign trade in relation to the Leontief paradox, these empirical results being developed more fully in a paper prepared jointly with Elinor B. Yudin, "Skills, Human Capital and U.S. Foreign Trade," International Economics Workshop, Columbia University, 1965 (mimeographed).

[5] An early exception was Edwin Chadwick's effort more than a century ago to estimate the increase in productivity of workers attributable to education. See William L. Miller, "The Economics of Education in English Classical Economics," *Southern Economic Journal,* January 1966.

CHART 1

Wage and Nonwage Value Added per Employee in U.S. Manufacturing
by Major Industry Groups, 1965

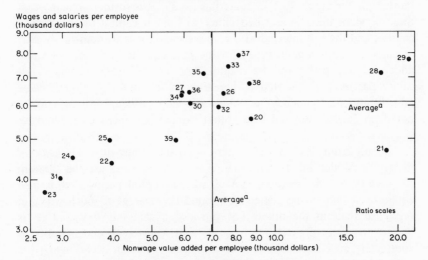

Source: 1965 *Annual Survey of Manufactures*, U.S. Bureau of the Census.
Note: For names of industry groups, see Table 2.
a Average for all U.S. manufacturing industry.

modern agriculture and the abundance of modern industry without making large investments in human beings." [6]

The method used here for measuring, or at least approximating, inputs of both human capital and physical capital on a common basis will be briefly illustrated by reference to Chart 1 and then considered more fully along with various qualifications. The data plotted in the chart are from the U.S. Census of Manufactures and consist of "value added by manufacture" in twenty major industry groups, separated into (a) wages and salaries and (b) the remainder, each of these components being divided by total employment in each industry. Put very loosely, "value added by manufacture" is what remains after subtracting the value of materials consumed from the gross value of output in any given industry or industry group.[7] Differences from industry to

[6] Schultz, "Investment in Human Capital," p. 16. One may, however, detect an increasing emphasis on technical assistance, training programs, educational loans, and other contributions to human capital.

[7] A more precise definition of the concept as applied in the United States is: "Value added by manufacture is derived by subtracting the total cost of ma-

industry in value added per employee are here assumed to measure differences in the aggregate flows of services from the factors of production employed in the manufacturing process (and exclude therefore indirect factor inputs such as materials used). It is further assumed that these services may be ascribed either to human capital or to physical capital, and that, in interindustry comparisons, the wage-and-salary part of value added is a good proxy for the first and the remainder of value added a good proxy for the second. For convenience, the wage-and-salary part will be referred to hereafter in this study as "wage value added" and the remainder as "nonwage value added," but it is to be noted, as further stressed below, that salaries are included along with wages in the first.

This procedure assumes that there is no such thing in reality as completely "unskilled labor," and that, if average earnings are the same in two industries, the average level of human capital per worker is also equal, even though the dispersion around the average is much wider in one case than in the other. For purpose of analysis, however, it is helpful to think of the labor force as if it were composed of units of completely unskilled labor to each of which is added, according to the industry, varying amounts of skill or human capital (vertical axis of Chart 1) and of machinery and other physical assets (horizontal axis).[8] The higher the value added per employee, the more capital-intensive the industry on both accounts combined; the lower the value added per employee, the more labor-intensive the industry.

terials (including materials, supplies, fuel, electric energy, cost of resales, and miscellaneous receipts) from the value of shipments (including resales) and other receipts and adjusting the resulting amount by the net change in finished products and work-in-process inventories between the beginning and end of the year." Note that the costs subtracted from value of shipments do not include purchased services, to wit: "purchases of services from nonmanufacturing enterprises, such as contract costs involved in maintenance and repair, services of development and research firms, services of engineering and management consultants, advertising, telephone and telegraph expense, insurance, royalties, patent fees, etc." (Citations are from *1963 Census of Manufactures,* Vol. I, Summary and Subject Statistics, U.S. Bureau of the Census, 1966, pp. 22–23.)

[8] The approach taken here thus differs from the traditional way of measuring the relative labor or capital intensity of different industries in terms only of physical capital per worker or the share of payroll in value added by manufacture. Such measures do not differentiate between labor of different qualifications and implicitly treat managers, scientists, engineers, foremen, and workers of varying skills all on the same basis. Victor R. Fuchs, however, arrived at results broadly similar to those given here by using both the share of wages in value added and average wage per production worker as guides to the relative labor intensity of different industries. See his *Changes in the Location of Manufacturing in the United States Since 1929,* New Haven, 1962, pp. 164–167 and Table 6:11.

Array of U.S. Industries by Value-Added Criterion

On this approach, the industry groups falling in the lower left sector of Chart 1 may be thought of as intensive in the use of relatively unskilled labor, since they are below the United States average in both wage and nonwage value added per employee. Their products include not only textiles and clothing but also lumber and wood products, furniture, leather and leather goods, and a miscellaneous group comprising a wide variety of items. These main industry groups are relatively homogeneous in that very few of their component industries fall outside the boundaries indicated. An interesting exception in the textile group is tufted carpets, a mechanized product which contrasts with the more labor-intensive woven carpets.

Industries in the upper right sector of the chart include two which are extremely capital-intensive by both criteria employed here—chemical products and petroleum refining. Also far to the right in the chart is the tobacco industry, ranking very high in nonwage value added, though low on the wage scale. Here again there is a high degree of homogeneity in the component industries of these major groups. An exception of some relevance for present purposes is the labor-intensive manufacture of cigars, which contrasts with the much larger and more capital-intensive cigarette branch of the industry.

The eleven remaining major industry groups fall closer to the over-all average of wage and nonwage value added for all U.S. manufacturing. They are also much more diverse in composition by these criteria, as indicated by the supplementary detail for selected three- , four- , and five-digit industries in Table 2. Some of the latter fall well within the capital-intensive sector—for example, blast furnaces and steel mills, primary nonferrous metals, automobiles, tires and tubes, pulp mills and paperboard mills, hydraulic cement, flat glass, alcoholic beverages, flour mills, sugar refining, and some other food processing industries. Other components fall well within the labor-intensive sector, including a number of items of interest in the present analysis—rubber shoes, motorcycles and bicycles, cutlery and various other metal products, pleasure craft and other small boats, glass containers, chinaware and pottery, ceramic tiles, canned seafood, canned fruit and vegetables, paper and paperboard containers, and various kinds of printed matter and printing services.

This allocation leaves a number of other industries and products near, or beyond, one or the other of the limits suggested by Chart 1 for the labor-intensive sector, among them being metal castings and stamp-

TABLE 2

Supplementary Detail on Employment and Value Added in U.S. Manufacturing by Main Industry Groups and Selected Subgroups, 1965

SIC Code	Industry Group or Subgroup	Total Employment (thousands)	Value Added by Manufacture ($ million)	Value Added per Employee (percentage of national average)		
				Total	Wages and Salaries	Other
	U.S. manufacturing, total[a]	16,900.6	222,283	100	100	100
20	Food and kindred products	1,635.0	23,383	109	91	124
2013	Meat processing plants	48.3	611	96	102	91
2031	Canned and cured seafoods	15.7	191	93	68	114
2033	Canned fruits and vegetables	99.7	1,174	90	66	110
2041	Flour Mills	20.7	403	148	105	186
2062	Cane sugar refining	11.2	276	188	124	243
2071	Confectionery products	65.2	723	84	74	94
208	Beverages	210.5	4,141	150	104	189
20943	Animal and marine oil products, including fats	2.0	24	84	77	123
21	Tobacco manufactures	75.1	1,768	179	77	269
2111	Cigarettes	35.9	1,366	289	90	463
2121	Cigars	20.9	220	80	59	98
22	Textile mill products	891.5	7,469	64	72	57
2211	Weaving mills, cotton	205.4	1,624	60	70	51
225	Knitting mills	231.2	1,644	54	63	46
2271	Woven carpets and rugs	10.6	109	78	83	74
2272	Tufted carpets and rugs	26.6	376	108	76	135

(continued)

TABLE 2 (continued)

SIC Code	Industry Group or Subgroup	Total Employment (thousands)	Value Added by Manufacture ($ million)	Value Added per Employee (percentage of national average)		
				Total	Wages and Salaries	Other
23	Apparel and related products	1,311.8	8,427	49	61	39
24	Lumber and wood products	569.7	4,388	59	73	46
25	Furniture and fixtures	407.7	3,620	68	81	56
26	Paper and allied products	605.6	8,400	105	104	107
2611	Pulp mills	14.3	336	178	124	226
2621	Paper mills, except building	131.7	2,043	118	118	117
2631	Paperboard mills	64.8	1,391	163	119	202
264b	Paper and paperboard products	155.7	1,908	93	94	92
2647	Sanitary paper products	19.1	418	166	104	221
265	Paperboard containers and boxes	208.7	2,136	78	96	62
2661	Building paper and board mills	11.3	169	114	104	123
27	Printing and publishing	962.8	11,888	94	104	85
2732	Book printing	37.3	396	81	108	57
275	Commercial printing	321.1	3,304	78	106	54
2771	Greeting card manufacturing	24.6	254	78	87	71
278	Bookbinding and related work	47.4	404	65	83	49
2791	Typesetting	21.0	223	81	129	39
28	Chemicals and allied products	776.2	19,721	193	117	260
29	Petroleum and coal products	143.5	4,154	220	126	303

(continued)

TABLE 2 (continued)

SIC Code	Industry Group or Subgroup	Total Employment (thousands)	Value Added by Manufacture ($ million)	Value Added per Employee (percentage of national average)		
				Total	Wages and Salaries	Other
30	Rubber and plastics products, n.e.c.	461.3	5,657	93	99	88
3011	Tires and inner tubes	88.7	1,602	137	132	142
3021	Rubber footwear	30.0	247	63	76	51
3069	Rubber products, n.e.c.	139.2	1,594	87	100	76
3079	Plastics products, n.e.c.	201.4	2,189	83	86	79
31	Leather and leather products	332.5	2,325	53	66	42
32	Stone, clay, and glass products	598.8	7,922	101	97	104
3211	Flat glass	25.3	463	139	132	145
3221	Glass containers	61.5	680	84	95	74
3241	Cement, hydraulic	34.3	837	186	115	247
3253	Ceramic wall and floor tile	12.6	112	68	85	53
326	Pottery and related products	41.6	376	69	86	53
33	Primary metal industries	1,242.6	18,759	115	121	110
331	Steel rolling and finishing	638.4	10,507	125	127	124
332	Iron and steel foundries	224.7	2,562	87	112	64
333	Primary nonferrous metal	52.5	1,225	177	115	232
335	Nonferrous rolling and drawing	174.3	2,565	112	117	108
336	Nonferrous foundries	74.6	804	82	105	62
34	Fabricated metal products	1,160.2	14,208	93	103	84
34211	Cutlery, scissors, shears, etc.	7.3	63	72	84	61
3423	Hand and edge tools	35.2	456	98	99	98
3425	Hand saws and saw blades	5.7	81	108	104	112

(continued)

TABLE 2 (continued)

SIC Code	Industry Group or Subgroup	Total Employment (thousands)	Value Added by Manufacture ($ million)	Value Added per Employee (percentage of national average)		
				Total	Wages and Salaries	Other
	Fabricated metal products (cont'd)					
3429	Hardware, n.e.c.	97.4	1,290	101	106	96
343	Plumbing and heating, except electric	70.8	855	92	99	86
344	Structural metal products	344.6	3,976	88	103	75
3451	Screw machine products	39.0	419	82	103	63
3452	Bolts, nuts, rivets, and washers	62.2	848	104	113	95
3461	Metal stampings	147.0	1,655	86	102	72
35	Machinery, except electrical	1,651.5	22,819	105	116	95
3552	Textile machinery	41.2	412	76	98	57
3572	Typewriters	18.6	298	122	102	139
3599	Miscellaneous machinery	147.7	1,662	86	104	69
36	Electrical machinery	1,604.5	20,222	96	105	88
3631	Household cooking equipment	20.9	268	98	98	97
3632	Household refrigerators	48.7	748	117	115	118
3633	Household laundry equipment	21.0	386	140	109	167
3634	Electric housewares and fans	40.9	542	101	84	116
3635	Household vacuum cleaners	6.5	131	153	102	198
3636	Sewing machines	6.9	90	99	117	84
3639	Household appliances, n.e.c.	13.9	229	125	104	145
3642	Lighting fixtures	62.2	740	90	93	88

(continued)

TABLE 2 (continued)

SIC Code	Industry Group or Subgroup	Total Employment (thousands)	Value Added by Manufacture ($ million)	Value Added per Employee (percentage of national average)		
				Total	Wages and Salaries	Other
	Electrical machinery (cont'd)					
3651	Radio and TV receiving sets	102.5	1,213	90	86	93
3661	Telephone, telegraph apparatus	101.9	1,362	102	113	92
367	Electronic components	317.7	3,321	79	91	69
3694	Engine electrical equipment	43.2	584	103	109	97
37	Transportation equipment	1,732.4	27,727	122	128	116
371	Motor vehicles and equipment	821.9	16,495	153	131	171
372	Aircraft and parts	642.3	8,493	101	133	72
3732	Boatbuilding and repairing	28.1	213	58	78	41
3742	Railroad and street cars	40.7	539	100	114	88
3751	Motorcycles, bicycles, and parts	11.2	107	72	90	57
38	Instruments and related products	327.7	5,046	117	110	124
382	Mechanical measuring devices	99.6	1,362	104	109	100
3841	Surgical and medical instruments	15.2	189	95	95	95
3851	Ophthalmic goods	22.3	215	73	82	66
38611	Still picture equipment	17.9	227	107	137	80
38613	Motion picture equipment	7.6	69	77	116	41
38615	Photographic sensitized film and plates	26.5	626	200	152	244
3871	Watches and clocks	29.0	340	89	90	89
3872	Watchcases	3.5	29	63	86	43

(continued)

TABLE 2 (concluded)

SIC Code	Industry Group or Subgroup	Total Employment (thousands)	Value Added by Manufacture ($ million)	Value Added per Employee (percentage of national average)		
				Total	Wages and Salaries	Other
39	Miscellaneous manufacturing	410.0	4,380	81	81	82
391	Jewelry and silverware	48.1	520	82	88	77
3931	Musical instruments and parts	23.6	231	74	86	64
394	Toys and sporting goods	119.7	1,088	69	72	67
395	Pens, pencils, and office supplies	33.4	378	86	86	87
396	Costume jewelry and notions	52.1	479	70	84	91

Source: *Annual Survey of Manufactures, 1965: General Statistics for Industry Groups and Industries*, U.S. Bureau of the Census, Washington, 1966; *1963 Census of Manufactures: Industry Statistics*, U.S. Bureau of the Census, Washington, 1966.

Note: All five-digit items are from *1963 Census of Manufactures* and, in the last three columns, are related to the national averages for that year. N.e.c. = not elsewhere classified.

[a]Operating establishments only, excluding administrative and auxiliary units. National averages in 1965 used as base in last three columns are total value added per employee, $13,152; wages and salaries, $6,136; other, $7,016.

[b]Excluding SIC No. 2647, sanitary paper products.

ings; hardware and tools; plumbing and heating equipment; household fans, automotive electrical equipment, radio and television sets, and other light electrical goods; sewing machines and typewriters; various types of machinery; surgical and medical instruments; some measuring or scientific instruments; and watches and clocks.[9]

As will be noted later, most of the items just enumerated are marginal also in the sense that exports by less developed countries form only a very small part of international trade in these goods. They are nevertheless of particular interest, since these products could be next in line for the achievement of an export potential by some of the less developed countries as the growth of their experience and capacity in manufacturing permits them to move beyond the more strongly labor-intensive types of production. And one may further observe that, to judge by the data for these industries in the last two columns of Table 2, the development of labor skills (including managerial experience and technical abilities) seems no less important than the growth of physical capital, if this kind of evolution is to occur.

The Content of Value Added

Taken literally, the assumption that interindustry variations in value added by manufacture per employee reflect differences in the aggregate value of services rendered by human and physical capital would imply fully competitive factor and product markets in which the marginal contribution of these services is precisely matched in each case by the rewards paid. This condition is, however, only imperfectly realized at best because of various market interferences, some short-run and others of longer duration. These need to be noted as well as certain deficiencies or peculiarities of the statistics which may also affect interindustry difference in value added per employee.

Among the short-run influences, the business cycle is no doubt the most important and pervasive through its influence on profits and, to a lesser extent, on wage rates. Since some industries are more sensitive than others to cyclical fluctuations, interindustry differentials in value added per employee may reflect the phase of the business cycle pre-

[9] Some of these items are included in the above list on the basis of similar data from earlier U.S. censuses of production because of changes in the products in recent years. Thus, typewriter production now includes fewer manual and more electric models, with the result that value added per employee in this industry in 1965 was 22 per cent above the national average for all manufacturing, whereas in 1947 it was 12 per cent below the average. Domestic output in such cases would no longer be indicative of the factor intensities of imported types.

vailing at the time the observations are made as well as capital intensities. In fact, however, comparison of value added per employee in the prosperous year 1965 and in the recession year 1958 shows a high, positive correlation, the coefficient of correlation for 406 industries at the four-digit level being 0.94 (R^2 adjusted = 0.87). One may therefore conclude that, except perhaps in more extreme circumstances, the meaningfulness of the value-added approach to the measurement of capital intensity does not require major qualification for the effects of the business cycle.

Profit rates may vary from industry to industry for numerous other reasons. As Stigler says, "The sources of disequilibrium are infinitely varied. . . . All leave their impact upon the rates of return, and we can, in fact, turn our analysis around and define the fluctuations in an industry's profit rate as the measure of the extent and duration of disequilibrium." [10] Among the causes of disequilibrium, differences in the extent of concentration—i.e., in the relative importance of a few large companies—are frequently thought to have a substantial effect on interindustry differences in rates of return and profit margins, "monopoly profits" being enjoyed by the more strongly concentrated industries. To the extent that this is so, the profit element in nonwage value added would tend to vary across industries with the extent of concentration.[11]

Not only profit differentials but also wage differentials may arise because of greater monopolistic tendencies in one industry than in another. Workers in some industries are much more strongly organized than in others, and one would expect unionization to have an effect on relative wage levels.[12] Differences in wages also occur because some

[10] George J. Stigler, *Capital and Rates of Return in Manufacturing Industries,* Princeton University Press for National Bureau of Economic Research, 1963, p. 64.

[11] A monograph in preparation by Norman R. Collins and Lee E. Preston ("Concentration and Price-Cost Margins in Manufacturing Industries") notes "a significant, although weak association between concentration and corporate profits" in most previous analyses based primarily on U.S. concentration data for 1954. Their own analysis of 1958 data leads them to report a significant association (though, paradoxically, weaker at the more detailed four-digit industry level than at the broad two-digit level). Noting that 1954 and 1958 were both years of mild recession and also that profits of smaller firms show greater cyclical instability than those of large firms, Collins and Preston consider that the association between concentration and profits may be a recession phenomenon (though not unimportant for that reason), but do not exclude other possibilities pending the results of analysis of the data for 1963.

[12] In connection with his study of the service industries for the National Bureau, Victor R. Fuchs finds that differences in unionization (measured as the fraction of total employment in each industry covered by collective bargaining agree-

industries are growing faster than others and seek to attract labor; thus for short periods observed wages are disequilibrium values. Still other differences in wages are to be explained because nonmonetary utilities or disutilities are greater in some industries than in others, or perhaps simply because tradition irrationally bestows higher earnings on some activities than on others.[13]

The essential question is, however, whether or not the various influences noted in the labor and capital markets are so strong and pervasive as to impair the general usefulness of value added per employee as a guide to the capital intensity of different industries.

Before this topic is further explored, still another question needs to be clarified; that is, how much violence is done to reality in proceeding as if all contributions to value added in manufacturing could be attributed either to human capital or to physical capital.[14] Since it is obtained as the difference between the cost of material inputs and the value of output, value added by manufacture is not regularly and systematically broken down in the Census of Manufactures into its main components. The only important exception is payroll of operating establishments, which permits the division here made between wage and nonwage value added.[15]

Conceptually, there should not be any difficulty about seeking to relate wages to the gross return on human capital. The problem would

ments) help to explain earnings differentials among industries. His provisional "best" estimate is that, over the range from 20 to 60 per cent of unionization, an increase of one percentage point in unionization is associated with an increase of approximately 0.8 cent in hourly earnings, taking 138 goods and services industries together. Fuchs qualifies his results by noting that they may not measure the effects of unionization alone but may also reflect quality differences among workers not adequately taken into account in his analysis.

[13] At a meeting of the OECD Study Group in the Economics of Education, J. Sandee of the Central Planning Office, The Hague, maintained that "people are paid according to what they 'ought' to have, rather than according to what they individually produce"; among the more decisive influences he mentioned "custom and tradition, arbitrary decisions copied by whole industries, relative trade union strengths [and] considerations of 'fairness.'" "Comments on Mr. Edward F. Denison's Paper," in *The Residual Factor and Economic Growth,* OECD, Paris, 1964, p. 75.

[14] In considering this question we need not be concerned (at least for the time being) with the contribution of natural resources, since value added by manufacture excludes the input of materials.

[15] The Census reports show, for each industry, both total payroll for all employees and total wages for production workers only, along with the aggregate numbers in each case. It is the more comprehensive series which is used here, so that throughout this study "average wage" should be understood to mean average earnings per employee, covering both wage earners and salaried personnel.

seem to be concentrated rather in the catchall residual, nonwage value added, which would include not only the gross return on physical capital but payments to various other factors as well (except those subtracted out with material inputs). Indeed, as indicated by the estimates in Table 3 for manufacturing as a whole in 1957, these payments even include several streams of rewards to labor not in the regularly reported payroll item. These are items 2, 3, and 4 in the table, i.e., wage supplements, payrolls of central administrative offices and other nonmanufacturing divisions of multiunit companies, and the estimated labor income of proprietors of unincorporated manufacturing businesses.[16]

Of the remaining items in the table, those numbered 5 to 10 would all seem to have a fairly close connection with capital assets. This may even be true of some of the elements (such as royalty payments and patent fees), though not of others (notably advertising, further discussed below) in the ultimate residual group III in the table. Capital-related payments thus seem to account for close to $40 billion, or about 60 per cent, of nonwage value added in 1957. On the assumption that other elements in nonwage value added are randomly distributed by industries, it would seem reasonable to think of interindustry differences in nonwage value added per employee as largely reflecting differences in the intensity of capital inputs, and to try to test this relation.

The separation between wage and nonwage value added may be, however, unduly restrictive for purposes of measuring the industry pattern of capital inputs per employee. As noted, nonwage value added includes certain elements (such as item 4 in Table 3) which may be identified with human capital, though without necessarily following the same industry distribution as the payroll of operating establishments. This may hold also for some of the elements of the final residual, notably, contract research and possibly legal and other professional services. It may not be a disadvantage therefore that nonwage value added is conceptually broader than physical capital, though there is little possibility of relating it empirically to any of the other inputs. One can only conjecture that some of these inputs may have a systematic relation, not necessarily the same as that of physical capital, to different

---

[16] An industry breakdown is available only for item 2, wage supplements, and in this case only for 1957 as the result of a special survey of selected costs (see *1958 Census of Manufactures*, Vol. I, pp. 9–3—9–23). Payments of the nature covered by item 3 of the table, as well as many of those indicated for the residual group III, are company-type expenditures and cannot be reported on an establishment basis by companies consisting of more than one establishment. It must be assumed, however, that these expenses are reflected in value of shipments and, hence, in value added by manufacturing establishments.

TABLE 3

Partial Breakdown of Value Added in All U.S.
Manufacturing Enterprises, 1957
($ billion)

Total value added by manufacture	147.8
I. *Payroll and Other Rewards to Labor, Total*	91.9
1. Payroll of operating establishments	76.4
2. Supplements to payroll	6.0
3. Payroll in central administrative offices, sales departments, and auxiliary establishments	7.0
4. Imputed salaries of proprietors of unincorporated firms[a]	2.5
II. *Expenses Related to Physical Assets, Total*	37.5
5. Pretax corporate profits	22.1
6. Depreciation	7.3
7. Maintenance and repair services purchased from other firms	4.5
8. Property taxes	1.5
9. Insurance	.7
10. Rents	1.4
III. *All Other Expenses, Total*[b]	18.4

Source: *1958 Census of Manufactures,* Vol. I, pp. 13 and 14, supplemented by information provided by the Industry Division, Bureau of the Census, except as noted in footnote a with respect to item 4.

[a]Rough estimate based on unpublished tabulations for Irving Leveson's National Bureau study of self-employment derived from *U.S. Census of Population and Housing: 1960, 1/1,000.* According to these tabulations, self-employment income received by proprietors of unincorporated manufacturing businesses in 1959 amounted to some $4 billion. Allowing for returns to property and allowing also for growth from 1957 to 1959, this implies that returns to labor of proprietors were between $2 billion and $3 billion in 1957.

[b]This item, obtained by difference, is presumed to include expenditures for advertising, publicity, legal services, travel and communications, royalty payments, patent fees, purchases of research and advisory services from outside firms, other professional services, bad debts, entertainment, and miscellaneous other expenses.

industries. To the extent that they do, it would enhance the usefulness of total value added per employee as a guide to capital intensity, broadly viewed, even though the division of the total into its wage and nonwage components yields only an imperfect measure of inputs of human and physical capital separately considered. It will be seen in the following two sections that, in fact, the two components appear to provide reasonably good indications of these inputs.

Wages and Human Capital

Recognizing that undifferentiated man-years were a crude way of measuring labor inputs into different industries, Leontief introduced in his second article on U.S. factor proportions a table showing labor requirements distributed by five broad skill groups in export industries and in import-competing industries.[17] This comparison showed a significantly larger concentration of higher skills in the first than in the second array of industries. He made the further point, relevant to the methodology followed in this analysis, that "The measurement of labor inputs in terms of wages paid reflects the same distinction, insofar as it amounts to weighting in the process of aggregation the man-years of each skill group by its respective average annual wage rate." [18]

Leontief did not apply either of these measures to his factor proportions analysis, but he did remark in passing that his table on skill levels confirmed and possibly explained Kravis' findings that average wage rates in U.S. export industries were systematically higher than those prevailing in import-competing industries.[19] Kravis had found that hourly wages in 330 U.S. manufacturing industries in 1947 were higher the greater the ratio of exports to domestic production and, conversely, were lower the greater the ratio of imports to domestic production.[20] The difference in average hourly wages was 15 per cent in 46 leading export industries compared with 36 leading import-competing industries (weighted by the amount of trade in 1947 in each case).

Taking her cue from these results, Helen Waehrer confirmed by various tests that average wages were significantly higher also in 1960

[17] W. Leontief, "Factor Proportions and the Structure of American Trade: Further Theoretical and Empirical Analysis," *Review of Economics and Statistics,* November 1956, p. 399.

[18] *Ibid.,* p. 394.

[19] *Ibid.,* p. 399, note 8.

[20] Irving B. Kravis, "Wages and Foreign Trade," *Review of Economics and Statistics,* February 1956, pp. 14–30.

in export industries than in import-competing industries.[21] In explanation of these differences, Mrs. Waehrer offered the dual hypothesis (a) that average wages varied from industry to industry with skills, and (b) that skills were higher in export industries than in import-competing industries. To test this hypothesis, she constructed two measures of skill with data from the 1960 Census of Population, an "occupational index" and an "educational index," and related each of them to average earnings, computed from the 1960 Survey of Manufactures, in 35 broad industry groups significantly involved in foreign trade.[22] She found a significant correlation between each of these indexes and earnings and also, by either index, a substantially higher level of skills in export industries than in import-competing industries.

The first part of Mrs. Waehrer's hypothesis being of primary interest for present purposes, it is preferable to consider her data relating the two skill indexes to average annual wages in all of the 59 industry groups distinguished by the Census of Population for the manufacturing sector.[23] Each of the indexes suffers from certain limitations as a measure of skill or human capital. The occupational index varies from industry to industry only with differences in the distribution of employees between occupations treated as skilled and those treated as unskilled, and wide variations in skill may be concealed within each of these two very broad categories. The educational index covers only formal schooling, not on-the-job training and experience. Moreover, strict comparability cannot be assured in compressing the industrial classification used in the Census of Manufactures, the source of the

[21] "Inter-industry Skill Differences, Labor Earnings and United States Foreign Trade, 1960" (unpublished Ph.D. dissertation, Columbia University, 1966).

[22] The "occupational index" is defined as the percentage of employees in each industry falling in six occupational groups selected by Mrs. Waehrer as skilled (professional and technical workers; managers, officials, and proprietors; clerical and kindred workers; sales workers; craftsmen and foremen; and service workers) out of a total labor force including two groups treated as unskilled (operatives and kindred workers, and laborers except farm and mine). Her "educational index" is defined as the median years of formal schooling completed by employees in each industry weighted by the sex composition of the industry. Since Mrs. Waehrer was interested in studying the wage structure of export industries and import-competing industries, she confined her selection of industries to those in which exports or imports were above the over-all average ratios to the value of shipments in all manufacturing industry. Those meeting this criterion included 22 defined as export industries and 22 defined as import-competing industries, with an overlap of nine, i.e., a total of 35 out of the 59 industry groups into which manufacturing is divided in the Census of Population.

[23] Mrs. Waehrer has kindly made available her computations for the 24 industry groups additional to those counted as export industries or as import-competing industries and reported on in her dissertation.

earnings data, into the fifty-nine industries given in the Census of Population. Not only are the classifications different but also the individual employee, in responding to the Census of Population questions, may place himself in a different industry than that given by his employer's plant report to the Census of Manufactures.

Since there is no apparent reason to suspect a systematic bias in these various deficiencies, all the more interest attaches to the correlation coefficients obtained: 0.78 between annual earnings and the occupational index, and 0.76 between annual earnings and the educational index (59 observations), both measures being significant at the 1 per cent level of confidence and attesting to a meaningful association between wages and skills across industries. The variables used in the correlation of earnings and the occupational index are plotted in Chart 2 and are identified by industries (along with those plotted in Chart 3) in Appendix Table A-1.

The two skill indexes prove to be a poor guide to earnings in newspaper publishing and printing, as the occupational index is also for other kinds of publishing and printing. These two industries account for the extreme deviations in the upper right area of Chart 2.[24] Since neither of them could be regarded as typical of manufacturing, it has seemed useful to recompute the regressions excluding these industries. The result is to raise the correlation coefficient to 0.85 for the occupational index and to 0.79 for the educational index.

Yet a third measure of variations in the quality of labor among the same 59 manufacturing industries is available as a by-product of the National Bureau's study of productivity in the service industries. This measure takes the form of estimates of "expected" hourly earnings in 1959 on the basis of data given by the one-in-a-thousand sample from the Census of Population in 1960. These are the average earnings that would be found for each industry if each worker's earnings were equal to the national average for his particular color, age, sex, and level of education (workers being classified into 168 cells according to these characteristics). Significant differentials in national average earnings associated with each of these variables suggest that they reflect, at least in part, differences in human capital.[25]

---

[24] Part of the explanation, at least, is that newsboys, who form a large part of total employment in the newspaper business as reported by the Census of Population, are counted by the later as "sales workers" and, in turn, enter into the skilled category of Mrs. Waehrer's occupational index.

[25] See Victor R. Fuchs, *Differentials in Hourly Earnings by Region and City Size, 1959,* New York, NBER, 1967. Regarding the color variable, Fuchs notes (p. 5) that "The white-nonwhite differences are probably due in part to market

CHART 2

Average Annual Earnings and the "Occupational Index"
in 59 Industry Groups in the United States, 1960

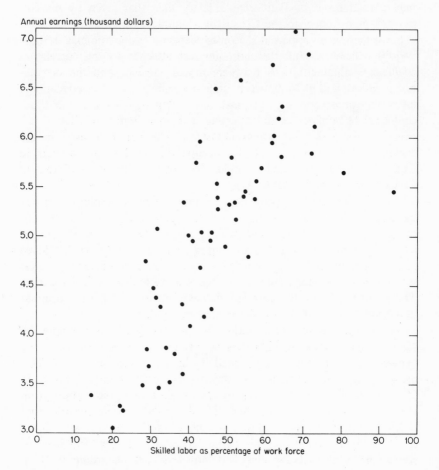

Annual earnings (thousand dollars)

Skilled labor as percentage of work force

Source: See Appendix A.

Chart 3 relates the "expected" average hourly earnings in the 59 industries to actual average annual earnings in 1959, derived from the same Census of Population sample. The reason for choosing the annual rather than the hourly series as the variable for analysis is that all other wage series used in this study from censuses of manufactures for

discrimination, but color is relevant to quality because of the likelihood that, at given levels of education, nonwhites have received poorer-quality schooling and less on-the-job training than have whites."

CHART 3

*Average Annual Earnings and "Expected" Hourly Earnings
in 59 Industry Groups in the United States, 1959*

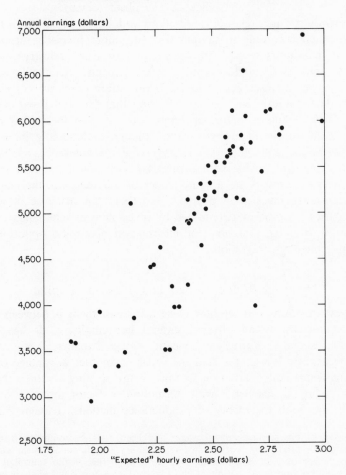

Source: See Appendix A.

the United States and other countries are on an annual basis,[26] and it
is these figures which need to be tested as a guide to the intensity of

[26] The U.S. Census of Manufactures, as well as those for most other countries,
reports total payroll and total numbers for all employees and for production
workers separately, but gives total man-hours for the latter group only. One
must therefore choose between (1) working with average annual earnings or (2)
applying the derived man-hours per production worker to salaried employees
also. Neither course is fully satisfactory, but probably there is little difference

different industries in inputs of human capital. Correlation coefficients computed between both hourly and annual earnings and expected hourly earnings are 0.79 and 0.84, respectively, both results being significant at the 1 per cent level of confidence (59 observations).

A slightly stronger relation is found, on both bases, when the variables are weighted according to sample size (or, more precisely, according to total man-hours worked in the sample for each industry), which tends to reduce the influence of erratic elements attributable to the small coverage of some industries. This procedure raises the correlation coefficient for hourly earnings to 0.81 and that for annual earnings to 0.85. These results give further support to the hypothesis that inter-industry differences in average wages, though undoubtedly influenced by unionization and other forces, largely reflect differences in human capital. They are in line with Schultz's hypothesis that "most of the differences in earnings are a consequence of differences in the amounts that have been invested in people," and that "the structure of wages and salaries is primarily determined by investment in schooling, health, on-the-job training, searching for information about job opportunities and investment in migration." [27]

Nonwage Value Added and Physical Capital

The next question is to see how close a relation there is between non-wage value added and physical capital per employee. It has been suggested above that the first concept, though broader, is not therewith necessarily less useful than the second. Another advantage of the nonwage-value-added criterion is that, being a "flow" rather than a "stock" figure, it fits better with the notion of factor inputs into production and with the theory of production functions. Though the use

for present purposes, since annual wages and hourly wages computed from the aggregates for production workers are very closely correlated. A linear correlation coefficient of 0.98 is found for 412 U.S. industries at the four-digit level in 1963, and a linear correlation of the two variables for 100 Indian industries in 1961 yields the same coefficient, both results being significant at the 1 per cent level of confidence.

The interindustry variance is greater, however, in annual than in hourly earnings in U.S. manufacturing and is positively related to interindustry differences in skills. This result arises largely because of the generally shorter hours worked by female than by male employees and the relative concentration of female employment in apparel and other low-skill industries. This explains why a higher correlation coefficient is obtained with annual earnings than with hourly earnings as the dependent variable.

[27] T. W. Schultz, "Reflections on Investment in Man," *Journal of Political Economy*, Supplement, 1962.

of the estimated stock of capital is a more conventional measure of the physical capital intensity of different industries, the stock figures may not closely reflect the flow of services from capital into the production process.[28]

The uncertainty regarding the stock figures is compounded by the familiar vintage problem, i.e., the fact that available data on capital assets include equipment and buildings acquired at various times past and at different price levels and written down according to depreciation practices varying among industries and influenced by changing tax laws. It can be argued that it is better to think of the flow of services rendered by a stock of capital as being spread evenly over its lifetime, and hence to use the original undepreciated book values. This procedure, however, fails to meet the problem that investment outlays have to be recouped much faster from some types of equipment than from others and faster from equipment in general than from buildings.

Fortunately, the data on capital assets in different industries at the end of 1957 obtained by a special survey in connection with the 1958 Census of Manufactures make it possible to use the figures both before and after deducting depreciation and depletion. Inventories can also be added in and an allowance made for rented assets on the basis of data reported on rents paid.[29] The outcome is that a meaningful association is found between nonwage value added per employee and physical assets per employee, with assets measured either gross or net. Using the logarithms of these variables for 276 four-digit industries, the coefficient of correlation is 0.81 on the first basis and 0.80 on the second, both results being significant at the 1 per cent level of confidence.[30]

[28] For a discussion of the problems encountered in working with data on the stock of capital as inputs into production, see Edward F. Denison, *The Sources of Economic Growth in the United States and the Alternatives Before Us,* New York, 1962, pp. 94–98.

[29] The gross-assets series used here consists of the sum of (1) gross book value of fixed assets at the end of 1957, (2) inventories at the end of 1957, and (3) rentals paid during 1957 multiplied by 7 to approximate the capital value of the rented assets. The net series used consists of the foregoing minus the sum of (4) accumulated depreciation to the end of 1956 and (5) depreciation charged during 1957. For a fuller statement of sources and methods, see Appendix A.

[30] There is no economic theory to determine a priori the correct functional form, arithmetic or logarithmic, for these correlations. Use of the arithmetic form presumes that there is a relation between the absolute differences from industry to industry in each of the two variables (i.e., physical assets per employee and nowage value added per employee), and use of the logarithmic form presumes that there is a relation between the percentage differences from industry to industry in each of the variables. Appendix A gives the results of a test for linearity and a test for homoscedasticity, or homogeneity of variance, undertaken to help in judging the appropriate form of correlation.

CHART 4

Nonwage Value Added and Net Physical Assets per Employee
in U.S. Manufacturing by 122 Three-Digit Industries, 1957

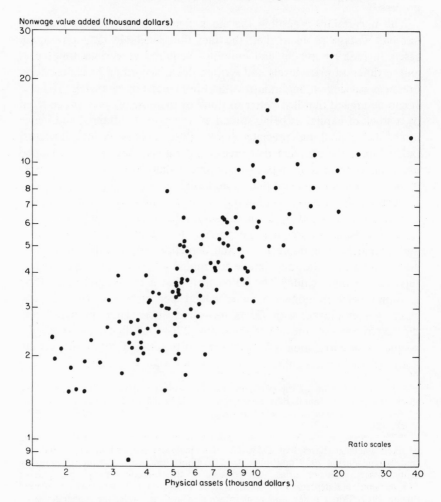

Nonwage value added (thousand dollars)

Ratio scales

Physical assets (thousand dollars)

Source: See Appendix A.

The net-assets series is plotted against nonwage value added per employee in Chart 4 (covering 122 industries at the three-digit level), and both of these series are reproduced in Table A-2 (also covering three-digit industries only).[31]

[31] At the three-digit level (122 industries) the coefficients of correlation are 0.80 with assets on a gross basis and 0.81 with assets on a net basis.

Advertising and Other Influences on Value Added

Advertising expenditures are, as previously mentioned, among the purchased services reflected in nonwage value added by manufacture, and differences from industry to industry in the one may help to explain differences in the other. This influence could scarcely be a dominant one, since total advertising expenditures reported to the Internal Revenue Service by manufacturing corporations for 1957–58 amounted to $4.4 billion, not all of which would be allocated to their manufacturing establishments and included in the $55.9 billion of nonwage value added shown (for 1957) in Table 3.[32] Advertising outlays are, however, concentrated in certain industries, notably foods, tobacco, drugs and chemicals, and electrical appliances and machinery, these four major groups accounting for almost half of the total cited for 1957–58. Whether considered as current expenditures or as an indication of likely past advertising and of the return realized on investment in good will, advertising may make up more of value added in the industries in question than it does in others and, in such cases, would weaken the reliability of value added per employee as a measure of capital intensity.

This supposition seems to be borne out by Table 4, covering industries in which nonwage value added per employee exceeds by a wide margin (i.e., by more than two standard errors) what would be expected on the basis of their physical assets. These industries all belong to the groups just mentioned. Their advertising expenditures, with the sole exception of electric lamps, also appear very high in relation to physical assets, on the basis of data drawn from Internal Revenue sources. Unfortunately, the two sets of data are not closely comparable, not only because of differences in coverage but also because of the more summary nature of the IRS classification. As a result, the rate of advertising outlays in breakfast cereals, chewing gum, and cigarettes, for example, would no doubt be greatly understated in the data for the broader groups with which these products are merged in the IRS list. If allowance is made for these effects, it seems clear that advertising expenses help to explain the wider deviations noted, on the high side, in nonwage value added compared with physical assets.[33] The number of such

[32] On the other hand, the figure of $4.4 billion would not include advertising by unincorporated manufacturing firms. Data are from *Statistics of Income— 1957–58, Corporation Income Tax Returns*, Washington, 1960, p. 26.

[33] It would be more to the point to show advertising per employee, rather than in relation to assets, but employment is not reported on the corporate tax returns underlying the Internal Revenue statistics. The Bureau of the Census has, however, compiled from its own (establishment) records 1958 employment figures for "matched corporations" accounting for 91 per cent of total receipts of corporations in the IRS universe. (See especially Table 7 in *Enterprise Statistics:*

TABLE 4

Manufacturing Industries with Exceptionally High Nonwage Value Added per Employee (1957) and High Advertising Expenditures (1957–58) in Relation to Physical Assets

| | Data on Establishment Basis Used in Census of Manufactures | | | Data on Company Basis Used in Internal Revenue Reports | | | |
| | Nonwage Value Added per Employee | | | | | | |
SIC Number and Industry Name[a]	Actual Average (dollars) (1)	Indicated by Assets (dollars) (2)	Ratio of 1 to 2 (per cent) (3)	IRS Number and Industry Name[b]	Advertising Expenditures ($ million) (4)	Physical Assets ($ million) (5)	Ratio of 4 to 5 (per cent) (6)
All manufacturing	4,876	—	—	All manufacturing	4,424	130,205	3.4
2043 Cereal breakfast foods	13,190	4,229	312	207 Cereal preparations	26	165	15.8
2052 Biscuits and crackers	7,460	3,279	228	204 Bakery products	111	874	12.7
2073 Chewing gum	16,579	6,596	251	206 Confectionery and related products	54	416	13.0
2091 Leavening compounds	17,747	5,972	297	208-9 Other food and kindred products[c]	243	1,357	17.9
2111 Cigarettes	24,158	9,921	244	211 Tobacco products, excl. cigars[d]	210	2,086	10.1
2834 Pharmaceutical preparations	16,440	6,030	273	282 Drugs and medicines	255	1,012	25.2
2841 Soap and glycerin	20,449	7,624	268	283 Soap and glycerin cleaning and polishing preparations	173	494	35.0
2842 Cleaning and polishing products	13,529	5,948	227				
2893 Toilet preparations	17,589	5,045	349	285 Perfumes, cosmetics, and other toilet preparations	108	164	65.9
3584 Vacuum cleaners	9,438	4,234	223	362 Electric appliances	25	272	9.2
3651 Electric lamps (bulbs)	7,898	3,214	246	365 Electric lamps	0.4	13	3.1
3663 Phonograph records	8,442	3,587	235	366 Radio, radar, and television equipment and phonographs	100	1,371	7.3

Notes to Table 4

Source: For nonwage value-added data, see Appendix A. Data on advertising and physical assets are from *Source Book of Statistics of Income* for 1957-58.

ªStandard Industrial Classification prior to 1957 revision.

ᵇAdaptation of SIC by Internal Revenue Service.

ᶜCombined from No. 208, "other food, including manufactured ice and flavoring syrups," and No. 209, "food and kindred products, not allocable." It is to be noted that these two miscellaneous subgroups account for about 16 per cent of fixed assets and about 30 per cent of advertising in the food group in 1957–58 and are very much broader than SIC 2091, with which they are paired in this table.

ᵈListed as "other tobacco products."

deviations is relatively few, though a similar relation to advertising would no doubt be found for some other industries, including some of the apparel group, if less extreme deviations were also examined.

Some of these industries, as well as others showing relatively high nonwage value added per employee, would also have large research and development outlays and large central office expenses.[34] High rates of return on capital are a further important influence. Thus, Stigler estimated the rate of return, after tax, in 1957 at 7.28 per cent in tobacco products, 5.60 per cent in motor vehicles, 4.68 per cent in chemicals, and 4.71 in electrical machinery and equipment, compared with an average rate of return of 3.81 in all manufacturing industry.[35]

1958, Part 3, "Link of Census Establishment and IRS Corporation Data," Series ES 3, No. 3, Washington, 1964.) On the basis of these figures, it may be roughly estimated that advertising expenditures per employee in 1957–58 were in the order of $2,500 in drugs and medicines, $4,000 in soap and other cleaning and polishing preparations, and $3,500 in perfumes, cosmetics, and toilet preparations (these calculations being confined here to those industries for which the product coverage in the IRS series does not appear to be significantly wider than that of the four-digit items from the Census of Manufactures with which they are matched in Table 4).

[34] Research and development work done outside the manufacturing establishment may be (1) purchased as a service from other firms, or (2), in the case of multiestablishment firms, conducted by the central office and costs allocated back to the individual producing units. In either event, the costs would tend to be reflected in higher nonwage value added in these units. Similarly, other central office expenses would be allocated to the producing units and reflected in their value added.

[35] George J. Stigler, *Capital and Rates of Return in Manufacturing Industries,* Princeton for NBER, 1963 (see especially Table 2 of errata statement issued July 6, 1964). It should be noted that the rates of return in Stigler's study are computed in relation to all corporate assets (except investments in other companies) and would be larger in relation to physical assets only.

Differential rates of return on investment may also help to explain downward deviations in observed compared with expected nonwage value added per employee. As may be seen in Table A-2, the textile and wood products industries figure prominently in this group, a position consistent with Stigler's estimated average rate of return in 1957 of only 1.38 per cent in textile mill products and 1.16 per cent in lumber and wood products. In addition, the amount of value added reported by textile manufacturing establishments producing "gray goods" may be held down by the allocation of profits from finishing the fabric (i.e., bleaching, dyeing, and printing) to sales or head offices.[36] And in some of the wood products industries value added may appear relatively low because of the inclusion of timber holdings in assets. More generally, multifirm companies benefiting from depletion allowances in their tax returns may find it advantageous to shift profits from the manufacturing to the raw-material phase of their business, a factor which would tend to reduce value added in petroleum refining and in various of the primary metal industries and nonmetallic mineral industries.

These various explanations and qualifications, along with those noted previously, need to be kept in mind in any attempt to measure and compare the capital intensity of different industries, but they do not argue uniformly in favor of the use of either the stock or the flow series. The fact that the two series are significantly correlated does, however, tend to strengthen confidence in both of them. Support of nonwage value added per employee as a measure of capital intensity in different industries is particularly helpful in view of the greater availability of this kind of information for other countries, and for past periods in the United States, through censuses of manufactures.

Supporting Data from India

Assets data for another country of special interest in this study, India, are available by detailed industry breakdown and can be compared with nonwage value added per employee in the same manner as for the United States. These variables for 115 Indian industries in 1961 are given in Chart 5.[37] In logarithmic form, the coefficient of

[36] For a brief description of the way the production process is divided and organized, see section on "Dyeing and Finishing Textiles, except Wool Fabrics and Knit Goods," *1963 Census of Manufactures*, Vol. II, Pt. 1, pp. 22C—1–4.

[37] Two of the 117 industries used in the comparison of India and the United States in the next chapter (see Chart 13) are omitted here. Their inclusion would raise the correlation coefficient quoted above to 0.87 (or to 0.91 in a linear regression). This result is attributable, however, to the undue influence of one

CHART 5

*Nonwage Value Added and Net Productive Assets per Employee
in 115 Manufacturing Industries, India, 1961*

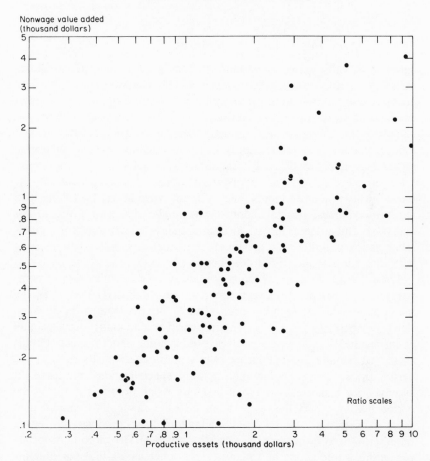

Source: See Appendix A.

of the omitted industries, petroleum refining, for which both productive assets
and nonwage value added per employee are extremely high in India—$33,827
and $8,244, respectively. The second omitted industry, carpet weaving, is at the
other end of the scale and is very low in productive assets per employee in
India, $585, and lower still, relatively speaking, in nonwage value added, $61
(though data for 1962, which have subsequently become available, indicate that
the relative size of these two variables—$609 and $155, respectively—is much
closer to that given by the regression equation).

correlation between these two variables is 0.78.[38] These results thus provide additional support for the use of nonwage value added per employee as a guide to interindustry differences in the intensity of capital inputs.

Indirect Inputs and the Role of Natural Resources

The use of value added by manufacture as a guide to capital requirements per employee is subject to the possible criticism that it takes into account only direct inputs into manufacturing. Perhaps, as Leontief endeavored to do in his oft-cited computations of physical capital per employee in United States foreign trade,[39] we should also include indirect capital and labor inputs into growing, digging, or otherwise producing the materials used in manufacture. This still would not make flour or meat or cement labor-intensive and probably none of the metals, whose material inputs tend to be intensive in capital (along with natural resources, which Leontief was unable to incorporate in his analysis). But some other products might show rather different capital-labor ratios if indirect factor inputs into materials are counted along with direct inputs into the processing or manufacturing phase.

Even if true, the point is scarcely relevant to a consideration of comparative advantage in different manufacturing industries insofar as the materials needed are readily transportable internationally. In all such items competition takes place in the world's commodity markets, and countries which do not themselves produce the materials can import them. To include indirect factor inputs in these cases fits ill with the very purpose of explaining international specialization and trade. It assumes, for instance, that Japan or Hong Kong produces not only the cotton textiles which they export but also the raw cotton embodied in these exports, or that the United Kingdom itself produces the crude oil entering into its exports of refined products.[40] The more appropriate procedure would surely be to count only direct inputs into manufactur-

---

[38] With reference to footnote 30 above, see Appendix A for the results of tests for linearity and for homoscedasticity made to assist in determining whether the arithmetic or the logarithmic form of correlation is appropriate.

[39] Leontief, "Domestic Production and Foreign Trade," and "Factor Proportions and the Structure of American Trade."

[40] In the summary record of an international conference on these and related issues, Bertil Ohlin is reported as "very worried that 98 per cent of reasoning in international trade theory was based on the assumption that the whole of a good was produced in one country. Countries did import raw materials and export semimanufactures." From Roy Harrod (ed.), *International Trade Theory in a Developing World*, London, 1963, p. 398.

ing in considering the influence of factor intensities on the location of such industries.[41]

Resource-Oriented Manufacturing Industries

Some primary products are, however, too perishable or too bulky to bear transportation costs over long distances without first undergoing some processing. This is particularly true of certain foodstuffs, notably fresh fish, fruit, and vegetables.[42] In such products the location of the processing industries is determined far more by the availability of the material inputs on the spot than by the relative requirements and supplies of capital and labor for processing the materials. At least for these industries, therefore, one needs to push the question back one stage and ask what determines the location of primary production. An answer must allow for the influence of soil, climate, and other natural conditions and encounters the familiar difficulty of distinguishing and measuring the contribution of natural resources on the same basis as that of labor and capital.[43]

In passing, it may be recalled that the unavoidable absence of natural resources in Leontief's simplified two-factor model is one of the most crucial and most criticized features of his analysis of factor proportions in United States foreign trade, and one which leaves his paradoxical findings of uncertain significance.[44] The problem is, fortunately, of much more limited importance in the present inquiry, which omits primary products altogether and focuses on labor-intensive manufactures. At least a rough and impressionistic judgment can be attempted for those few labor-intensive manufactures which also appear to be strongly resource-oriented. These items will be included in the trade flows

[41] This is also the view expressed by Donald B. Keesing in "Labor Skills and International Trade: Evaluating Many Trade Flows with a Single Measuring Device," *Review of Economics and Statistics,* August 1965, pp. 287–294.

[42] Even in these groups select qualities destined for high-income markets may move to distant points by swift air or surface transport.

[43] This problem is explored at length by Jaroslav Vanek in *The Natural Resource Content of United States Foreign Trade, 1870–1955,* Cambridge, Mass., 1963. Vanek found it necessary to work with what he defined as "resource products" rather than with resource requirements.

[44] This view was strongly expressed in several early commentaries on Leontief's results, including those by Boris C. Swerling, "Capital Shortage and Labor Surplus in the United States," *Review of Economics and Statistics,* August 1954; Norman S. Buchanan, "Lines on the Leontief Paradox," *Economia Internazionale,* November 1955; Irving B. Kravis, "Availability and Other Influences on the Commodity Composition of Trade," *Journal of Political Economy,* April 1956; and M. A. Diab, *The United States Capital Position and the Structure of its Foreign Trade,* Amsterdam, 1956.

examined in Chapter 4 only if the availability of low-cost labor seems to be decisive in determining the location of the primary production to which the processing is tied by transportation costs.

For present purposes, it seems plausible to assume that the natural conditions governing the supply of fish, fruit, and vegetables are not peculiar to only a few of the less developed countries, compared with others or with more developed countries, and that the production of these inputs as well as their processing into transportable form is decisively influenced by the supply of low-cost labor.[45] These products in canned or preserved form, along with certain other food products less closely tied to the local production of material inputs, are accordingly treated here as labor-intensive. The same assumption is not made, it may be noted, with respect to meat and meat products, which are supplied mainly by Argentina among the less developed countries and reflect a heavy natural-resource input into range-fed cattle. In this case and others like it, it is the resource factor that determines the location of the primary production and, therewith, the location also of the processing industry.

Outside the food group, there are only a few other industries where the location of labor-intensive manufacturing seems to be fairly closely tied to local sources of the material inputs. These concern mainly various extracts and materials of vegetable origin usually classed with chemicals: tanning extracts; medicinal and pharmaceutical products; and essential oils, perfume, and flavoring materials (items 532, 541, and 551 of the Standard International Trade Classification). Only with regard to the last of these groups is it here assumed that the supporting primary production is predominantly influenced by the supply and cost of labor, though even in this case some of the important commodities in the group are unique to certain localities.

[45] Peru's striking success since the early 1950's in developing the production and export of fish meal (included here in the selection of labor-intensive manufactures) has, of course, been conditioned upon the usually abundant supply of anchovy brought near its shores by the Humboldt Current. But low labor costs would seem to be decisive in making the product competitive with other low-unit-value animal feedstuffs such as soyabean and meat meal.

3

INTERNATIONAL COMPARISONS
OF FACTOR INTENSITIES

The Phenomenon of Factor-Intensity Reversals

The evidence for the United States examined in the preceding chapter indicates that value added per employee in manufacturing provides a reasonably good guide to the capital intensity of different industries, reflecting inputs of human as well as physical capital. It may be asked, however, whether any pattern of industries by factor intensity discerned for the United States would hold true for other countries. Doubt on this score is natural, given the lower wage rates and higher capital costs generally prevailing in other countries, especially the less developed ones. All industries will no doubt tend to use more labor in relation to capital in poor, low-wage countries than in richer ones, at least in auxiliary services if not in basic production processes.[1] But if this substitution tendency were stronger in some industries than in others, the ranking of industries by factor intensity would also differ from country to country.[2] And if the tendency were widespread, it would mean that—contrary to the "strong-factor-intensity" hypothesis underlying the factor proportions theorem—one could not confidently rank industries according to their requirements of labor and capital, nor look at the relative factor endowments of different countries for clues to the likely composition and direction of their foreign trade.[3]

[1] In *The Economics of Underdeveloped Countries* (New York, 1966, pp. 188–191), Jagdish Bhagwati gives an illuminating discussion of various ways in which, with a given production process, the amount of labor per unit of capital can be varied.

[2] R. F. Harrod was one of the first, if not the first, to point out the possibility or, as he saw it, the likelihood of this result. See his "Factor-Price Relations under Free Trade," *Economic Journal,* June 1958, pp. 245–255.

[3] For a review of the literature on this subject, see Michael Michaely, "Factor Proportions in International Trade: Current State of the Theory," *Kyklos* XVII, fasc. 4, 1964, pp. 529–550.

Plausibility is added to the notion of factor-intensity reversals by the ready observation that technology seems to be much more fixed in some industries than in others.[4] Thus, the coefficients describing the relative amounts of capital and labor used in making steel or refining petroleum might be rather rigid, but methods of rice production could vary from extremely labor-intensive to highly capital-intensive. With regard to this last example, however, it should also be noted that illustrations of wide variability in factor combinations given in the literature are almost always taken from agriculture and rarely, if ever, from industry.[5]

What was largely regarded as a theoretical curiosity took on new force with the appearance of Leontief's paradox. One way of explaining his results, but one which Leontief himself did not propose, was to accept them as casting doubt on the strong-factor-intensity hypothesis.[6] That is to say, the goods comprising United States imports might be, as ordinarily expected, more labor-intensive than other foreign goods when produced abroad, even though similar ("import-competing") goods produced in this country were found to be relatively capital-intensive in Leontief's analysis.[7]

[4] See, for example, Jack Baranson, "Is There a Direct Route to Development?" *Challenge,* July 1964.

[5] See the cases cited by Charles P. Kindleberger in *Foreign Trade and the National Economy* (New Haven, 1962), p. 76. Lloyd G. Reynolds in a discussion at the 1965 meetings of the American Economic Association made the same point (including, however, the textile industry): "Our examples of labor-using adaptation seem always to come from agriculture, where factor proportions are notoriously flexible, or from textile production" (*American Economic Review,* May 1966, p. 113).

[6] This view is expressed with some emphasis in a note on "The Leontief Paradox" by S. R. Merrett in the *Economic Journal,* September 1965, page 641: "I suggest," he writes, "that Leontief's nonsense conclusion (that America imports capital-intensive goods) derives not from the conjunction of an invalid argument with true premises, but from the conjunction of a valid argument with a false premise. It is a simple and significant proposition that there is more than one way of producing most goods. This . . . is what makes the Heckscher-Ohlin theory almost valueless."

Kindleberger writes in a somewhat similar vein with regard to Leontief's findings: "What he proves is not that the United States is capital-scarce and labor-abundant, but that the Heckscher-Ohlin theorem is wrong." He adds: "When goods change their factor intensities from country to country, depending on factor endowments and factor prices, the Heckscher-Ohlin theorem falls to the ground." (*Foreign Trade and the National Economy,* pp. 75, 76.)

[7] Haberler suggests that the explanation of Leontief's results is that he operates, in fact, not from a two-factor but from a many-factor model. These include not only labor and capital but also various other factors such as "natural resources," "management," and "entrepreneurship," even though these other factors cannot be included, at least so far, in Leontief's statistical measurements. "The existence of factors other than those explicitly treated," Haberler states, "implies that the production functions, *in terms of labor and capital,* are not

Different Elasticities of Substitution

More specific evidence supporting the possibility of factor intensity reversals between countries has been developed by Bagicha S. Minhas, making use of a "Constant Elasticity of Substitution" (CES) production function developed earlier in collaboration with Arrow, Chenery, and Solow.[8] The underlying hypothesis is that, in any given industry, capital would be substituted for labor in a constant relation to increases in the ratio of labor costs to capital costs, but that the rate of substitution would vary from one industry to another depending essentially on the range of technological choices available for combining the two factors. In other words, a higher level of wages in relation to capital costs would always produce some tendency to substitute capital for labor, but at a slower rate in, say, steel than in textiles.

These possibilities are illustrated, in a purely hypothetical manner, in Chart 6. The amount of capital per worker (K/L) is measured on the vertical axis, and the ratio of wages to capital costs (w/r) on the horizontal axis. Both scales being logarithmic, a straight line portrays a constant elasticity of substitution and its slope measures the elasticity. Low elasticities are here assumed for both petroleum refining and leather products, the first remaining strongly capital-intensive and the second strongly labor-intensive throughout. A higher elasticity of substitution is assumed for furniture and a still higher elasticity for food products, the latter ranking lowest in capital intensity in the extreme left area of the chart but even surpassing petroleum refining in the extreme right area.

On the further assumptions indicated in the chart regarding the relative ratios of wages to capital costs in Southern Asia, Japan, Western Europe, and the United States, the ranking of industries in descending order of capital intensity would vary as follows from one area to another:

	Southern Asia	Japan	Western Europe	United States
Petroleum refining	1	1	1	2
Furniture	2	2	3	3
Food products	4	3	2	1
Leather products	3	4	4	4

necessarily homogeneous and that the production functions are not the same in different countries" (Gottfried Haberler, *A Survey of International Trade Theory,* Princeton, 1961, pp. 21–22).

[8] *An International Comparison of Factor Costs and Factor Use,* Amsterdam, 1963, and "Capital-Labor Substitution and Economic Efficiency" by K. J. Arrow, H. B. Chenery, B. S. Minhas, and R. M. Solow, *Review of Economics and Statistics,* August 1961.

CHART 6

Hypothetical Illustration of Factor-Intensity Reversals with Constant
Elasticity of Substitution Between Capital and Labor

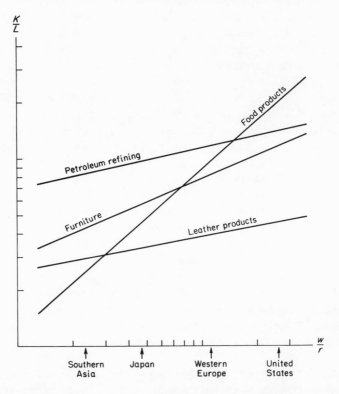

Reasoning from this type of analysis and with estimates of elasticities
of substitution developed from international cross-sectional data for a
limited number of industries, Minhas states that it is impossible to
characterize industries as labor-intensive or capital-intensive without
regard to differences in the ratio of wages to capital costs, and further
that, in the case of any two industries with different elasticities of substitution, "the reversal of relative factor-intensity is as inevitable as the
meeting of two straight lines with different slopes." [9] The only question,
he adds, is whether the reversal occurs within the observable range of
relative factor prices.

[9] A fuller theoretical analysis of these possibilities is given by Harry G. John-
son, "Factor Endowments, International Trade and Factor Prices," *Manchester
School of Economic and Social Studies,* September 1957 (reprinted in Johnson's
International Trade and Economic Growth, Cambridge, Mass., 1961).

The capstone to Minhas' argument is a comparison of the ranking of twenty industries by capital intensity in the United States and Japan, capital intensity being measured by the stock of fixed capital per worker. If the rankings of industries were not similar between countries, this would indicate that factor-intensity reversals had occurred. The comparison between the United States and Japan is of special interest because of the broad range of industry in the two countries along with wide disparities in the relative amounts and prices of labor and capital. Table 5, reproduced from Minhas' study, shows the rankings of the twenty industries in each country based first on total inputs of capital and labor and then on direct inputs only. The comparison based on total inputs, which Minhas favors, shows a Spearman rank correlation coefficient of only 0.328, far from enough to support the strong factor-intensity hypothesis. The comparison based on direct inputs only yields a much higher coefficient of 0.730, but, he says, sufficiently far from unity "to provide room for reversals in relative capital-intensity to take place" (page 41).

Minhas concludes therefore that the phenomenon of factor reversals is "general enough to be empirically important" (page 40) and "robs the factor proportions theory of any predictive significance in regard to the direction of trade" (page 50). He also makes an "empirical observation" which, if valid, would have major implications for investment policy in less developed countries:

The observation is that the labor abundant, low wage countries would tend to hold comparative advantage in those industries which have low elasticities of substitution between capital and labor *even though* those very industries happen to be relatively capital-intensive at the prevailing relative cost of labor and capital.[10]

This advice seems to mean that the less developed countries should not hesitate to invest even in very capital-intensive industries, the reason given being that more developed countries "may be able to take advantage of the relative cheapness of capital relatively more in those industries which have higher elasticities of substitution between capital and labor." In terms of the hypothetical examples given in Chart 6 and, presumably, with an eye toward relative wage and capital costs in the distant future, Southern Asia might find it advantageous on Minhas' line of argument to invest in industries typified by petroleum refining, while the United States would do better in those typified by food products.

Since this view has an evident interest for less developed countries

[10] P. 48 (italics in the original).

TABLE 5

Ranking of U.S. and Japanese Industries by Capital
Intensity According to B. S. Minhas

Name of Industry	Ranks Based on Total Capital and Labor Requirements		Ranks Based on Direct Capital and Labor Requirements	
	U.S.	Japan	U.S.	Japan
Petroleum products	1	1	1	1
Coal products	2	2	2	2
Agriculture	3	20	3	14
Grain-mill products	4	19	9	6
Processed foods	5	13	10	7
Chemicals	6	5	6	4
Nonferrous metals	7	4	4	3
Iron and steel	8	3	5	5
Paper and products	9	11	7	15
Nonmetallic mineral products	10	9	8	11
Textiles	11	15	18	12
Transport equipment	12	10	11	9
Machinery	13	6	12	10
Rubber and products	14	12	14	16
Shipbuilding	15	7	13	8
Lumber and wood	16	17	15	17
Industry, n.e.c.	17	16	17	20
Printing and publishing	18	8	16	18
Leather	19	18	19	19
Apparel	20	14	20	13

Source: Bagicha Singh Minhas, *An International Comparison of Factor Costs and Factor Use,* Amsterdam, 1963, p. 40.

in search of guiding principles for their investment decisions, it may be useful to consider the reasons for the author's failure to find a stronger relation between the rankings of United States and Japanese industries.

The Natural Resource Factor Again

The unavoidable omission of natural resources from both direct and indirect inputs is no less crucial to Minhas' two-factor model, and to the conclusions drawn from it, than it is to Leontief's. In commentaries published about the same time, Gary Hufbauer and David Ball have challenged the inclusion of agriculture as one of the twenty industries figuring in Minhas' comparison of factor intensities in the United States and Japan (Table 5), given the vastly different endowments of the two countries in farmland.[11] They expressed the same doubts regarding two other industries, grain mill products and processed foods, which also have a high resource content when total (indirect as well as direct) inputs are counted. Omitting all three of these industries, both critics found that the Spearman rank correlation coefficient moved up from only 0.328 to 0.765, based on total factor inputs. The correlation coefficient is further raised to 0.833 if only agriculture is omitted and the calculation is based on direct factor inputs only.

Ball offered a further comparison of capital intensities in United States and Japanese industry on the basis of data given by Arrow, Chenery, Minhas, and Solow in their paper on the "Constant Elasticity of Substitution" production function.[12] He found a rank correlation of 0.603 for all twenty-seven industries covered in the source, including eighteen in manufacturing, six in primary production, and electric power, transport, and trade. As the nonmanufacturing industries were eliminated from the test, the coefficient was progressively raised and, for the eighteen manufacturing industries plus electric power, reached 0.920. These computations were also on the basis of direct inputs.[13]

[11] Hufbauer's criticism is given in an appendix, "Factor Intensity Reversals," to his book *Synthetic Materials and the Theory of International Trade* (Cambridge, Mass., 1966), based on his doctoral dissertation at Cambridge University in 1963. Ball's paper, "Factor-Intensity Reversals in International Comparison of Factor Costs and Factor Use," is in the *Journal of Political Economy*, February 1966. Mention should also be made of a doctoral dissertation by Seiji Naya containing a critical appraisal of Minhas' results ("The Leontief Paradox and the Factor Structure of Japanese Foreign Trade," University of Wisconsin, 1965).

[12] See footnote 8.

[13] Minhas also based his argument in part on fitting the CES production function to selected industries, but these were of illustrative value only and, as Min-

In brief, Hufbauer's and Ball's reappraisal of the data for the United States and Japan indicates that the phenomenon of factor intensity reversals becomes a good deal less common than first appeared, once the comparison is limited to manufacturing industry and based on direct factor inputs only.[14] Their approach, it will be noted, is consistent with that taken here, which will be applied in the next section to other international comparisons on the basis of the value-added criterion.

More recent evidence on the phenomenon of factor-intensity reversals has been presented by Merle Yahr. Using estimates of elasticities of substitution developed from international cross-sectional data for two- and three-digit ISIC industries, she tests directly whether there are significant differences among them, considering each level of industry aggregation separately. The general conclusion that emerges from these tests is that there are no statistically significant differences among the elasticities of substitution.[15]

Problems of International Comparison

For purposes of international comparison, the use of value added per employee as a guide to interindustry variations in capital intensity has the great advantage that the basic data needed are available from censuses of manufactures for a considerable number of countries and frequently for more than one year. Various problems arise, however, in using and interpreting these statistical resources. Those having to do with differences in market forces will first be noted, and then others more specifically concerned with the comparability of the data.

has seemed to recognize, of interest largely because of the "fewness of the cases in which factor-intensity reversals are shown" (Minhas, *Factor Costs and Factor Use*, p. 39). Leontief examined this part of Minhas' analysis in detail and, on the basis of supplemental computations, found that the evidence "does not confirm Minhas' emphatically stated conclusion" against the strong factor-intensity assumption ("An International Comparison of Factor Costs and Factor Use," review article, *American Economic Review*, June 1964, pp. 335–345).

[14] Minhas maintains (p. 41) that "if we restrict attention to direct factor inputs only we no longer remain within the bounds of a two-factor world and all sorts of extraneous things (like differences in the degree of vertical integration among industries) can affect the nature of the results." To the extent that he is right about the effects on the comparability of the data (and other problems in this regard are noted below), the significance of the correlations found would be enhanced.

[15] M. I. Yahr, "Estimating the Elasticity of Substitution From International Manufacturing Census Data" (unpublished Ph.D. dissertation, Department of Economics, Columbia University, 1967), pp. 100–101.

Differing Degrees of Market Freedom

In beginning the analysis of data for the United States in Chapter 2, it was noted that various kinds of interferences with competition in factor and product markets may affect the reliability of value added per employee as a measure of differences among industries in capital intensity. Without implying any normative judgment, there is some reason to suspect that these interferences are stronger in many foreign countries, particularly in some of the less developed countries, than in the United States.

For instance, it is fairly common practice in the less developed countries to provide loans, including loans by international agencies, at preferential rates of interest to industries selected for promotion as compared with the terms available to other borrowers. Such industries may also benefit by accelerated depreciation allowances or other forms of subsidy.

The influence of unionization or, perhaps still more, of minimum wages on the structure of wages across industries and across different groups of the population may be significantly greater in some of the less developed countries than in more advanced ones.

To the extent that, for these or other reasons, factor-price ratios are not the same for all industries in a given country, the ranking of industries by factor intensity would be disturbed compared with that which would otherwise prevail, without thereby constituting genuine cases of factor-intensity reversal.[16] A further difficulty for the value-added criterion in particular is presented by differential monopoly rents in different industries brought about by a combination of controls on new entries or on the expansion of existing enterprises and highly protective tariffs along with quantitative restrictions on imports. These conditions are frequently encountered in less developed countries, whether specifically intended as a form of aid to particular industries or arising out of the scarcity of investment funds and foreign exchange receipts.

---

[16] In commenting on an early draft of the present study, Jagdish Bhagwati has stressed to the author the likelihood that different industries will, in fact, face different factor-price ratios within the same country, particularly in some of the less developed countries. He has also pointed out in this connection that the fitting of CES production functions to selected industries across countries poses a weaker test of the strong-factor-intensity hypothesis than the correlation method relied on in this study. The first requires only the assumption that firms everywhere will seek to minimize costs. The second requires, in addition, the assumption that factor-price ratios (though differing among countries) are everywhere the same within a given country.

Differences in Statistical Concepts

The concepts employed in censuses of manufactures in different countries are broadly similar, but they are not identical. Gross value of output by manufacturing establishments is usually measured at factor cost, but sometimes, as in the West German census of 1958, is at market prices (including in the latter event excise and other indirect taxes and excluding subsidies). Items deducted from gross value to arrive at value added by manufacture generally include materials, supplies, fuel, and energy, but may differ in other respects. Depreciation is not usually subtracted out, but India does so (though reporting it separately and thus permitting adjustment). As may be seen in Table 3, above, the United States does not deduct purchased services, but recommendations adopted by the United Nations indicate that those of an "industrial nature," including maintenance and repairs performed by outside firms, should be deducted.[17]

Differences may also arise in what is included in wages and salaries and, therewith, in the separation made here between wage and nonwage value added. At least in principle, wages and salaries cover all payments made to employees whether in cash or in kind. It is not certain, however, that practice is uniform in this respect, and there seems to be still greater room for divergence in the treatment of various supplementary benefits, such as bonuses and contributions to social insurance. The earlier discussion of Table 3 makes it clear also that reported totals of wages and salaries may vary among industries and countries with differences in the prevalence of unincorporated enterprises and of multiestablishment firms. Moreover, the employment figures may inject some erratic elements into the derived averages of wage and nonwage value added per employee. This would be so if, for instance, seasonal or other part-time work is more common in certain industries in one country than in the same industries in another country.

Strict international comparability cannot therefore be expected in the available data on value added per employee in manufacturing. Were it not for these difficulties, the similarities found in the interindustry structure of value added might well be even closer than those reported below.

[17] *International Recommendations in Basic Industrial Statistics,* Series M, No. 17, Rev. 1, New York, United Nations, 1960, pp. 45–57. There is, however, room for serious doubt as to the feasibility of reporting and deducting such services unless the statistics are placed on a company (rather than establishment) basis, in which case they may lose greatly in precision by type of product covered.

Differences in Industries or Products Compared

Other and perhaps more serious problems arise with respect to the comparability of the industries or products specified in the various national censuses of manufacture. In principle, one would like to be able to make intercountry comparisons over a wide range of identical products. In practice, the smallest reporting unit is the manufacturing establishment, which can be classified according to its major product, but may make other products as well. The degree of product specialization is very high in the United States,[18] but may be less so in other countries, for which little information on this point is available. In any event, returns from individual establishments have to be combined into totals for industries and industry groups. What are ostensibly the same industries or groups in two countries—say, fertilizers or, at a higher level of aggregation, agricultural chemicals or, still higher, chemicals and allied products—may in fact differ significantly in composition of output. Even superficially, however, national classifications differ markedly in the kind and amount of industrial detail listed. International comparisons therefore necessarily entail further aggregation of items on one side or the other, or both, in the effort to achieve at least a nominal similarity of industries and groups, and therewith entail also a further loss of specificity.

The best chance of matching like with like no doubt lies in working at the lowest level of aggregation permitted by the data. This, however, may mean some sacrifice of reliability of the statistics reported, particularly those covering small industry groups in less developed countries (for which the reporting firms are likely to be either fewer in number or less able to comply closely with reporting requirements than firms in more fully developed branches of industry). Thus, the accuracy of the statistics is likely to be greater at higher levels of aggregation but, as noted, with greater uncertainty as to the comparability of the outputs covered. Given this dilemma, the course followed here is to give, first, some extremely broad comparisons for a large number of countries; then to provide a further industrial breakdown, though still at a high level of aggregation, for a more limited group of countries; and, finally, to give the most detailed breakdown possible in bilateral comparisons between the United States, on the one hand, and the United Kingdom, Japan, and India, on the other.

[18] John W. Kendrick, *Productivity Trends in the United States,* Princeton for NBER, 1961, pp. 406–407.

Analysis of Three Summary Groups

Chart 7 presents data for twenty countries on value added in three very broad groups of industry, exclusive of food, beverages, and tobacco.[19] The composition of the three groups has been determined by reference to the data for the United States presented in Chart 1. Thus, Group I consists of those industries which, in the United States, appear to be most labor-intensive by the criterion of value added—i.e., clothing, textiles, leather goods, furniture, other wood products, and miscellaneous manufactures. Group III includes just two major industry groups, chemicals and petroleum refining, which in the United States are the most capital-intensive of all. And Group II comprises machinery, electrical goods, basic metals, and various other major industry groups which are, on the average, relatively capital-intensive, though much less so than those in Group III, and (as noted for the United States in Chapter 2) some of their component industries fall within the labor-intensive sector.

At least as far as these three broad groups of industry are concerned, the pattern found for the United States with respect to value added per employee and its wage and nonwage components is fairly well confirmed by most other countries. The averages rise appreciably in almost all cases from Group I to Group II, and in all cases from Group II to Group III. In the first comparison Argentina and Colombia are the only exceptions. The distortion of the relative position of the industry groups in Argentina, compared with other countries, probably reflects the high degree of state intervention under Perón, notably in wage policies that favored the *descamisados* irrespective of skills. It is also interesting to observe, however, that the spread of average wages from Group I to Groups II and III is wider in the United States and Canada, and wider still in Japan, than it is in a number of other countries, including some of the less developed countries in addition to Argentina. As noted in Chapter 4, this subdued variability in wages may bear unfavorably on the ability of such less developed countries to compete in labor-intensive manufactures.

The percentage distributions of value added given on the left side of Chart 7 show a remarkably stable pattern for the developed countries. Among these countries, with one or two slight exceptions in each case, the industries in Group I account for some 20 to 25 per cent of

---

[19] The industries included in each group are identified at the top of the chart by their numbers in the International Standard Industrial Classification, the names of which are given in the note to the chart.

total value added in manufacturing, exclusive of food, beverages, and tobacco, those in Group II for 65 to 70 per cent, and those in Group III for 10 to 15 per cent. Not surprisingly, the share contributed by Group I, the labor-intensive industries, is much higher and exhibits more variability in the less developed countries depicted in the chart, usually falling in the range of 30 to 50 per cent and rising even higher in Egypt and Pakistan. The share of Group III is also generally higher in these countries, while that of Group II is usually not more than 50 per cent.[20]

If food, beverages and tobacco are also included in Group II,[21] the effect is rather uneven among the less developed countries. So far as can be judged by the reported data for these countries, the share of the food, beverage, and tobacco segment in total value added varies widely, and value added per employee in this segment is sometimes appreciably higher and sometimes appreciably lower than the corresponding over-all average. The coverage of these industries is, however, likely to be particularly uneven in less developed countries, depending, for instance, on the minimum size of reporting establishments and on how strictly small firms are made to report. For this reason, it has seemed preferable in the summary comparisons offered in Chart 7 to analyze the rest of manufacturing undisturbed by differences from country to country in the reported position of food, beverages, and tobacco. In any event, this omission chiefly affects the distribution of value added among the three main groups of industry presented and does not materially influence the comparisons made of interindustry differences in value added per employee.

Analysis of Thirteen Main Groups

Comparisons extending over all thirteen industry groups distinguished in *The Growth of World Industry* are given for nine countries in Charts 8–10. The countries selected include all of those, save Argentina,[22] with

[20] For a review of the literature on product-mix variations among countries at varying levels of development, see Yahr, "Estimating the Elasticity of Substitution," Chapter 6. Yahr also demonstrates that product-mix variations among countries are related to the skill levels of their labor forces; i.e., the underdeveloped countries specialize in industries requiring relatively more unskilled labor, and the developed countries specialize in industries requiring relatively more skilled labor.

[21] These industries (numbers 20, 21, and 22 of the ISIC) are treated as a single group in *The Growth of World Industry, 1938–1961: National Tables* (United Nations, 1963) and are therefore treated in the same way here.

[22] Argentina is less relevant as a test of the value-added criterion if, as suggested above with reference to Chart 7, the relative positions of different industries and labor groups were strongly influenced by policies under Perón.

CHART 7

Summary Analysis of Value Added by Manufacture in Twenty Countries: Three Groups of Manufacturing Industry Excluding Food, Beverages, and Tobacco

(Composition by ISIC code: I = 23–26, 29, 39; II = 27, 28, 30, 33–38; III = 31–32)

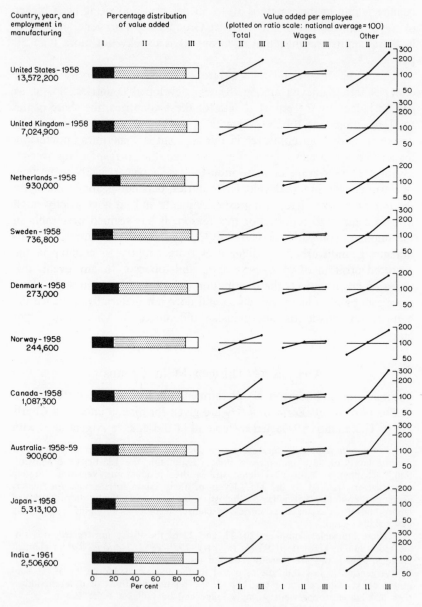

CHART 7 (*continued*)

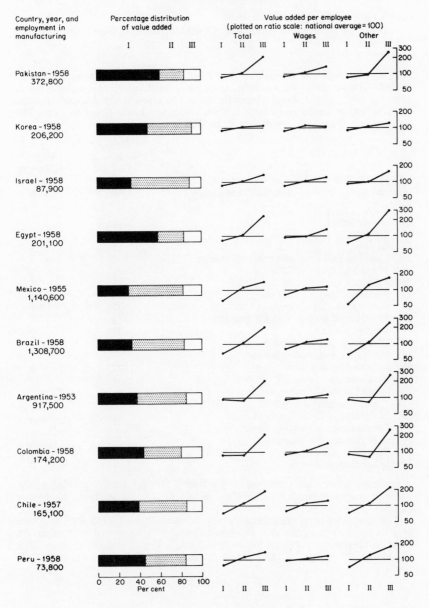

Country, year, and employment in manufacturing

Percentage distribution of value added

Value added per employee (plotted on ratio scale: national average = 100)

Total   Wages   Other

Pakistan - 1958
372,800

Korea - 1958
206,200

Israel - 1958
87,900

Egypt - 1958
201,100

Mexico - 1955
1,140,600

Brazil - 1958
1,308,700

Argentina - 1953
917,500

Colombia - 1958
174,200

Chile - 1957
165,100

Peru - 1958
73,800

Note on Sources of Data and Composition of Industry Groups in Charts 7–10

All data are from *The Growth of World Industry, 1938–1961: National Tables,* United Nations, 1963, and, for India, from the *Annual Survey of Industries, 1961,* Calcutta, 1964, Vol. I. Employment figures are as given in the national censuses of manufactures and in some cases exclude enterprises below a specified size. The composition of the industry groups is as follows:

Major (Two-Digit) Industry Groups in the *International Standard Industrial Classification*	Group to Which Assigned in Chart 7	Number Given in Charts 8–10
20 Food ⎫		
21 Beverages ⎬	Omitted	11
22 Tobacco ⎭		
23 Textiles	I	2
24 Clothing, footwear, and made-up textiles	I	1
25 Wood and cork products ⎫	I	3
26 Furniture and fixtures ⎭		
27 Paper and paper products	II	10
28 Printing and publishing	II	6
29 Leather and leather and fur products	I	4
30 Rubber products	II	9
31 Chemicals and chemical products ⎫	III	13
32 Petroleum and coal products ⎭		
33 Nometallic mineral products	II	8
34 Basic metals	II	12
35 Metal products, except machinery and transport equipment ⎫		
36 Machinery, except electrical	II	7
37 Electrical machinery, apparatus, appliances and supplies		
38 Transport equipment ⎭		
39 Other manufacturing	I	5

Bracketed groups are combined in the United Nations source specified above, and each such combination is therefore treated as a single group in the present analysis.

Two deviations from the general pattern followed in the United Nations source may be noted: (1) In the data for Brazil, group 35 is combined with group 34, affecting Charts 8–10. (2) In the wage and salary data for Sweden, group 34 is combined with groups 35–38, affecting Charts 9 and 10 (but not Chart 8).

CHART 8

Value Added per Employee in Thirteen Industry Groups, Nine Countries

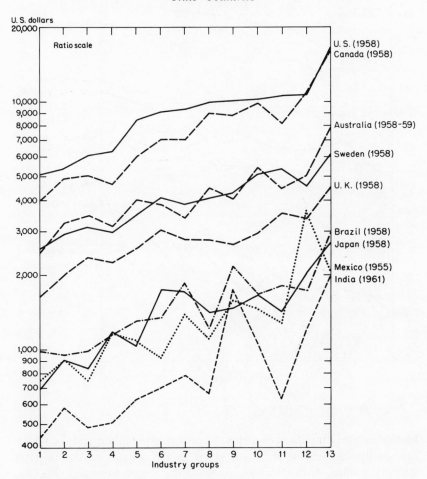

Note: See explanatory note following Chart 7.

CHART 9

Average Annual Wage in Thirteen Industry Groups,
Eleven Countries

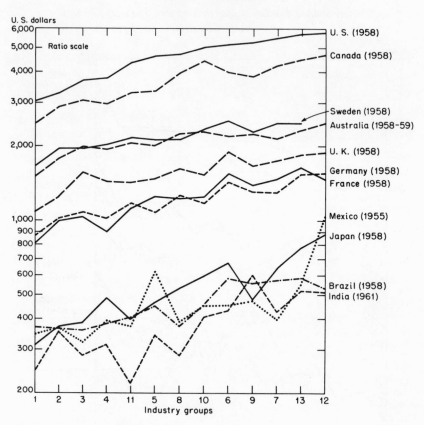

Note: See explanatory note following Chart 7.

employment in manufacturing close to or over one million and for which reasonably comparable data are given in the source on the thirteen industry groups. Unfortunately, none of the larger Continental European countries could be included,[23] but otherwise the nine constitute

[23] Value-added data are totally lacking for France and Italy in *The Growth of World Industry* and are given for West Germany on a market-price rather than factor-cost basis. Wage data for France and West Germany are, however, included in Chart 9. As previously noted, all three countries conducted censuses of manufacture in 1963, but the results became available only with great delay and too late for inclusion in this analysis.

CHART 10

Nonwage Value Added per Employee in Thirteen Industry Groups,
Nine Countries

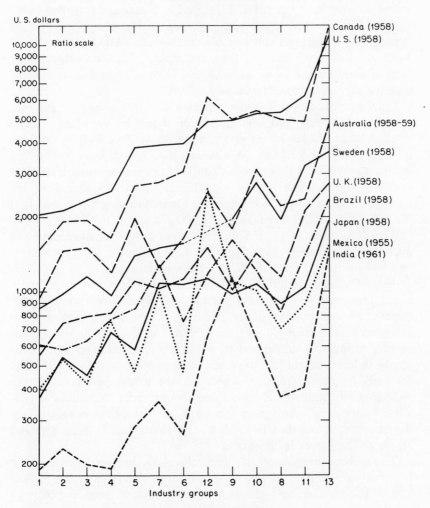

Note: See explanatory note following Chart 7.

an interesting selection. The United States, the United Kingdom, and
Sweden are highly developed economies of long standing and important
exporters of manufactures. Canada and Australia are also highly developed countries, as measured by real incomes or by the share of the

labor force outside primary production, but depend heavily on primary products for their exports. Japan, after the swift postwar growth of its production and exports of manufactures, can be regarded as a more recent addition to the group of developed countries and still shows similarities with the less developed countries in the composition of its exports and in the level and structure of its wages. Mexico, Brazil, and India are less developed countries, but differ from each other in the level of development so far attained, and none of them has yet become a major exporter of manufactured products.

Chief interest attaches to the shapes and slopes of the curves presented in the charts, and less importance should be attributed to their levels relative to each other, given the problem of converting data for other countries into dollars on a meaningful basis.[24] There can be no doubt, however, that the value-added data for the nine countries extend over a very wide range. Taken more literally than they should be, the average value added per employee in all manufacturing is some $9,000 for the United States as of 1958, $1,500 for Japan in the same year, and $800 for India in 1961. Similarly, wages and salaries per employee average approximately $5,000 for the United States, $500 for Japan, and less than $400 for India in the years indicated.

The differences just noted in average wages do not, of course, imply equal differences in labor costs per unit of output, given the wide differences among countries in the efficiency of labor. Nevertheless, these differences in average wages, along with manifest disparities in the relative supplies of skilled and unskilled labor, would seem to provide strong inducements in low-wage countries to substitute unskilled labor for skilled labor or physical capital to the extent permitted by the technological conditions of production. And if these technological possibilities are significantly greater in some industries than in others, one would expect to find the effect registered in differences in the shapes and slopes of the curves in the charts.

To facilitate comparison, all three charts are arranged in ascending order of the variables plotted for the thirteen industries in the United States. The sequence of industries varies somewhat from one chart to another, but the numerical identifications given in Chart 8 are retained in the other two. Visual inspection shows some sharp deviations,

[24] Conversions have been made at official exchange rates or, in the case of Brazil, at the "official" free rate in 1958 (138.5 cruzerios to the dollar). Note in particular that the position of Brazil relative to that of the United Kingdom and Japan seems highly suspect, especially in Chart 10, above, on nonwage value added per employee.

but nevertheless suggests in all three cases a fairly strong conformity to a common pattern. A measure of the degree of conformity is provided by Kendall's coefficient of concordance,[25] the coefficients obtained being given below together with the computed chi-squares test, indicating that all of the coefficients are significantly different from zero at the 1 per cent level of confidence:

	Coefficient of Concordance	Chi Square
Total value added per employee, nine countries	0.853	92.12
Wage value added per employee, nine countries	0.828	89.42
Ditto, including France and West Germany	0.843	91.04
Nonwage value added per employee, nine countries	0.829	89.53

The deviations observable in comparisons among the developed countries are all relatively minor, particularly in total value added per employee. And even here one would want to allow something for less than perfect comparability of outputs in the different industries as well as for the kinds of statistical aberration previously warned against.

Some of the deviations which can be observed in comparing the less developed countries with the United States and other developed countries are more disturbing. Value added per employee (along with nonwage value added per employee) seems very high in rubber products (No. 9 in the chart), compared with the rest of manufacturing, in India and, to a lesser extent, also in Brazil—a result suggesting that the production of tires and tubes, which figure prominently among rubber products in these countries, is less amenable than other industries to the substitution of unskilled labor for capital.[26] Value added per employee is also exceptionally high in basic metals (No. 12) in Mexico (and this observation extends to both the wage and the nonwage components) and in the chemicals and petroleum refining group (No. 13) in India.

Deviations in the other direction may be observed in the food, beverages, and tobacco group (No. 11) in India and, much less markedly, in Mexico, but not in Brazil, though the significance of intercountry differences in this group has already been questioned above. Perhaps a slight tendency for nonmetallic mineral products (No. 8) and some other items to fall out of line may also be detected.

[25] See Sidney Siegel, *Nonparametric Statistics for the Behavioral Sciences,* New York, 1956, pp. 229–239.
[26] The extraordinarily high figures for the rubber industry in India and some other less developed countries may reflect the success which they have had in inducing the large American and European tire manufacturers to establish plants in their area.

One can therefore find a few wide deviations and a number of minor ones in comparing the ordering of industry according to the value-added criterion in developed and less developed countries. But there is really nothing that could be regarded as a clear-cut swapping of places between industries on the left side and those on the right side of Chart 8 —that is, between those which, in the United States, rank as labor-intensive and those which rank as capital-intensive. On the contrary, the major deviations noted—rubber products in India and Brazil, basic metals in Mexico, and chemical and petroleum products in India—are in the direction of accentuating the difference. This evidence is thus consistent with the observations based on the more summary data given in Chart 7.

Detailed Bilateral Comparisons

Finally, three bilateral comparisons are undertaken in much finer detail by industries, entailing the establishment of at least a rough concordance between the U.S. classification and that employed by each of the other countries considered. This approach is taken with a view to providing closer comparability of the industries examined than can be assumed with respect to the very broad groups hitherto studied. At best, however, the data compared still relate to the output of apparently similar industries rather than to identical products.

The United Kingdom, Japan, and India have been selected for these comparisons because of the availability of the statistics needed and because of the interest offered by their contrasting economic situations in relation to each other and to the United States. India is of special importance in this analysis since it is still very low in the scale of economic development and in wage levels, and yet, with its great size, has a larger manufacturing sector and probably a better census of manufactures than any other less developed country.

The number of industries entering into these bilateral comparisons varies, depending on the amount of industrial detail originally reported by the partner country, on the extent to which two or more of its items have had to be combined in the effort to establish comparability with the United States, or vice versa, and on the number of items which, in some cases, have been deleted for lack of a clear counterpart in the U.S. statistics. It should be noted that the amount of industrial detail reported in the U.S. *Census of Manufactures* is very great, comprising 417 four-digit items in the 1963 census. The Japanese census of 1962 is even more detailed, providing 501 items, and has the further advantage for present purposes of being laid out on lines similar to the U.S. Standard Industrial Classification. After the combinations and deletions made for the reasons indicated, 178 items have been used in comparison with the United States.[27] The British census of 1958 contains fewer items, 109 in all, of which 103 have been retained for comparison.[28]

The Indian census is based on the International Standard Industrial Classification but in more detailed form, giving altogether 194 items. In addition, however, to those industries which have had to be left out because of no clear U.S. equivalent, others have been deleted because of a preponderance of repair work as distinguished from manufacturing proper. After combination of some other items in the interest of comparability, 117 Indian industries remain for present purposes.

United States and United Kingdom

The United States and the United Kingdom show a strong similarity in the pattern of value added per employee in different industries, plotted in Chart 11 in logarithmic form.[29] The correlation coefficients given in Table 6 (all of which are significant at the 1 per cent level of confidence) indicate further that this close relation is found also in both wage and nonwage value added in the two countries. Roughly three-quarters of the interindustry differences in these variables in the United Kingdom [30] may be held to be "explained" by the United States pattern. To the extent that, on evidence such as that examined in Chapter 2, the United States pattern reflects variance in the intensity of human and physical capital inputs in different industries, these influences would also go far toward explaining the English pattern. Other forces, such as the rate of unionization and of advertising, may, however, also show a similar industrial pattern in the two countries and to this extent would help to explain the relations observed.

[27] Appendix B provides more specific information on these points, and Tables B-1, B-2, and B-3 give the names of industries and the variables used in all three bilateral comparisons.

[28] Unfortunately, the results of the 1963 census of manufacture in the United Kingdom were not available in time for use in this study.

[29] It will be noted that all three of the bilateral correlations given here are in logarithmic form. As stated in Chapter 2, footnote 30, there is no basis in economic theory for determining in advance whether this form or the arithmetic form is appropriate. To assist in this determination, tests for linearity and for homoscedasticity have been made; the results of these tests are given in Appendix B.

[30] $\bar{R}^2$, adjusted for the number of observations, is 0.775 for value added per employee, 0.719 for wage value added per employee, and 0.728 for nonwage value added per employee.

CHART 11

*Value Added per Employee in 103 Manufacturing Industries,
the United Kingdom and the United States*

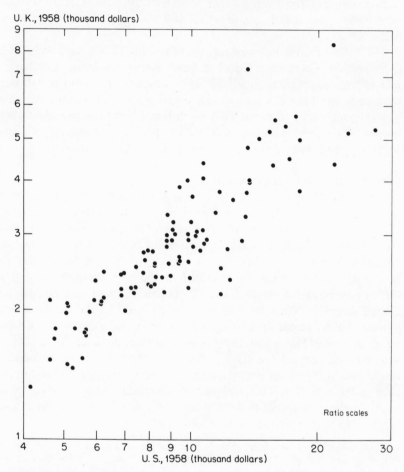

Source: See Appendix B.

United States and Japan

The comparison with Japan gives appreciably lower coefficients of correlation (though still significant at the 1 per cent level of confidence) than that with the United Kingdom for each of the three variables, but the United States pattern may nevertheless be said to "explain" over half of the interindustry variance in value added per employee in

TABLE 6

Coefficients of Correlation Obtained in Detailed Log Correlation Analysis of Value Added, Wage Value Added, and Nonwage Value Added per Employee, in the United States and the United Kingdom, Japan, and India

Countries Compared and Year of Census	Number of Industries in Correlation	Value Added per Employee		
		Total	Wage	Other
U.S. (1958) and U.K. (1958)	103	0.882	0.849	0.855
U.S. (1962) and Japan (1962):				
Maximum list of industries	178	0.753	0.778	0.690
Excluding nine extreme derivations	169	0.806	0.782	0.743
U.S. (1963) and India (1961):				
Maximum list of industries	117	0.600	0.494	0.599
Less industries with employment under 1,000	100	0.622	0.520	0.635
Less industries with employment under 2,000	83	0.634	0.553	0.658
Excluding also seven extreme deviations	76	0.786	0.518	0.785

Source: See Appendix B.

Japan.[31] Much of the remaining variance is attributable to nine industries in which, as indicated by Chart 12, value added per employee in Japan deviates exceptionally widely from the United States pattern. In seven of these industries the deviation is on the high side, and it may be significant that total value added in the seven industries in Japan is also extraordinarily high in relation to reported payrolls, at least as judged once more by corresponding data for the United States. Expressed the other way round, the percentage share of payroll in total value added in these industries in the two countries is as follows:

[31] The adjusted $\bar{R}^2$ is 0.57 for value added per employee, 0.60 for wage value added, and 0.47 for nonwage value added.

CHART 12

Value Added per Employee in 178 Manufacturing Industries, Japan and the United States

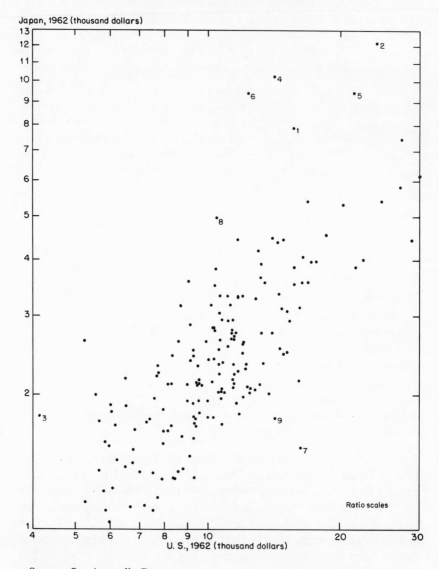

Japan, 1962 (thousand dollars)

U. S., 1962 (thousand dollars)

Source: See Appendix B.

Note: Numbered points identify industries in which value added per employee in Japan deviates by two standard errors of estimate or more from the value indicated by the regression equation. The industries and their percentage deviations are as follows: (1) sugar, +124; (2) petroleum refining, +128; (3) leather gloves, +84; (4) flat glass, +222; (5) hydraulic cement, +98; (6) steam engines and turbines, +236; (7) electric lamps, −58; (8) radio and television sets, +107; (9) photographic equipment, excluding film, −45.

	Japan	U.S.
Petroleum refining	12.8	30.6
Hydraulic cement	16.5	29.1
Sugar	17.0	36.7
Flat glass	17.4	51.6
Steam engines and turbines	13.1	60.0
Radio and television sets	14.8	47.0
Leather gloves	28.6	72.7

In several of these industries the share of payroll is so low as to leave the accuracy of the Japanese figures open to question,[32] though in some cases the return on capital may be exceptionally high in Japan.[33]

Of the two instances of very wide negative deviation in Japan marked in Chart 12, one concerns an industry, electric lamps, for which non-wage value added per employee in the United States has been found to be high in relation to physical assets (Table 4). It may be, therefore, that the factor intensity of the industry is better indicated by its ranking in Japan, which would place it in the labor-intensive category. The other industry, photographic equipment, would also be in this category by its relative position in Japan, and may provide an example of significant factor-intensity reversal between the two countries. Even here, however, it may be the product itself which is adapted, rather than the technology of producing the same product, to differing conditions of factor supply and factor costs, since American and Japanese cameras can probably be regarded as rather different instruments catering to different buyers.[34]

[32] The share of payroll in value added by manufacture is, however, generally much lower in Japan than in the United States (32 per cent against 50 per cent in manufacturing as a whole in 1962), partly because a greater part of labor compensation is in noncash forms.

[33] In response to an inquiry from the author as to possible reasons for the large deviations in question, Hirotaka Kato (Kanagawa University) suggests that some of those on the high side, notably in petroleum refining and hydraulic cement, may reflect a markedly higher degree of industrial concentration in Japan than in the United States, and he further notes, with respect to deviations in the opposite direction, a much higher concentration in electric lamps in the United States than in Japan.

[34] There are, of course, numerous lesser shifts of position. Among the industries which, by the value-added criterion, would rank as more labor-intensive in Japan, relative to the rest of Japanese industry, than in the United States are cotton cloth and other woven goods, carpets, canned fruits and vegetables, rubber footwear, ceramic wall and floor tile, primary batteries, medical instruments, and toys and sporting goods. Shifts in the opposite direction include yarn, lace goods, certain agricultural chemicals, leather handbags and purses, some types of office machines, industrial trucks and tractors, and storage batteries.

United States and India

The analysis for the United States and India, taking the full list of industries selected for comparison, produces lower correlation coefficients than those found for the United States and Japan. A number of the industries compared are still in an embryonic state in India, however, and may constitute a less representative sample, or provide less accurate statistical reports, or use different production processes, than would more fully developed industries. Progressively higher coefficients of correlation are found by eliminating, first, industries employing fewer than 1,000 and, next, those employing fewer than 2,000.

Inspection of the data plotted in Chart 13 shows that seven industries account for very wide deviations from the pattern indicated by value added per employee in the United States. Given the exceptionally wide gaps separating these industries from the other observations, it is pertinent to note that their exclusion from the regression analysis results in a marked increase in the correlation of value added per employee in the two countries (Table 6). This is also true of nonwage value added, but not of wage value added.

As indicated by the chart,[35] all seven of the industries singled out are relatively capital-intensive in the United States, according to the value-added criterion. Three of them—petroleum refining, tires and tubes, and dyestuffs—are even more so in India in relation to the general run of its industry. As suggested earlier in the analysis of Charts 8–10, these industries seem to exhibit a very low elasticity of substitution of unskilled labor for capital, though it is also likely that the relatively high value added in India includes a large element of monopoly-rent attributable to restrictions on imports and on new entries into production in these fields. The remaining four industries are much more labor-intensive in India than in the United States, relative in each case to the rest of manufacturing industry. There is room for doubt, however, as to the comparability of wines and spirits and perhaps also perfumery products [36] between the two countries, though this may be less true of such items as milled rice and salt.

These last two products would therefore seem to furnish the principal instances of possible reversals of factor intensity emerging from this comparison of manufacturing in the United States and India. Another,

[35] See also Table 2.

[36] The perfumery industry in India includes a relatively large amount of processing of essential oils for export. Even rice and salt would differ between the two countries in packaging for the consumer and perhaps also in sanitary controls.

CHART 13

Value Added per Employee in 117 Manufacturing Industries, India and the United States

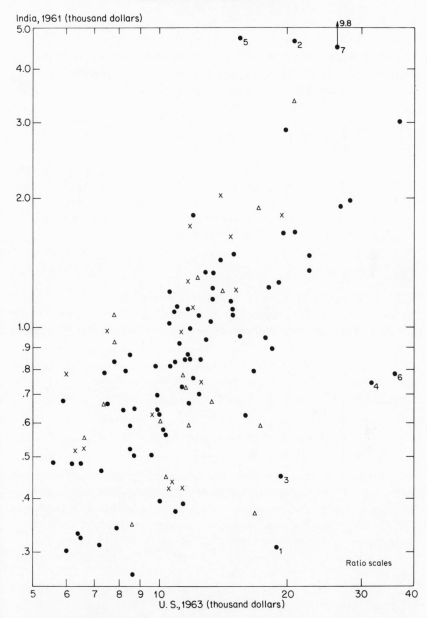

Source: See Appendix B.

Note: Industries with employment under 1,000 in India are marked △, and those with employment from 1,000 to 2,000 are marked ✕. Numbered points identify industries in which value added per employee in India deviates by two standard errors of estimate or more from the value indicated by the regression equation. The industries and their percentage deviations are as follows: (1) rice mills, −77; (2) dyestuffs, +225; (3) salt, −66; (4) spirits and wine, −66; (5) tires and tubes, +331; (6) perfumes, cosmetics, and other toilet preparations, −67; (7) petroleum refining, +455.

less sharp but perhaps of greater potential commercial significance, is flat glass, whose position in the Indian scale contrasts remarkably with that which the Japanese statistics would indicate. There are, of course, numerous other more moderate shifts of position, as is evident from the dispersion of observations in Chart 13. The ones clustered in the lower left area of the chart are of particular interest, including as they do apparel, woven carpets, chinaware, glass products, and castings and forgings. These are all products which are labor-intensive in the United States and still more so, relative to the rest of industry, in India. But this kind of moderate shift in comparison with United States factor intensities gives little support to the idea that factor-intensity reversals are a common and significant feature of the international economy.

To sum up, the international comparisons made in this chapter tend to support the general validity of the strong-factor-intensity hypothesis and, more particularly, the relevance of the United States pattern of factor intensities to other countries at very different levels of development and with very different factor-price ratios. By the criterion of value added per employee, some industries appear to be more labor-intensive in one or more foreign countries, and others less so, than in the United States. But few of these shifts could be regarded as clear and significant reversals of factor intensity. They are consistent with Samuelson's impressionistic judgment some years ago that "the phenomenon of goods that interchange their roles of being more labor intensive is much less important empirically than it is interesting theoretically." [37]

Technological Advance and Factor Intensities:
The Case of Cotton Textiles

Apart from any influence which may be exerted by differences in factor-price ratios, the interindustry pattern of factor intensities may change because the rate of technological advance is faster in some industries than in others, leading to new combinations of the factors of production. And these changes may be registered sooner in some countries than in others, depending on technological leadership, entrepreneurial initiative, and the conditions of competition.

In recent years a good deal of attention has been given to the rate of technological progress and changing factor proportions in textiles, especially cotton textiles. Thus, *A Study on Cotton Textiles,* prepared

---

[37] Paul A. Samuelson, "A Comment on Factor Price Equalisation," *Review of Economic Studies,* Vol. XIX (2), No. 49, 1951–52, pp. 121–122.

by the GATT Secretariat,[38] states that "the industry is continually improving its performance through a shift to new types of equipment embodying technical advances and innovations at every stage of production," and that "the cotton industry in the industrialized countries and some of the less-developed exporting countries is undergoing fundamental changes. Use is being made of huge investments for this new equipment," the GATT study reports, and it adds: "A modern cotton industry is regarded as being among the most highly capital-intensive of the manufacturing industries."

How far this and other similar assessments are correct is important for reasons that transcend the identification of labor-intensive manufactures for analytical purposes. For one thing, technological advance in textiles is thought to have been stimulated by the rapid growth of exports by some of the less developed and other low-wage countries. Developments in the industry could therefore be regarded as illustrative of the kind of competitive response which, in still other products, could slow down or even thwart the growth of exports by less developed countries. Second, the prospect of a highly capital-intensive cotton textile industry is sometimes invoked as a reason why, in the meantime, imports from less developed countries should be curbed. Commercial policy is thus summoned to the support of economic projections.

This last view, with its reborn-infant-industry implications, is most strongly expressed in a report prepared by the Special Committee on Textiles of the OECD and published under the title *Modern Cotton Industry—A Capital-Intensive Industry*.[39] "Only a few years ago," the Special Committee states, "it was usual for the textile industry to be cited by economists as one of the so-called 'labour-intensive' industries, i.e. those whose production depends primarily on manpower. Although this may still be true for certain branches of the textile industry, it is no longer so for cotton which is increasingly becoming a capital intensive industry with investments easily amounting to $20,000 per workplace." This transformation, the report goes on to say, is "practically complete in the United States and Japan, but still slowly proceeding in Europe."

Tariff barriers, the OECD Special Committee states, are not high

[38] General Agreement on Tariffs and Trade, Geneva, July 1966. The passages cited are from page 55.

[39] Published by the Organization for Economic Cooperation and Development, Paris, 1965. The quotations given here are from pages 95 and 131–133. Reasons for a modern and efficient cotton textile industry in the United States and Japan are given on page 17.

enough, with some exceptions, to provide effective protection to the cotton textile industry, "particularly against imports from low-cost countries," and "the impermanence of quotas, due to the rules at present governing international trade, offers the industry only temporary security." Turning to the restraints on imports applied under the Long-Term Cotton Textile Arrangement of 1962 (further discussed in Chapter 4), the Special Committee says that the Arrangement will be successful only if the imports affected by it "can be regulated in such a way as to encourage and speed up any structural adjustments required to enable the cotton industry in Member countries to flourish, i.e. eliminate any excess of capacity, continually modernize plant, introduce two- or three-shift working in Europe, and seek new outlets for industries confined to the domestic market." [40]

While the rate of technological innovation in cotton textiles is impressive,[41] it may be exaggerated to suppose that the process is significantly faster than in manufacturing as a whole and to conclude that the industry is becoming strongly capital-intensive. Certainly, the assertion of the OECD Special Committee that such a transformation is "practically complete" in the United States and Japan is not borne out by the data already presented for these two countries.[42] Further data are given in Table 7 on the evolution in recent years of cotton weaving, the most important branch of the cotton textile industry. New investment per employee increased rapidly during the first half of the 1960's both in absolute terms and in relation to the average for all manufacturing, but nevertheless remained below that average.[43] Value added per

[40] The argument was summed up as follows by *The Economist* (London) in its issue of February 19, 1966 (pp. 723–725): "How do European textile manufacturers survive? On the almost universal assumption that their governments have in effect an obligation to protect them; and currently by basing their case for protection on the grounds that their much battered industries are now becoming so capital intensive, through re-equipment, that underdeveloped competitors like Pakistan will soon lose the advantage of their lower wages."

[41] See the section on textile mill products (pp. 148–154) in *Technological Trends in Major American Industries,* U.S. Department of Labor, February 1966.

[42] See particularly Table 2 (U.S. SIC code No. 2211) and Table B-2 (Japanese code No. 2031). Value added per employee in cotton weaving mills, in relation to the average for all manufacturing, is even lower in Japan than in the United States, being in the order of 43 or 44 per cent in each of the years 1961 to 1964.

[43] Congressman Thomas B. Curtis, ranking Republican member of the Joint Economic Committee, questioned the desirability of investing so much in the industry in a report delivered to the House of Representatives on August 29, 1966, in which he expressed strong opposition to the restrictions on imports imposed under the international Long-Term Cotton Textile Arrangement. His comments on the risk of overinvestment were as follows:

"The great increase of productive capacity for the U.S. textile industry is one

TABLE 7

Capital Expenditures, Value Added, and Employment in Cotton Weaving Mills (SITC 2211), 1947, 1954, 1958, and 1961–65

Year	New Capital Expenditures ($ million)	Value Added ($ million)	Total Employment (thousands)	Averages per Employee[a]			Percentage of Average in All U.S. Manufacturing	
				New Capital Expenditures (dollars)	Value Added (dollars)		New Capital Expenditures	Value Added
1947	79	1,449	330	239	4,388		56.9	84.4
1954	55	1,135	296	186	3,833		35.5	51.2
1958	48	1,079	243	199	4,431		32.0	48.3
1961	81	1,282	228	355	5,619		57.1	53.8
1962	115	1,346	224	513	6,020		79.4	54.3
1963	113	1,257	209	542	6,013		76.8	50.8
1964	138	1,404	204	678	6,896		83.7	55.1
1965	169	1,624	205	821	7,910		84.4	60.1

Source: *1963 Census of Manufactures* and *1965 Annual Survey of Manufactures.*
[a]Averages computed from data before rounding.

employee has also risen, but in 1965 was still only 60 per cent of the average for all manufacturing. Moreover, much of this increase may be attributed to the rise in profits in cotton textiles resulting from the strengthening of demand, particularly military demand, and from the elimination in August 1964 of the two-price system for raw cotton, which had discriminated against domestic buyers in favor of exports.[44] It cannot be assumed, therefore, that the rise in value added per employee can be projected on into the future.

It might be expected that if there were a basic trend toward a capital-intensive industry, it would be reflected in appreciably higher averages for some parts of the industry, or for some parts of the country, than for others. Yet an examination of nine product classes in weaving at the five-digit level available in the *1963 Census of Manufactures* shows none in which value added per employee was above 63 per cent of the average for all manufacturing. Similarly, the data for individual states and regions in the 1963 census provide only one instance, and that a minor one,[45] where the value added per employee in weaving was as high as 73 per cent of the average for all manufacturing and no other higher than 54 per cent.

In brief, the evidence considered for the United States is consistent with the view that there has been heavy investment in modernization in

of the key elements of concern about the future of that industry. The wiser policy would seem to be to unshackle import competition now, through more liberal administration of the Long-Term Arrangement, especially in those categories where unmet demand is greatest, rather than to allow our economic resources to be diverted to expanding portions of an industry which may prove to be uneconomic. The real danger is that the capacity being created will only increase pressure to protect this new capacity later even though it be inefficient. It is no favor to the wage earner to entice him into a job which has an unstable economic base."

[44] The after-tax return on capital in the textile industry (as reported by the Federal Trade Commission and the Securities and Exchange Commission) had been as high as 19.5 per cent in 1947 (accounting for the exceptionally high value added per employee in that year shown in Table 7). The rate fell to 12.6 per cent in 1950, 5.7 per cent in 1955, and was as low as 5.0 per cent in 1961 and 6.0 per cent in 1963. It then strengthened to 8.4 per cent in 1964 and 10.8 per cent in 1965 (*Statistical Abstract of the United States, 1966*, p. 497).

The elimination of the two-price system for raw cotton cut the price to domestic mills from 35.50 cents per pound in July 1964 to 27.64 cents in August. At the same time, the so-called mill margin (that is, the difference between the price paid by textile mills for raw cotton and the price at which they sell gray cloth to finishing mills) rose from 25.09 cents to 33.19 cents and continued to rise to 38.72 cents in May 1966 (from speech by Representative Thomas B. Curtis in the House of Representatives, August 29, 1966).

[45] That is, the Middle Atlantic region, accounting for only 1.2 per cent of total value added in cotton weaving in the United States in 1963.

the last few years in cotton textiles, but it gives little reason to think that the industry is becoming capital-intensive compared with manufacturing in general and ceasing to be appropriate to the factor endowments of the less developed countries. According to the criteria applied in this study, cotton textiles and the textile industry in general still rank among the most labor-intensive of the manufacturing industries, and they will be so treated in the analysis of trade in the next chapter.

The contrary view that a fundamental change in textiles is under way may rely unduly on comparisons with the industry's own past characteristics and performance, and fail to allow for the progress made by manufacturing in general. The illustrations frequently given of developments in the industry also suggest a tendency to confuse the technological optimum with average practice at any one time.

4

TRADE IN
LABOR-INTENSIVE MANUFACTURES

Selection of Labor-Intensive Items

Application of Value-Added Criterion

Judged by the criterion of value added per employee, both in the United States and in other countries, a number of industries have been found to be clearly capital-intensive and a number of others clearly labor-intensive. This is true of such major industry groups as chemicals and petroleum products on the one hand and textiles and wood products on the other. It is true also of many of the component industries of other major groups. As always, the problem of classification concerns mainly the observations in an intermediate position—in this instance, those industries which, at the finest level of industrial detail given, are near the national average on the value-added scale.[1]

The general rule followed in this study has been to count as labor-intensive all manufactures which meet both of two conditions. The first is that, in value added per employee in the United States, they do not exceed the national average for all manufacturing by more than 10 per cent. The second is that, in total imports by developed from less developed countries in 1965, they add up to at least $100,000 at the three-digit level of the Standard International Trade Classification (SITC). This approach, while tending to exclude the most clearly capital-intensive items, applies the test of the market (as reflected in imports) to items at or near the over-all national average in recognition that

[1] If all four-digit items from the *Census of Manufactures* are arrayed in ascending order of value added per employee, they present a continuum with no sharp breaks such as those suggested by the arrangement of two-digit major industry groups according to wage and nonwage value added in Chart 1, above. It may be noted that in this chapter the value-added criterion is applied without the distinction between the wage and nonwage components made in Chapters 2 and 3, which were concerned with testing the variable as a guide to the intensities of different industries in human and physical capital.

value added per employee in the United States is not an infallible guide to factor intensity. It also recognizes that close comparability between industrial and trade classifications is hard, and sometimes impossible, to achieve. The case for some additional flexibility in applying the value-added criterion is strengthened by several instances noted where the averages derived from the U.S. censuses of manufactures may overstate the relative capital intensity of the imported items.[2]

Setting some minimum level such as $100,000 as a cutoff point helps to eliminate small, erratic elements from the trade statistics, but does not avert the need to detect and exclude irrelevant elements at still higher values of trade. Returned merchandise seems to be the chief offender, notably various kinds of machinery and equipment brought back from use in oil exploration and development, and is sometimes reported in a manner indistinguishable from regular imports. The principal problems of this nature seem to be found in the United Kingdom's statistics.[3]

Unfortunately, other imperfections in the trade statistics require the omission of two items which rank as labor-intensive by the value-added criterion and hold a certain actual or potential export interest for some of the less developed countries. One of these is cut diamonds, now coming only from Israel among the less developed countries, but expected to come eventually from Sierra Leone and other diamond-producing countries which are endeavoring to establish their own diamond-cutting industries. The other item is yachts and other small craft built in Hong Kong and Singapore and exported chiefly to the United States. The trouble is that the Standard International Trade Classification (the basis for the trade statistics assembled by the United Nations) does not distinguish cut from uncut diamonds nor small craft from larger vessels (the latter including, in some cases, mere changes of registry).[4]

[2] Thus a lower capital intensity by the value-added test has been found for electric lamps, batteries, and cameras in the Japanese census and for perfume and flat glass in the Indian census.

[3] See Appendix D.

[4] The United States does distinguish cut from uncut diamonds in its import statistics, and these imports from Israel amounted to $42,134,000 in 1965. Other developed countries' imports of diamonds from Israel (doubtless consisting mainly, if not entirely, of cut diamonds) as reported to the U.N. Statistical Office were as follows in 1965: United Kingdom, $11,504,000; Switzerland, $4,123,000; Germany, $8,574,000; France, $2,892,000; Belgium, $14,642,000; Japan, $7,384,000; Canada, $1,982,000; other developed countries, $470,000. It is uncertain, however, how much of these imports in each case—notably in Belgium —ends up as domestic sales and how much is re-exported. For instance, U.S. imports of cut diamonds from Belgium—$73,923,000 in 1965—may have in-

Summary Statement of Items Selected

Table 8 gives a summary list of the manufactures selected as labor-intensive, condensed into twenty-four subgroups and four main groups, together with matching data on imports in 1965 by the United States and by other developed countries from all sources and from the less developed countries. As will be clear from the much fuller presentation in Appendix C, the selection and matching have been carried out in considerable detail, so that, as far as possible, imports from the less developed countries might be set against total imports, or against United States production, of similar items. Assume, for instance, that imports of "transportation equipment" (SITC 73) from the less developed countries consist in fact of bicycles (7331), or that imports of "domestic electrical equipment" (725) consist only of space-heating equipment (72505). In these cases, it should be more meaningful with respect to market shares or market potentials to make the comparison at the more disaggregated levels.

Appendix C also indicates, however, the difficulties encountered in matching the U.S. Standard Industrial Classification with the Standard International Trade Classification and the lack of complete success in doing so. Problems of comparability arise throughout the list, but are likely to be most serious with respect to the last four subgroups of Group 2 in the table—various metal products, scientific instruments and the like, electrical apparatus, and nonelectrical machinery and equipment. The products included in these subgroups are of marginal labor intensity, judged by their relatively high average value added per employee, and imports from the less developed countries are very small compared with total imports and with U.S. production. The chances are that imports from the less developed countries in these subgroups are, in fact, much more limited in range than total imports or domestic production, despite the elimination of items not meeting the criteria previously indicated and other efforts to ensure comparability. The four subgroups (to be referred to for convenience as "marginally labor-intensive") will accordingly be excluded from some of the comparisons

cluded stones originally imported from Israel. Even this uncertainty (further complicated by doubts regarding the accuracy of some of the figures) does not reveal the real problem of dealing meaningfully with the trade in cut diamonds, which lies in the fact that they are, presumably, almost as "fungible" as gold.

With respect to yachts, and other pleasure boats and small craft (U.S. Schedule A, Nos. 7350020 and 7350040), the United States imported $2,941,000 of these items from Hong Kong and $260,000 from Singapore, Taiwan, and the Philippines in 1965. Export figures of these countries indicate that sales to developed countries other than the United States were negligible.

TABLE 8

Condensed List of Manufactures Selected as Labor-Intensive: U.S. Production and Imports and Imports of Other Developed Countries, 1965

| Product Group and Subgroup | United States Production | | | Value of Imports | | | |
| | Value Added by Manufacture ($ million) | Value of Shipments ($ million) | Value Added per Employee (index)a | United States | | Other Developed Countries | |
				Total ($ million, f.o.b.)	From LDC's ($ million, f.o.b.)	Total ($ million, c.i.f.)	From LDC's (c.i.f.)b
Labor-intensive manufactures, total	72,593	140,841	75.0	5,696.6	1,009.8	27,558.9	1,571.8
Total, excluding marginal items (*)	42,679	89,541	64.8	3,655.0	942.5	14,392.8	1,517.0
1. *Textiles, clothing, and accessories*	14,758	33,945	53.7	1,052.9	286.3	5,316.5	534.0
Yarn and thread	865	2,405	60.0	63.6	5.9	1,035.1	31.1
Cotton fabrics, woven	1,967	4,219	61.2	134.5	61.5	642.0	122.2
Other woven fabrics, excl. jute products	1,866	4,862	71.9	236.0	9.2	1,244.8	12.4
Textile small wares and specialties	1,772	4,363	63.2	67.3	12.9	563.7	35.8
Carpets and other floor covering	133	331	74.4	54.3	15.7	415.1	120.7
Clothing and accessories, excl. goods of leather, rubber, and plastic	8,155	17,765	47.4	497.1	181.1	1,415.8	211.7
2. *Other light manufactures, excl. food*	48,424	86,076	86.0	3,281.8	269.4	16,845.6	250.9
Footwear and other leather rubber, and plastic goods	3,169	5,813	57.6	337.2	54.2	913.7	43.5
Glassware, china, and pottery	1,307	1,962	81.4	111.7	3.1	324.6	2.0
Furniture	3,051	5,923	64.3	59.9	6.8	338.1	4.1
Books and other printed matter	3,954	6,569	78.5	58.5	4.2	436.8	2.7
Games, toys, sporting goods, and musical instruments	1,563	2,941	77.6	368.5	25.8	650.3	40.9
Jewelry and silverware	500	971	81.6	61.8	17.6	233.0	42.2

(continued)

TABLE 8 (concluded)

Product Group and Subgroup	United States Production			Value of Imports			
				United States		Other Developed Countries	
	Value Added by Manufacture ($ million)	Value of Shipments ($ million)	Value Added per Employee (index)[a]	Total ($ million, f.o.b.)	From LDC's, f.o.b.)	Total ($ million)	From LDC's, c.i.f.)[b]
Costume jewelry and notions	4,966	10,597	79.3	242.6	90.3	783.2	60.7
Optical goods, cameras, watches and instruments*	1,289	2,062	92.9	200.9	3.0	658.9	5.8
Cutlery, hardware, and other metal products*	3,507	6,341	91.3	340.4	14.1	1,466.3	12.1
Electrical apparatus and appliances*	14,666	24,100	91.5	703.5	46.3	3,600.1	27.0
Nonelectrical machinery and equipment*	10,452	18,797	102.0	796.8	3.9	7,440.8	9.9
3. *Labor-intensive food manufactures*	2,748	6,674	89.7	268.3	112.4	1,773.2	380.0
Fish and fish products	221	574	95.5	124.4	44.6	705.5	193.4
Fruit and vegetables	1,303	3,332	90.5	117.4	65.3	884.5	175.0
Miscellaneous food products and cigars	1,224	2,768	87.8	26.5	2.5	183.2	11.5
4. *Labor-intensive industrial materials*	6,663	14,146	66.4	1,093.6	341.7	3,623.6	406.9
Products of jute and other coarse fibers	142	406	58.5	238.2	194.6	228.2	122.0
Leather and tanned or dressed furs	363	892	80.6	78.7	20.5	539.0	77.7
Lumber, plywood, and other simple wood products	3,802	8,948	58.3	648.8	115.8	2,019.9	204.4
Building materials of clay, stone, etc.	2,356	3,900	83.8	128.0	10.8	836.4	2.9

Source: Appendix C.
[a] All U.S. manufacturing = 100.
[b] Includes Canadian and Australian imports on f.o.b. basis.

made below, which would otherwise be unduly influenced by the high values which these subgroups have in total imports and in domestic production.

Valuation of Imports C.I.F. and F.O.B.

A quite different problem of comparability of the data arises from the fact that U.S. import statistics generally reflect values at the principal markets in the exporting country and do not include the freight and insurance charges required to bring the merchandise to the United States, whereas these charges are typically included in the import values recorded by other countries (the first method of valuation being usually described as "f.o.b." and the second as "c.i.f."). Canada and Australia along with the United States are the principal exceptions to the general rule and the only ones of interest for present purposes.

How much difference freight and insurance charges may make in recorded import values under the two systems has long been the subject of more or less informed guesses and of a few detailed studies.[5] Recently, intensive inquiries have been undertaken both by the Tariff Commission and by the Bureau of the Census. On the basis of the Tariff Commission's report,[6] covering imports in 1965 distributed among 190 items, it may be estimated that these charges would add about 11 per cent to the reported values given in Table 8 for U.S. imports of labor-intensive manufactures from the less developed countries. The differentials for the four main product groups would be as follows: group 1, 7.0 per cent; group 2, 11.6 per cent; group 3, 9.2 per cent; group 4, 15.5 per cent. (See Appendix E.)

Given the size of these differentials, it is scarcely possible to continue to combine f.o.b. figures for some countries and c.i.f. figures for others in the same tables without attempting to achieve closer comparability. In principle, the adjustment might be made in either direction —that is, by applying appropriate adjustment factors either to increase the recorded import values of the United States, Canada, and Australia

[5] Probably the most careful study was that undertaken by Carmellah Moneta for the National Bureau and reported on in her article, "The Estimation of Transportation Costs in International Trade," *Journal of Political Economy,* February 1959, pp. 41–58.

[6] The Tariff Commission's report is in the form of an attachment to a press release of February 7, 1967, entitled "C.I.F. Value of U.S. Imports" (mimeographed). The Commerce Department issued a release on December 20, 1966, with findings of the Bureau of the Census based on imports in the first six months of 1966 grouped in twenty-one categories (too broadly defined to be directly applied to the data examined in the present study).

to an approximate c.i.f. basis or to reduce those of other countries to an approximate f.o.b. basis.

The first course would have the advantage of making U.S. import figures more comparable with domestic production and consumption data, if that were the main purpose to be served. But such an adjustment would compound the error already present in the statistics insofar as the trade figures are taken as a measure of the foreign exchange earnings of the less-developed countries, since only a negligible part of the freight and insurance charges accrues to them.

From this point of view, the alternative course of reducing the recorded import values of other countries is clearly preferable. In the absence, however, of adjustment factors directly relevant to the body of trade data collected here for foreign countries, this course entails the use of the differentials found for the United States and raises questions as to their applicability to other countries whose imports from the less developed countries differ in greater or less degree from those of the United States in composition by product and origin. This doubt may be relieved in some measure by the use of the separate adjustment factors for each of the four main groups of products, though much the same results would be obtained, both over all and for individual importing countries, by the application of a uniform 10 per cent reduction throughout (as is, in fact, done in adjusting the historical series in Chart 14, below).[7]

No high degree of accuracy can therefore be claimed for the adjusted data presented in this chapter [8]—only that, as long as the direction of the difference between U.S. and foreign recorded import values is as clear as it is, the revised figures are probably superior to the unrevised ones both for comparisons with the United States and

---

[7] That the revisions made are not exaggerated is suggested by the c.i.f./f.o.b. adjustment of 14.6 per cent for 1965 and 16.3 per cent for 1964 made in the German balance-of-payments estimates with respect to imports from non-European developing countries. (See *Monthly Report of the Deutsche Bundesbank,* June 1966, pp. 54–55.) This figure applies, of course, to an assortment of goods heavily weighted with unmanufactured or processed materials, but it does not seem out of line with the differential of 15.5 per cent reported above for labor-intensive industrial materials (group 4), the over-all German adjustment factor expressed on the same basis (i.e., as a percentage of the f.o.b. value of imports from non-European developing countries) being 17.2 per cent for 1965 and 19.3 per cent for 1964.

[8] The figures given in Table 8 and in the basic tables in Appendixes C and D are, however, as recorded and are therefore a mixture of f.o.b. import values for the United States, Canada, and Australia and c.i.f. import values for other developed countries.

for measuring the foreign exchange receipts of the less developed countries. There is indeed reason to think that these adjustments err on the side of caution. The Tariff Commission's release observes that an allowance for freight and insurance would not alone provide comparability and adds: "The value used by most foreign countries for duty and statistical purposes includes not only freight and insurance charges, but additional costs (such as buying commissions), which are not ordinarily included in U.S. values.[9] It is not feasible to collect reliable statistics on these additional costs on imports into the United States, but they are known to range from an insignificant amount to as much as the charges for freight and insurance, or even more."

Characteristics of the Trade

Probably the most important generalizations that can be made about imports of labor-intensive manufactures by developed from less developed countries are, first, that these imports are small and, second, that they have been growing rapidly in recent years.

Another broad generalization is that the trade is rather uneven in its composition by products and in its distribution by both exporting and importing countries. By product, textiles and clothing make up a particularly large share of the total, though some other light manufactures have recently been rising more rapidly. Among the countries of origin, Hong Kong holds an extraordinary position, and, all together, the less developed countries of the Far East are paramount over other areas as suppliers of labor-intensive manufactures to developed countries. Among the latter, the United States, the United Kingdom, and West Germany account for by far the greater part of these imports, and they also take the greater part of imports of labor-intensive manufactures from Japan and other low-wage countries.

These characteristics will first be examined on the basis of detailed trade statistics for 1964 and 1965 [10] and then, in the section "Market Potentials," below, the growth of the trade since 1953 will be considered on the basis of more summary data.

[9] The additional costs referred to are, however, generally paid to parties in the exporting country. It could be held that such costs should properly be included in f.o.b. valuations and that, if the information needed were available, any further adjustment for these costs undertaken in the interest of comparability should take the form of an addition to U.S. recorded import values rather than that of a subtraction from the c.i.f. import values of other countries.

[10] Compiled for this project by the Statistical Office of the United Nations.

Relative Size of Imports

A noteworthy feature of Table 8 is the small size of U.S. imports of labor-intensive manufactures from the less developed countries in relation to U.S. production of similar goods. The value of U.S. output (or "value of shipments") in 1965 of all the items listed in the table was $141 billion. Imports of these items from all sources in 1965 were equal to only about 4 per cent, and those from less developed countries only 0.7 per cent, of that amount. The ratio of imports from less developed countries was particularly low for the last four items of group 2 in the table (marked by asterisks). Exclusive of these items, identified above as marginally labor-intensive, total imports were about 4.1 per cent, and imports from the less developed countries about 1 per cent, of domestic output. Products of jute and other coarse fibers were exceptional in that imports from the less developed countries were almost half as large as domestic manufacturing production. The corresponding ratio was about 8 per cent for fish products, 4.7 per cent for carpets, and 2.3 per cent for leather and tanned or dressed furs. It was between 1 and 2 per cent for a few other items—cotton fabrics, clothing, jewelry and silverware, canned fruit and vegetables, and lumber, plywood, and other simple wood products. Otherwise, the ratios for individual items imported from the less developed countries were below, in most cases far below, 1 per cent of domestic output.

The foregoing comparisons are possible for the United States as a by-product of the selection method followed. A similar comparison, if it could be made, would probably yield a slightly higher ratio of imports from the less developed countries to the domestic production of other developed countries considered as an entity, but with sharp contrasts among the members of the group. This is suggested by Table 9 (derived from the OECD report on cotton textiles cited in Chapter 3) relating 1963 imports of textile products from Asian countries other than Japan to consumer expenditures on clothing in individual developed countries.

Looked at in relation to total imports of labor-intensive manufactures, the share supplied by the less developed countries is much larger in this country than in other developed countries—about 18 per cent for the United States in 1965 versus 6 per cent for other developed countries taken as a whole, or 25.8 per cent and 10.5 per cent, respectively, exclusive of the four marginal items in group 2. This observation has to be set against the much more limited role which imports in general play in the U.S. economy than in most other countries. Even

TABLE 9

Imports of Textiles, Clothing, and Accessories (Including Jute Products) by Developed Countries of the OECD from Asian Countries Other Than Japan, 1963

Importing Country	Value of Imports (million dollars) (1)	Amount per Capita (dollars) (2)	Consumer Expenditure on Clothing (million dollars) (3)	Col. 1 as Per Cent of Col. 3 (4)
United States	332.8	1.757	32,945[a]	1.0[a]
EFTA, total, excl. Portugal	295.7	3.5846	7,871[b]	3.5[b]
United Kingdom	228.5	4.246	5,180	4.4
Sweden	20.6	2.708	1,115	1.8
Norway	7.0	1.908	479	1.5
Denmark	15.0	3.200	443	3.4
Switzerland	17.8	3.064	n.a.	n.a.
Austria	6.8	0.948	654	1.0
EEC, total	141.3	0.800	17,943	0.8
West Germany	94.2	1.635	6,445	1.5
France	8.0	0.167	6,482	0.1
Italy	11.5	0.228	2,686	0.4
Netherlands	19.1	1.598	1,364	1.4
Belgium-Luxembourg	8.5	0.885	966	0.9
Japan	3.6	0.037	2,748	0.1
Canada	38.5	2.034	2,161	1.8

Source: *Modern Cotton Industry,* Organization for Economic Co-operation and Development, Paris, 1965, pp. 68-70.

Note: Products included are those in SITC·items 65 and 841. Countries of origin include Mainland China (not included in other tables in this analysis).

[a]Including footwear and jewelry.

[b]Excluding Switzerland.

TABLE 10

Imports of Labor-Intensive Manufactures, Other Manufactures, and Unmanufactured Commodities by Developed From Less Developed Countries, 1965

Product Group	Value, f.o.b.[a] ($ million)
Imports from less developed countries, total	25,600
Labor-intensive manufactures, total	2,438
Other manufactures, total	5,537
Sugar, meat, other food products, beverages, and tobacco	1,200
Animal and vegetable oils and fats	680
Petroleum products	1,600
Nonferrous metals	1,700
Chemical elements and compounds	251
Pig iron, iron and steel powders, sponge iron, ferro-alloys, etc.	55
Other iron and steel products	19
Pulp and paper	22
Cement and lime	7
Other manufactures	3
Unmanufactured commodities, total	17,625
Coffee, cocoa, and tea	2,825
Cereals, live animals, other foods and feeding stuffs, and tobacco	2,600
Cotton, wool, and other textile fibers	1,300
Crude petroleum, coal, and coke	6,525
Metalliferous ores	1,800
Hides and skins, oilseeds, lumber, rubber, and other crude materials[b]	2,575

Source: Derived from tabulations prepared by United Nations Statistical Office.

[a]Imports of countries reporting on a c.i.f. basis have been adjusted to an approximate f.o.b. basis by use of differentials given in Tariff Commission's release of February 7, 1967, "C.I.F. Value of U.S. Imports."

[b]Includes gem diamonds both uncut and cut (no distinction being made in the Standard International Trade Classification).

so, the ratios (again exclusive of the four marginal items) seem very small in most cases—between 3 and 8 per cent in all of the smaller European countries and Canada. In France, despite its long-standing economic ties with African countries and the tariff preferences extended to them, the 1965 ratio is only 12.3 per cent, or slightly larger than in West Germany with 11.1 per cent and much less than in the United Kingdom with 19.4 per cent. These ratios will be further considered in connection with Table 12, below.

As a final comparison, on the basis of the 1965 trade returns, labor-intensive manufactures make up less than one-tenth of total imports of the developed countries from less-developed countries. Coffee, cocoa, and tea alone bulk larger in the total, and crude petroleum 2.7 times larger, as may be seen in Table 10. Labor-intensive manufactures are less than half as large as other products classed in the table as "manufactures," the latter being more capital-intensive and generally having an evident natural-resource orientation. The only items of which the latter is not true are of negligible consequence in the trade.

It is noteworthy, however, that developed countries' imports of labor-intensive manufactures from the less developed countries rose by almost 11 per cent from 1964 to 1965 in contrast to an increase of less than 4 per cent in all other products. This relative gain was achieved despite the fact that the defensive balance-of-payments measures taken by the United Kingdom toward the end of 1964 and, more particularly, the tightening of restrictions on textiles seem to have fallen with special severity on its imports of labor-intensive manufactures from some of the Commonwealth countries (Table 11).[11] Developed countries other than the United Kingdom raised their imports of labor-intensive manufactures from less-developed countries by 17.5 per cent in 1965.

Product Composition of the Trade

Textiles, clothing, and accessories included in group 1 made up about one-third of 1965 imports of labor-intensive manufactures by developed from less developed countries. If burlap and other coarse fiber products from group 3 are also counted in the textile group, the latter accounted for some 44 per cent of the total.

The concentration of the trade by product is therefore pronounced, but it is perhaps less extreme than sometimes suggested by the attention given to textile imports from low-wage countries. Comparison of the

[11] In contrast to the decline of more than 10 per cent from 1964 to 1965 in the United Kingdom's imports of labor-intensive manufactures from less developed countries, its imports of these goods from all other sources, excluding the marginal items, were virtually unchanged.

TABLE 11

Imports of Labor-Intensive Manufactures by Developed from Less Developed Countries: Distribution Among Four Main Groups of Products in 1965 and Increase from 1964

(per cent)

Importing Country	All Items	Group 1 Textiles, Clothing, and Accessories	Group 2 Other Light Manufactures, Except Food	Group 3 Labor-Intensive Food Manufactures	Group 4 Labor-Intensive Industrial Materials
Imports in 1965 ($ million, f.o.b.)					
Developed countries, total	2,438	787	495	459	698
United Kingdom	429	180	73	54	121
Total, excl. U.K.	2,009	607	421	404	577
United States	1,010	286	269	112	342
Other developed countries	1,000	320	152	292	236
Increase from 1964 (per cent)					
Developed countries, total	11.3	10.4	26.8	4.6	7.7
United Kingdom	-10.7	-20.8	-11.1	6.0	1.6
Total, excl. U.K.	17.5	24.9	36.9	4.4	9.0
United States	21.5	34.0	44.3	-3.0	8.6
Other developed countries	13.7	17.8	25.6	7.6	9.6

Source: Appendixes D and E.

1965 results with those for 1964 indicates, moreover, that the concentration may be diminishing, the textile items in group 1 having increased by 10.4 per cent compared with an over-all increase close to 27 per cent by the wide assortment of light manufactures included in group 2. Both figures are strongly influenced by the British measures noted above. Developed countries other than the United Kingdom increased their imports in group 1 by about 25 per cent and those in group 2 by 37 per cent from 1964 to 1965. The corresponding increases for the United States alone were 34 per cent and 44 per cent, respectively.

The increase in 1965 was much more modest, however, in labor-intensive food manufactures and industrial materials, groups 3 and 4. The very low rate of increase in the food group reflects the poor anchovy catch by Peru during the 1965 season, which interrupted the rapid growth of its fish meal exports in recent years.

Distribution by Importing Countries

Of total imports of labor-intensive manufactures by developed from less developed countries in 1965, the United States accounted for 41.4 per cent (Table 12). The United Kingdom was next with 17.6 per cent, and West Germany third with 12.7 per cent. Together, these three countries took almost 72 per cent of the total. The United Kingdom's share had been as high as 22 per cent in 1964, but was reduced in 1965 with the absolute decline in its imports from the less developed countries, while those of the United States and West Germany continued to rise.

Rapid increases are also indicated in Table 12 for several countries —Sweden, Austria, Japan, Australia, and New Zealand—whose imports are relatively small. Others, including the European Common Market members except West Germany, show small shares in total imports of labor-intensive manufactures from the less developed countries, small ratios to their own imports of like products from all sources, and low rates of increase.

Table 13 points to considerable differences in the distribution of the main product groups among importing countries. The share of the United States is particularly high—more than half of the total—in the rapid-growth items included in group 2. The Common Market countries take a relatively large part—twice as much as the United States— of the food products in group 3. The United States, the United Kingdom, and West Germany account for three-quarters of total imports of textiles, clothing, and accessories, group 1, from the less developed countries. All three show considerable variety in the product compo-

TABLE 12

Imports of Labor-Intensive Manufactures by Individual Developed Countries from Less Developed Countries in 1965: Ratio to Imports of Similar Items from All Sources, Percentage Distribution Among Importing Countries, and Increase from 1964

Importing Country	Imports in 1965 from LDC's ($ million, f.o.b.) (1)	Percentage of Imports from All Sources, Excluding Marginal Items[a] (2)	Percentage Distribution Among Importing Countries (3)	Percentage Increase over 1964 Imports from LDC's (4)
Developed countries, total	2,438	13.9	100.0	11.3
United States	1,010	25.8	41.4	21.5
EFTA, total, excl. Portugal	574	11.9	23.6	-5.8
United Kingdom	429	19.4	17.6	-10.7
Sweden	44	5.8	1.8	23.9
Norway	13	4.3	.5	2.1
Denmark	32	6.4	1.3	9.4
Switzerland	43	6.2	1.8	7.5
Austria	14	4.0	.6	16.5
EEC, total	580	8.9	23.8	13.0
West Germany	309	11.2	12.7	24.2
France	127	12.3	5.2	4.8
Italy	47	8.3	1.9	2.0
Netherlands	65	5.8	2.7	1.8
Belgium-Luxembourg	32	3.0	1.3	-4.1
Japan	66	22.6	2.7	19.2
Canada	87	7.6	3.6	9.9
Australia	94	18.3	3.8	18.4
New Zealand	27	15.8	1.1	19.9

Source: Appendixes D and E.

[a] The items excluded (from both numerator and denominator) in computing the percentages in column 2 are those marked by an asterisk in Table 8.

TABLE 13

Imports of Labor-Intensive Manufactures by Developed from Less Developed Countries in 1965:
Percentage Distribution Among Importing Countries by Four Main Groups of Products

Importing Country	All Items	Group 1 Textiles, Clothing, and Accessories	Group 2 Other Light Manufactures, Except Food	Group 3 Labor-Intensive Food Manufactures	Group 4 Labor-Intensive Industrial Materials
United States	41.4	36.4	54.5	24.5	48.9
United Kingdom	17.6	22.9	14.8	11.8	17.3
Other EFTA	6.0	8.7	5.9	5.2	3.6
West Germany	12.7	16.8	5.9	22.5	6.4
Other EEC	11.1	5.1	9.1	26.0	9.4
Canada, Australia, and New Zealand	8.5	9.5	6.1	3.1	12.7
Japan	2.7	.6	3.7	7.0	1.6

Source: Appendixes D and E.

sition of their imports from the less developed countries. The United Kingdom's imports are, however, more concentrated on Commonwealth countries, which enjoy preferential entry to the British market, than those of the United States and West Germany. The much smaller total of French imports of labor-intensive manufactures from the less developed countries is composed to the extent of two-thirds of food products, leather, and lumber, chiefly from Africa. Japan's imports of labor-intensive manufactures from the less developed countries are extraordinarily small by almost any standard and, in conjunction with the data in Table 15, below, indicate that in these products Japan's role vis-à-vis the less developed countries is, at least for the time being, far more that of a competitor than that of a customer.

Distribution by Exporting Countries

Hong Kong alone supplied 28 per cent of total imports of labor-intensive manufactures by developed from less developed countries in 1965, outranking India and the whole of Latin America with less than one-fifth each (Table 14). The extraordinary role of Hong Kong is not sufficiently indicated by the over-all percentage just cited: Its share in labor-intensive food products and industrial materials (groups 3 and 4) was negligible, reflecting its lack of land and other natural resources, but it supplied half of the textile group and more than half of other light manufactures (groups 1 and 2).

Other less developed countries of the Far East brought the combined share of that area to two-thirds of the total. Extraordinarily rapid rates of increase from 1964 to 1965 were shown by several of these countries, notably South Korea and Taiwan. It may be noted that their highest rates of increase were in the miscellaneous light manufactures included in group 2, and this was generally true of the less developed countries in other regions as well.

No less remarkable than the vigor shown by the exports of some of the small Far Eastern countries is the failure of some of the larger less developed countries, with an earlier beginning of industry, to compete on a significant scale in the markets of the developed countries for labor-intensive manufactures. These countries include Argentina, Brazil, Chile, Mexico, the Philippines, Egypt, Algeria, and Morocco.[12] With

---

[12] Peru forms a striking contrast because of the rapid development of its production and exports of fish meal in recent years (though, as noted above, temporarily interrupted by the poor anchovy catch in 1965).

It is also relevant to the discussion of policies in Chapter 5 to note that several of these countries have had the advantage of preferential entry to markets in developed countries—the Philippines in the United States and Algeria and

TABLE 14

Imports of Labor-Intensive Manufactures by Developed from Less Developed Countries by Four Main Groups of Products and by Countries of Origin: Value in 1965 and Increase from 1964

(value in 1965 in $ million, f.o.b.; increase from 1964 in percentages)

Country of Origin	Groups 1–4, Total		Group 1 Textiles, Clothing, and Accessories		Group 2 Other Light Manufactures, Except Food		Group 3 Labor-Intensive Food Manufactures		Group 4 Labor-Intensive Industrial Materials	
	Value in 1965	Rise from 1964	Value in 1965	Rise from 1964	Value in 1965	Rise from 1964	Value in 1965	Rise from 1964	Value in 1965	Rise from 1964
Less developed countries, total	2,438	11.4%	787	10.4%	495	27.1%	458	4.6%	698	7.6%
Far East, excl. Japan, total	1,644	15.0	629	9.5	391	29.6	124	24.2	500	10.3
India	443	7.8	101	-7.0	38	20.4	6	26.1	298	12.1
Pakistan	68	17.1	20	6.7	5	3.3	1	33.4	41	24.6
Hong Kong	690	18.1	391	13.6	285	25.0	6	14.4	8	19.1
Taiwan	137	34.1	29	23.1	24	80.7	52	51.3	32	3.4
Philippine Islands	85	-4.1	25	-9.8	10	22.5	14	8.5	37	-9.4
South Korea	58	91.6	31	87.9	10	268.2	2	131.3	15	47.1
Other Far East	164	4.8	33	-8.6	19	45.0	43	4.5	70	4.6
Western Hemisphere, total	451	2.6	34	24.1	68	17.3	236	—	113	-4.5
Mexico	91	-1.1	5	13.2	24	12.5	24	6.3	37	-13.4
Brazil	70	30.8	7	188.6	14	30.5	11	58.7	37	13.1
Argentina	16	-30.3	—	-95.2	5	30.1	6	-34.5	4	-31.4
Chile	17	-7.1	—	—	—	-38.5	15	-13.0	2	225.9
Peru	147	-1.3	—	-25.3	1	-17.0	145	-1.4	1	40.4

(continued)

TABLE 14 (concluded)

Country of Origin	Groups 1–4, Total		Group 1 Textiles, Clothing, and Accessories		Group 2 Other Light Manufactures, Except Food		Group 3 Labor-Intensive Food Manufactures		Group 4 Labor-Intensive Industrial Materials	
	Value in 1965	Rise from 1964	Value in 1965	Rise from 1964	Value in 1965	Rise from 1964	Value in 1965	Rise from 1964	Value in 1965	Rise from 1964
Western Hemisphere (cont.)										
Colombia	18	36.4%	5	53.4%	6	50.8%	—	−60.7%	6	24.8%
Jamaica	19	1.1	8	−6.7	3	18.5	7	5.9	2	−5.7
Other Western Hemisphere	74	1.6	9	54.1	14	3.9	27	7.8	24	−15.3
Africa, excl. South Africa and Egypt	167	6.6	7	32.9	23	21.1	62	−4.4	75	11.1
Morocco, Algeria, and Tunisia	59	−2.5	6	41.3	8	−1.0	40	−8.1	5	7.0
Countries associated with EEC	53	18.3	1	16.9	7	55.7	13	0.2	32	20.5
Other Africa	55	7.2	—	−22.5	8	25.0	10	6.8	37	4.7
Middle East, total	175	7.7	117	10.3	13	22.3	36	−3.1	9	5.1
Iran	92	15.1	82	20.8	1	65.1	9	−20.7	—	−100.0
Israel	50	6.2	16	1.6	7	7.7	19	7.0	8	12.9
Egypt	22	−9.5	17	−16.3	3	71.7	2	−5.0	—	−100.0
Other Middle East	11	−1.3	2	−16.8	2	18.9	6	1.4	1	−22.3

Source: From basic tabulations prepared by United Nations Statistical Office; see Appendix D, below.

the exception of Brazil, whose exports in 1965 gave some promise of renewed growth, these countries also failed to share in the general rise in exports of labor-intensive manufactures from the less developed countries in 1965. Their participation is especially weak in group 2, which includes some of the more rapidly growing items. Nor should it be supposed that the minor role played by these countries as exporters of labor-intensive manufactures to the developed countries is to be explained by a more impressive performance in capital-intensive manufactures. As previously noted in connection with Table 10, exports of such manufactures by the less developed countries, apart from strongly resource-based products, are exceptional. Some of the exceptions are, however, of possible interest in the present connection. They include $15,758,000 of iron and steel exported by Mexico to the United States; $1,002,000 of tires and tubes exported by Israel to Western European countries as well as smaller amounts from Morocco, India, and the Philippines; $363,000 of trucks from Morocco to France; and $90,000 of insulated wire and cable exported by Argentina to the United States.

Imports from Other Low-Wage Countries

The major role of Hong Kong in the trade highlights the problem of defining just what is a "less developed" or "developing" country and, in particular, whether or not Hong Kong should be considered as belonging to the group. Undoubtedly, its circumstances have been unusual in several key respects, though the point loses in relevance as some of the other less developed countries begin to make headway in exporting manufactures.

The problem of definition may be simpler if one speaks instead of "low-wage countries." In this event a number of other countries would need to be brought into the analysis as exporters. They would include, as a minimum, the whole of Southern Europe with the exception of Italy—that is, Portugal, Spain, Yugoslavia, Greece, and Turkey. And it is probably appropriate to include also Japan, which, though certainly not an undeveloped country and perhaps no longer a low-wage country compared with many others, still shows some of the same attributes and faces some of the same export problems and opportunities as countries in the less developed and low-wage categories.[13]

Table 15 shows that imports of labor-intensive manufactures from

Morocco in France. Their poor performance in exporting manufactures either to these countries or elsewhere sugggests that other influences may be more important than preferences.

[13] See Leon Hollerman, "Japan's Place in the Scale of Economic Development," *Economic Development and Cultural Change,* January 1964, pp. 139–157.

TABLE 15

*Imports of Labor-Intensive Manufactures by Developed Countries from
Less Developed Countries and from Other Low-Wage Countries, 1965*
($ million, f.o.b.)

	From Less Developed Countries	From Other Low-Wage Countries		
		Total	Japan	Southern Europe, excluding Italy
Developed countries, total, excluding Japan	2,372	2,979	2,347	633

By Product Group

1. Textiles, clothing, and accessories	782	710	566	144
2. Other light manufactures, except food	477	1,587	1,429	158
3. Labor-intensive food manufactures	427	386	185	201
4. Labor-intensive industrial materials	687	296	166	131

By Importing Country

United States	1,010	1,648	1,523	125
EFTA, total, excl. Portugal	574	440	249	192
United Kingdom	429	252	145	107
Sweden	44	65	37	28
Norway	13	18	10	7
Denmark	32	34	21	14
Switzerland	43	49	29	20
Austria	14	22	7	14
EEC, total	580	548	254	294
West Germany	309	290	143	146
France	127	82	34	48
Italy	47	61	15	45
Netherlands	65	68	37	31
Belgium-Luxembourg	32	47	23	24
Canada	87	166	149	16
Australia	94	147	143	5
New Zealand	27	30	29	1

Note: In this table Japan is included with "other low-wage
countries" and excluded from "developed countries."

these other low-wage countries by developed countries other than Japan were somewhat larger in 1965 than imports of corresponding items from the less developed countries; that, by product, these imports from the other low-wage countries were much more heavily concentrated in group 2; and that, by importing country, they were much more heavily concentrated in the U.S. market.

These characteristics are, however, largely determined by Japan, which supplies by far the greater part of the goods covered by Table 15, especially those in group 2, and sells more to the United States than to all other developed countries combined. Exports of labor-intensive manufactures by the Southern European countries are rather differently made up by product groups and go chiefly to other European countries. A relevant question is whether the small part of labor-intensive imports from the less developed countries, or from Japan, taken by the countries of Western Europe other than the United Kingdom and West Germany is to be explained by the intensity of their trade relations with their low-wage neighbors of Southern Europe. The size of the trade flows mirrored in Table 15 is clearly too small to support such an explanation.

Market Potentials

Past Growth, 1953–65

The rate of growth in imports of labor-intensive manufactures by developed from less developed countries in recent years has probably been much faster than had been expected. For instance, in a study published in 1964, Bela Balassa projected an annual rate of increase of 5.5 per cent in exports of manufactures by less developed to developed countries over the period from 1960 to 1975, prices being assumed to remain constant.[14] By contrast, the total of the labor-intensive items plotted in Chart 14 (slightly less comprehensive in coverage than Tables 11–15) shows imports in 1965 four and one-third times as large as in 1953, an increase of about 13 per cent per annum compounded. This is at current prices, and the annual rate of increase might be one or two percentage points less at constant prices.[15] Balassa's group of manufactures

[14] Bela Balassa, *Trade Prospects for Developing Countries,* Homewood, Illinois, 1964, p. 66 and Tables A3.1.1 and A12.

[15] There is no price index ready to hand for this small segment of world trade, and it would be difficult to construct a meaningful one (even if the necessary price information were available) in view of the considerable changes in composition and quality of the items over the period. The *Monthly Bulletin of Statistics of the United Nations* (issues of December 1966 for the period 1957–65 and December 1960 for the period 1953–57) indicates a rise of some

CHART 14

Imports of Labor-Intensive Manufactures
by Developed from Less Developed Countries, 1953–65

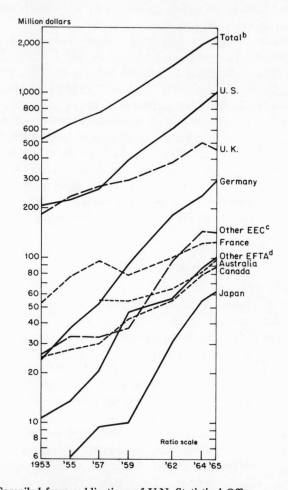

Source: Compiled from publications of U.N. Statistical Office.

a Imports of countries reporting on a c.i.f. basis have been adjusted to an approximate f.o.b. basis by a uniform reduction of 10 per cent.

b Excluding Australia, Japan, and Switzerland.

c Belgium-Luxembourg, Italy, and the Netherlands.

d Austria, Denmark, Norway, and Sweden (Switzerland and Portugal not included).

is somewhat broader than that given by the criterion of labor intensity employed here, but that does not seem to be the reason for the difference between projected and actual results. If one takes his list of items and adjusts the reported trade figures in the manner indicated in his study,[16] actual imports of manufactures by developed from less developed countries in 1965 equaled the mean of his higher and lower projections for 1975 and were almost 2.3 times actual imports in 1960 (unadjusted for price changes). In other words, the increase foreseen for 15 years was approximately realized in 5 years. As Table 16 shows, the strength of actual performance in relation to the projections was pervasive, extending to most product groups and geographic areas.

Structure of Wages in Less Developed Countries

One of the conditions for a continued rapid growth of the trade is that the structure of wages in less developed countries not be such as to nullify their comparative advantage in labor-intensive products. A few years ago Lloyd Reynolds suggested that "interindustry wage dispersion tends to reach a maximum some time during the early stages of industrialization and to diminish gradually after that point." [17] This is what one would expect under free-market conditions, assuming that skills are relatively short and unskilled labor abundant in newly developing countries, and that these disparities in supply are gradually overcome.

Recently, however, a growing literature indicates that interferences of one kind or another tend to narrow wage differentials between industries or occupations in many of the less developed countries and so to raise costs in their more labor-intensive manufacturing branches. And it has already been observed in Chapter 3 that in several of these coun-

11 per cent in prices of *world* exports of manufactures, but this index is, of course, dominated by the exports of the industrially developed countries. If one assumes that, at constant prices, the 1965 total in Chart 14 would be, say three and three-quarters times higher than that for 1953, the annual rate of increase would be about 11.6 per cent compounded.

[16] The most important of these adjustments are (1) the rough conversion of imports where reported c.i.f. to an f.o.b. basis and (2) the exclusion of certain spurious elements in the reported import data such as returned construction equipment. See note to Table 16 and Appendix D. Balassa's projections are, however, in 1960 prices, whereas the 1965 actual values shown in Table 16 are in current prices. The U.N. *Monthly Bulletin of Statistics* for December 1966 indicates a rise of about 5.5 per cent in the unit value of world exports of manufactures from 1960 to 1965, but, for reasons stated in the preceding footnote, this index is not necessarily relevant to exports of manufactures by the less developed countries.

[17] L. G. Reynolds and C. H. Taft, *The Evolution of Wage Structure,* New Haven, 1956, p. 356.

TABLE 16

Imports of Manufactures by Developed from Less Developed Countries: Imports in 1960 and 1965 and Balassa's Projections for 1975

($ million)

Product Group	Imports in 1960 (current prices)					Imports in 1965 (current prices)				
	All Developed Countries	North America	Western Europe	Japan	Oceania	All Developed Countries	North America	Western Europe	Japan	Oceania
Chemicals	119	54	59	5	1	267	109	131	22	5
Leather and footwear	81	14	64	2	1	132	36	90	5	1
Veneer, plywood, wood and cork manufactures, and paper	50	25	23	–	2	140	97	39	1	3
Textile yarn, cotton fabrics, and clothing	316	145	151	–	20	622	285	297	2	38
Jute manufactures	175	103	34	1	37	279	192	46	–	42
Floor coverings and other textile products	102	39	59	1	3	217	65	142	3	7
Silver, precious stones, pearls, and jewelry	94	28	64	2	–	277	95	161	20	1
Machinery and metal manufactures	42	20	21	–	1	252	117	108	25	2
Other manufactured goods	96	53	37	1	5	284	173	89	10	12
Total	1,075	481	512	12	70	2,470	1,169	1,103	87	111

(continued)

TABLE 16 (concluded)

Balassa's Projections for 1975 – Average of High and Low
(1960 prices)

Product Group	All Developed Countries	North America	Western Europe	Japan	Oceania
Chemicals	227	100	111	15	1
Leather and footwear	154	36	106	10	3
Veneer, plywood, wood and cork manufactures, and paper	268	179	84	—	5
Textile yarn, cotton fabrics, and clothing	658	281	332	—	45
Jute manufactures	217	121	50	1	45
Floor coverings and other textile products	246	79	156	4	7
Silver, precious stones, pearls, and jewelry	291	88	190	9	4
Machinery and metal manufactures	132	62	66	—	3
Other manufactured goods	253	138	97	4	14
Total	2,446	1,084	1,192	43	127

Notes to Table 16

Source: 1960 imports and 1975 projections from Bela Balassa, *Trade Prospects for Developing Countries*, Homewood, Ill., 1964; 1965 imports from United Nations, *Commodity Trade Statistics, 1965,* New York, 1966.

Note: See Balassa, *Trade Prospects,* p. 368, for definition of product groups in terms of the SITC and p. 338 for explanation of items deleted or adjusted because of their questionable content. In addition to the items specifically mentioned by Balassa, a number of other items in the import data reported for 1965 have been eliminated or adjusted for similar reasons, i.e., in an effort to minimize risk of overstatement in the 1965 results given above. The most important deletion is imports of cut and uncut diamonds (SITC No. 667) by the United Kingdom in 1965; these imports were not reported by the United Kingdom prior to that year and, presumably, could not be included in Balassa's figures of imports in 1960 or in his projections for 1975. Other important items deleted or adjusted downward in addition to those mentioned by Balassa are as follows (SITC numbers): 7143, 7184, 7191, 7192, 7193, 7196, 7198, 7199, 7249, 7295, 7299. On the other hand, rather than omit the whole of SITC 735 (ships and boats), the data for 1965 given above include imports within this group from Hong Kong where they can be identified as yachts and other small craft.

Imports of areas other than North America in 1965 have been reduced by 8 per cent, i.e., the figure indicated by Balassa for converting from a c.i.f. to an f.o.b. basis.

tries the differentials appear very small in the three broad groups of industries distinguished in Chart 7, particularly between the first and second of these groups. Frequently the stress is placed on labor unions as the main force underlying the development of wages.[18] Legal minimum wages may, however, be a more general and powerful influence on the level and structure of wages in less developed countries to a degree not matched in more developed countries.[19] An authoritative analy-

[18] See particularly W. Arthur Lewis, "A Review of Economic Development," *American Economic Review,* May 1965, pp. 1–16, and Raymond F. Mikesell, "Inflation and Growth: Observations from Latin America," in Paul L. Kleinsorge, ed., *Public Finance and Welfare Essays in Honor of C. Ward Macy,* Eugene, Ore., 1966.

[19] In a study of Puerto Rico, Lloyd Reynolds notes that, as contrasted with the U.S. mainland, "Most workers in each industry earn very close to the minimum rate; and as the minimum is raised, which happens every year or two, the industry level is forced up by a proportionate amount" (minimum wages being set at different levels for each industry). Reynolds also holds that the decisive influence in pushing up wages is exercised by manufacturers and union leaders on the U.S. mainland (represented on the committees recommending minimum wages in each industry). See Lloyd G. Reynolds, "Wages and Employment in a Labor-Surplus Economy," *American Economic Review,* March 1965, pp. 19–39.

sis in the organ of the International Labour Office,[20] in discussing changes in wage differentials by skill in the less developed countries, attributes minimum-wage policies to widespread disapproval of the wage levels of unskilled workers that would otherwise obtain. But he adds that "if governments insist that unskilled wages should increase independently of the forces of demand for and supply of unskilled labour, there is a likelihood that unskilled wages may increase faster than skilled wages." The author then quotes an earlier article in the same review (1959), finding "an extreme uniformity of wage rates in Brazil" attributable to public intervention, particularly the minimum wage, and cites other evidence of a tendency for the skilled-unskilled wage differential to narrow in "many African countries" and "some Asian countries." "This," he explains, " is because legal minimum wages are relatively high in these countries and are raised from time to time irrespective of the underlying conditions." [21]

Several unfavorable economic consequences are associated with tendencies toward uniformity of wage rates irrespective of skills. One (noted in the ILO article cited above) is the discouragement of effort by workers to acquire higher skills. Another (stressed by Lewis) is the inducement to entrepreneurs to adopt more capital-intensive methods of production than they otherwise would or (according to Reynolds' observations of Puerto Rico) to save on labor in other ways, thus inhibiting the growth of employment. A third effect of particular relevance here is the brake on the diversification of exports: A country unable to compete abroad in capital-intensive manufactures may also find itself priced out of the market in more labor-intensive manufactures and thus forced to continue to rely on exports of primary products.

These considerations may help to explain why it is that some of the less developed countries, notably those with an earlier start on industrialization, have fared so poorly in exporting manufactures and why, in contrast, some others, particularly some of the countries of Southeast Asia, have made such rapid headway.

[20] "Wage Differentials in Developing Countries: A Survey of Findings," by Koji Taira, *International Labour Review,* March 1966, pp. 281–301. With respect to *interindustry* wage differentials, Taira says that it is impossible to say, at the present state of research, whether these differentials are or should be wider in developing than in developed countries, "Though there is some evidence that they have been narrowing in both groups of countries over time" (p. 284). Moreover, given the different skill requirements of different industries, one would expect his findings with regard to skilled-unskilled wage differentials to be reflected in interindustry differentials.

[21] P. 287.

Possible Areas of Rapid Growth

At least for those less developed countries which do strengthen their comparative advantage in labor-intensive manufactures, the very unevenness of the trade hitherto may provide a key to future growth sectors. Imports from less developed countries of many of the light consumer manufactures listed in Table 8, above, have scarcely scratched the surface of the market. This certainly seems true of the United States on even a rough comparison of domestic production and imports from the less developed countries. There are, indeed, very few manufactured products of which *total* U.S. imports from all sources make up a significant part of supply.[22] It seems plausible to expect that a growing, adaptable economy will absorb increasing amounts of these miscellaneous consumer goods from the less developed countries.

This may be true also of many other developed countries, in some of which imports of consumer manufactures from the less developed countries have scarcely begun to play a role. Restrictive import policies and practices are doubtless one explanation. But perhaps also a learning period is required, and the experience gained by some of the less developed countries in exporting to the larger and higher-cost U.S. market, and by those of the Commonwealth with their privileged access to the British market, may now be applied to the conquest of still other markets.

Some of the greatest opportunities for expansion may be offered by the marginally labor-intensive manufactures included in group 2 of Table 8. The field of components and parts for use in electronic products and perhaps also in machinery, automobiles, and other transportation equipment seems particularly interesting. American manufacturers of electronic goods have reached out not only to Japan and Puerto Rico but also to Hong Kong, Taiwan, and Korea for components or even complete products. One analysis of this development runs in terms of a "product cycle" and finds that, as an invention passes from the early development and growth phases on into a "mature stage," the production process becomes more standardized, requiring less of skilled management and of scientific and engineering know-how and making more use of relatively unskilled labor.[23] Growing competition among producers may then lead them to site procurement where labor costs

---

[22] See Tables 8 and C-1 of this study and, for more detailed comparisons, see *U.S. Commodity Exports and Imports as Related to Output, 1963 and 1964,* U.S. Bureau of the Census, 1966 (Tables 1C and 4B).

[23] Seev Hirsch, "The United States Electronic Industry in International Trade," *Economic Review* (London), November 1965.

are lower and, where necessary, to help start production by providing capital, technical advice, and orders.

If these gains are realized, they will entail at least a relative displacement of domestic production in the importing countries, but they will be partly also at the expense of imports from other developed countries. Japan can be expected to face a particularly sharp dual adjustment in low-wage manufactures—that is, a loss to the less developed countries in its sales of light consumer goods both in its own market and in other developed countries. The word "loss" is, however, ill chosen, since a shift in employment may be a precondition for the further growth of Japan's production and exports of more sophisticated goods, and also for the strengthening of its important trade relations with the less developed countries.[24] The minute amount of Japan's imports of manufactures from these countries at present probably gives little hint of what they may be five or ten years hence. Such a development appears to be heralded by current changes in productivity and labor costs in Japan, which have been described as follows:

Industries where possibilities for increasing productivity of labour are limited are being more adversely affected by increased labour costs and consequently are becoming less resistant to competition from abroad, in particular from developing countries. A movement of labour to economic sectors with high labour productivity is expected to continue at a rapid pace, thus leading to adjustment in the economic structure. It is a well-known fact that economic adjustment and economic growth are closely related. A smoother economic adjustment which facilitates better use of resources will bring about a faster economic growth and vice versa. Entrepreneurs and workers in a rapidly growing economy are quick to switch from relatively stagnant or deteriorating sectors to those that offer more favourable prospects. Japan's economy has proved to be highly capable of adjustment under its free market system and from all indications will continue to be so.[25]

[24] For an illuminating account of Japan's rather unhappy middle position at the United Nations Conference on Trade and Development, see Saburo Okita, "Japan and the Developing Nations," in *Contemporary Japan*, Vol. XXVIII, No. 2, 1965. Some idea of the pressures on Japan by its neighbors may be seen in the following excerpt from the joint communiqué issued after the Ministerial Conference for Economic Development of Southeast Asia, which met in Tokyo in April 1966: "It was also suggested that the limitation of market opportunities for the simpler manufactures of countries concerned was a handicap, and it was recognized that developed countries in the region as well as those outside, in addition to assisting in making capital and know-how available, should offer increased market accessibility" (from *Japan Report* [New York], April 15, 1966, p. 7).

[25] Tamotsu Takase, "Japan—A Market for Developing Countries—A Survey," *International Trade Forum* (GATT, Geneva), December 1965, p. 13.

5

COMMERCIAL POLICIES
OF DEVELOPED COUNTRIES

The assessment of market potentials concluding Chapter 4 may be too optimistic. How far the expansionary forces go depends heavily on the commercial policies of the developed countries with regard to imports of manufactures from less developed countries. It remains therefore to consider in this regard both the tariff structures of the developed countries and nontariff barriers which, in some cases, may have a far more restrictive effect.

Tariff Structures:
Nominal Versus Effective Rates

Table 17 offers a summary analysis of trade in four main product groups, imports in each group being broken down according to stage of manufacture. The selection of products is limited to those in which the raw materials, as well as manufactures, lend themselves to international trade, thus omitting items such as pottery and structural clay products.[1] They are limited also to those in which, on the criteria developed in this study, the manufacturing process is relatively labor-intensive, leaving out petroleum, aluminum, and steel, for instance.[2] The product groups included in the table thus seem to offer a choice as

---

[1] Similarly, there would seem to be little point in comparing imports of seafood, fruit, and vegetables in fresh and in processed or canned form, given the rather different varieties involved at each stage.

[2] An analysis by the FAO of trade in vegetable oils and materials, to take another example, notes several factors favoring location of the crushing industries in the importing countries, including not only the very low value added (tentatively assumed to be only about 15 per cent) and the capital-intensive nature of the operation but also the advantages in blending materials from a variety of sources ("Trade in Processed Agricultural Commodities," *Proceedings of the United Nations Conference on Trade and Development*, Vol. IV, *Trade in Manufactures*, United Nations, 1964, p. 167).

TABLE 17

Imports by Developed Countries from Less Developed Countries in 1965:
Selected Product Groups by Stage of Manufacture
($ million, f.o.b.)[a]

Product Group and Stage of Manufacture	United States	United Kingdom	Other EFTA[b]	West Germany	Other ECE[c]	Canada, Australia, and New Zealand	Japan
Textile Group, Excluding Coarse Fibers							
I. Cotton, wool, and other fibers	122.9	155.2	44.9	151.7	290.8	16.7	301.1
II. Yarn	5.9	8.4	6.9	8.0	1.5	5.1	—
IIIa. Fabrics, clothing, accessories	264.7	153.9	38.8	71.0	28.1	65.9	3.9
b. Carpets, other floor covering	15.7	20.0	22.6	52.5	10.4	4.5	1.0
Coarse-Fiber Group							
I. Fiber of jute, sisal, and manila	32.3	45.9	10.0	22.8	73.8	17.2	25.8
II. Yarn	1.2	1.8	.7	1.7	5.3	1.0	.4
III. Jute fabrics, cordage, sets, etc.	193.4	18.3	5.6	7.6	10.3	60.4	.1
Leather Group							
I. Hides and skins, undressed	39.2	13.1	3.9	15.0	60.6	1.0	6.6
II. Leather	20.4	31.4	3.2	10.3	19.0	.9	5.4
III. Shoes, luggage, handbags, gloves, etc.	40.1	15.1	3.8	5.7	3.8	4.9	.4
Wood Group							
I. Sawlogs, veneer logs, etc., in the rough	9.3	19.1	25.2	78.3	128.5	3.6	235.4
II. Lumber, simply worked, sawn, etc.	25.3	45.7	11.4	17.3	23.2	18.5	4.3
III. Plywood, furniture, and other wood manufactures	97.3	17.0	1.7	4.2	5.6	8.5	.6
Total, All Groups							
I. Crude materials	203.7	233.3	84.0	267.8	553.7	38.5	568.9
II. Intermediate products	52.8	87.3	22.2	37.3	49.0	25.5	10.1
III. Finished manufactures	611.2	224.5	72.5	141.0	58.2	144.2	6.0

Notes to Table 17

Source: Compiled from statistical publications of the United Nations.

Note: I = crude materials, II = intermediate products, III = finished manufactures.

[a]Imports of countries reporting on a c.i.f. basis have been adjusted to an approximate f.o.b. basis by use of differentials given in Tariff Commission's release of February 7, 1967, "C.I.F. Value of U.S. Imports."

[b]Sweden, Norway, Denmark, Switzerland, and Austria.

[c]France, Italy, the Netherlands, and Belgium-Luxembourg.

[d]Includes also shoes of materials other than leather.

to where manufacturing occurs along with a presumption that comparative advantage is on the side of the less developed countries.

The distinction by stage of manufacture in Table 17 is made in light of the standing complaint of less developed countries that the import tariffs of the developed countries tend to be graduated according to stage of manufacture so as to bear lightly, if at all, on imports of raw materials for use in manufacture and to penalize imports of processed or finished goods. To the extent that these influences prevailed, many of the less developed countries would have to remain hewers of wood and drawers of water.

Theoretical and empirical support for the view that the "escalated tariff structures" of the advanced countries are "a potentially powerful inhibitor of economic growth in the underdeveloped countries" has been developed by Harry G. Johnson, Bela Balassa, Giorgio Basevi, W. M. Corden, and others.[3] Their analyses make the point that *nominal* tariffs may be quite different from *effective* tariffs, the latter being related to value added by manufacture after taking account of duties paid on material inputs. When the rates specified in the tariffs are graduated according to stage of manufacture, the effective rates are higher, and frequently much higher, than the nominal rates.

Suppose, for example, that an import consignment of cotton cloth worth $500 is subject to an import duty of $100. Suppose further that

[3] See Harry G. Johnson, "The Theory of Tariff Structure, with Special Reference to World Trade and Development," in Johnson and Peter B. Kenen, *Trade and Development,* Geneva, 1965, pp. 9–29 (quotation from page 23); Bela Balassa, "Tariff Protection in Industrial Countries: An Evaluation," *Journal of Political Economy,* December 1965, pp. 573–594; Giorgio Basevi, "The United States Tariff Structure: Estimates of Effective Rates of Protection of United States Industries and Industrial Labor," *Review of Economics and Statistics,* May 1966, pp. 147–160; W. M. Corden, "The Structure of a Tariff System and the Effective Protective Rate," *Journal of Political Economy,* June 1966.

the same amount and quality of cloth produced at home would require $240 of yarn which, if imported, would bear a duty of $30. In this case the value added by weaving is $260, protected by a duty of $70.[4] The effective rate of duty, computed in relation to value added, is therefore 26.9 per cent as contrasted with the nominal rate of 20 per cent.

Moreover, it may be more meaningful to relate the duty only to the wage part of value added on the assumption that capital costs are not likely to be lower, and may well be higher, in less developed than in developed countries. On this basis, and assuming that payroll makes up 60 per cent of value added in the example chosen, the effective rate of protection would be about 45 per cent. This would be the amount by which labor costs per unit of output in the importing country could exceed those in the exporting country. The difference will be greater still to the extent that capital costs, transportation charges, and other costs work in favor of the importing country. (And, of course, the difference in earnings *per worker* will be much greater still when the difference in productivity of labor is as large as it typically is between less developed and developed countries.)

Table 18, drawn from a current study by Balassa, presents nominal tariff rates and estimates of the effective rates, on both of the bases just described, for most of the intermediate products and finished manufactures covered by Table 17.[5] These estimates necessarily involve an element of approximation regarding input coefficients and can perhaps best be regarded as illustrative rather than as precise measurements. In most cases the effective rates are much higher than nominal tariffs. Some extreme examples are wool yarn and wool fabrics in the United States, products of coarse fibers in the Common Market, and plywood in both. Precisely because of the high protection of wool yarn and fabrics in the United States, however, the estimated effective rate in this country on imports of wool clothing becomes negative. The effective rates in Japan are in most instances higher than in the United States or the Common Market. In the United Kingdom, the structure of protec-

---

[4] It is relevant to the history of economic doctrine to note that this example is drawn from a study of tariff protection and free trade published more than sixty years ago by the Austrian economist and former undersecretary of state Richard Schüller (*Schutzzoll and Freihandel*, Vienna and Leipzig, 1905). Dr. Schüller's concise presentation on pages 149–150 of his study contains the fundamentals of what is now being developed into a theory of tariff structures.

[5] Table 18 does not show crude materials, most of which are admitted duty-free by the industrially developed countries (thus contributing to the graduation of duties by stage of manufacture). The United States, as a major producer as well as consumer of crude materials, is something of an exception, duties being imposed on imports of both raw wool and raw cotton, for example.

TABLE 18

Nominal Tariff Rates and Estimated Effective Rates on Imports of Selected Intermediate Products and Finished Manufactures by the United States, the European Economic Community, and Japan
(per cent)

SITC No.	Product	Nominal Tariff Rates			Estimated Effective Rates on Value Added			Estimated Effective Rates on Value Added by Labor[a]		
		U.S.	EEC	Japan	U.S.	EEC	Japan	U.S.	EEC	Japan
	Intermediate Products									
6513	Cotton yarn and thread	13.1	10.0	5.6	32.8	31.4	13.9	46.0	44.0	19.5
6512	Yarn of wool and animal hair	23.0	5.7	10.0	53.2	16.1	29.6	74.5	22.5	41.5
611	Leather	9.6	7.3	19.9	25.7	18.3	59.0	48.1	34.3	110.4
243	Wood, shaped or simply worked	0.7	3.2	5.9	1.1	4.5	13.3	1.9	7.5	22.5
	Finished Manufactures									
652	Cotton fabrics, woven	17.5	15.0	10.5	31.2	27.5	20.0	43.4	38.5	27.8
6532	Woolen fabrics, woven	50.1	16.0	20.0	119.1	36.9	43.1	165.6	51.3	60.0
841b	Cotton clothing	26.6	18.5	21.0	48.1	28.1	40.3	77.4	45.2	64.8
841b	Wool clothing	22.1	20.5	22.0	-5.4	32.4	30.8	-8.7	52.2	49.6
8414	Clothing and accessories, knitted	25.6	18.6	26.0	48.7	41.3	60.8	68.5	58.1	85.5
6534	Jute fabrics, woven	2.8	23.0	25.0	7.0	62.2	67.5	9.9	86.6	94.0
6561	Jute sacks and bags	7.5	19.4	25.0	16.6	19.2	34.5	25.0	29.0	52.0
6556	Cordage, ropes, nets, etc.	4.0	14.3	19.2	11.3	41.9	57.2	32.7	121.8	166.4
851	Shoes	16.6	19.9	29.5	25.3	33.0	45.1	47.6	62.0	84.8
612 } 831	Other leather goods	15.5	14.7	23.6	24.5	24.3	33.6	34.3	34.0	47.0
6312	Plywood	17.1	15.0	20.0	43.7	32.5	44.2	87.5	65.0	88.4
632 } 821	Other wood products including furniture	12.8	15.1	19.5	26.4	28.6	33.9	46.4	50.3	59.6

Notes to Table 18

Source: Bela Balassa, "The Structure of Protection in the Industrial Countries and Its Effect on the Exports of Processed Goods from Developing Nations," United Nations Conference on Trade and Development, May 25, 1967 (TD/B/C.2/36).

Note: Rates relate to structure prior to completion of Kennedy Round of GATT negotiations.

[a]The estimated effective rate on value added by labor is the lower of two sets of estimates given by Balassa (the higher estimates allowing for higher capital costs in developing countries).

[b]Data relate to selected components of SITC No. 841.

tion is not very different from that of other developed countries as far as tariff rates imposed on imports from outside the Commonwealth are concerned. These rates are, however, of less relevance than those of other countries (and are accordingly omitted from Table 18), since imports from the Commonwealth, including such major suppliers as Hong Kong and India, are generally free of duty (though not necessarily free of other restraints, as in cotton textiles and jute products).

It is noteworthy that, though the United States tariff appears in general to be no less graduated or escalated than those of other countries and is sometimes held to be more so, the effect on the structure of its imports as reflected in Table 17 seems to be much less marked than in some other developed countries, especially some of the members of the Common Market and Japan. One important reason is that the United States is itself a major producer and exporter of some of the crude materials included in the table, notably, cotton, cattle hides, and hardwoods. This alone would tend to cause a higher ratio of manufactured to unmanufactured imports than would be true of most other developed countries. The same influence may affect the composition of imports by Canada, Australia, and New Zealand.

Nevertheless, imports of finished manufactures from less developed countries by most countries of Western Continental Europe look very small, and those of Japan altogether trivial, compared both with their own imports of crude materials and intermediate products and with imports of finished goods by the United States from less developed countries. Part of the explanation may be that, even if effective tariff rates in the United States are the same as in Europe or Japan, they may be less effective, in fact, in restricting imports of labor-intensive goods, if wage costs per unit of output in manufacturing these goods are higher here than in other developed countries.

Nontariff Barriers to Imports

There are, however, other more specific though sometimes less visible hindrances to the growth of the trade than those presented by tariffs. The most obvious, at least so far as they are reported, are quantitative restrictions. After taking note of some further, but slow, progress in removing these restrictions, a mid-1966 report by UNCTAD observes that "the area of exports still affected is considerable and includes a number of products of major export interest to developing countries." The report then summarizes the position as follows: "Out of 63 Brussels Tariff Nomenclature items of export interest to developing countries, quantitative restrictions on the following among them are still maintained in the developed countries, namely: France 56, Japan 24, Federal Republic of Germany 21, Denmark 15, Norway 14, Austria 13, Italy 10, United Kingdom 7, Switzerland 6, Sweden 3, United States 3, Netherlands 2, Belgium-Luxembourg 2, Canada 1." [6]

It is hard to judge the significance of these restrictions, since they may be nominal in some cases and rigorously enforced in others. It is even more difficult to judge the incidence and effect of other more subtle hindrances, such as administrative red tape or collusion among private producers and distributors within the developed countries, but the absence of trade is sometimes difficult to explain otherwise. Though it is difficult to separate from other influences noted, perhaps something should be allowed for the view that competition is keener in the United States market than in other developed countries,[7] and that American entrepreneurs are more active in seeking out foreign sources of supply.[8]

[6] United Nations Conference on Trade and Development, "Review of International Trade and Development, 1966," Summary of Report by the Secretary-General, July 20, 1966 (TD/B/82), p. 15. A revised version of the material on nontariff barriers, "cleared with the governments of the developed countries concerned," was issued on May 29, 1967 (TD/B/C.2/26). The revised report covers a much longer list (147 Brussels Tariff Nomenclature items) of "manufactures and semimanufactures of export interest to developing countries," but does not attempt to summarize the results in the manner of the earlier document cited above.

[7] This is, of course, a view that would be difficult to test empirically. Joe S. Bain in his study, *International Differences in Industrial Structure* (New Haven, 1966), finds "distinct differences in absolute sizes of principal manufacturing plants" between the United States and all of the other seven countries studied (United Kingdom, Japan, France, Italy, Canada, India, and Sweden) along with "strong tentative indications that inferior plant sizes abroad seem to be associated with the production of significantly larger shares of industry outputs in plants of inefficiently small scale" (p. 143). As one of several "very tentative hypotheses," he suggests that in many of the foreign countries in question, "there

Restraints on Imports of Cotton Textiles

The history of cotton textiles in recent years illustrates how the very growth of trade can be its own undoing through provoking restrictive measures by the importing countries. Following the swift increase in imports of cotton textiles from India, Hong Kong, and other Commonwealth sources in the 1950's,[9] the United Kingdom made a series of

are found generally, and especially as nurtured in markets which are cartelized or not very competitive, some inertia, lack of vigorous enterprise, lack of technological information (ignorance), dampened profit-seeking motivation, and a social resistance to technological change" (p. 147).

[8] Richard L. Barovick reports in the *Journal of Commerce,* August 12, 1966, that the large retailers in the United States "have become a major underpinning for the high level of consumer goods imports," and that some of them "have combed the world for the best combination of price and quality." To illustrate, he points out that Macy's maintains a network of fifteen full-time offices in Europe and the Far East, and that the Hong Kong office alone employs a staff of thirty-five to forty persons, "all of them engaged in developmental work." See also the article by Bruce Hyatt, "Reaching the Department Store Market in the United States: Guidelines for Developing Nations," in *International Trade Forum,* December 1966, GATT, Geneva, pp. 10–13.

[9] The rise in these imports is explained as follows by A. M. Alfred, the chief economist for Courtaulds Ltd., in a paper read at the Manchester Statistical Society on November 10, 1965 ("U.K. Textiles—A Growth Industry"):

"On the import side, you will know well that the U.K. textile industry, particularly the cotton sector, has suffered from an unforeseen consequence of the Imperial Preference Treaty negotiated at Ottawa in 1932. Under that treaty, it was agreed that cotton and wool textiles and made-up goods could enter the U.K. duty free if coming from the Commonwealth. At that time there was no textile activity of relevance in India, Pakistan or Hong Kong. In fact India (then undivided) imported 550 mn. yds. of cloth from the U.K. In 1964 the U.K. imported 450 mn. sq. yds., of cloth and made-up goods from India, Pakistan and Hong Kong—a reversal of a billion yards. This large volume arose because of the channelling of these Commonwealth exports into the only country into which they could come duty free."

After noting that these imports, together with imports from other underdeveloped countries made up 35 per cent of British consumption, compared with his estimates of 8 per cent for the United States and 9 per cent for the European Common Market, Mr. Alfred went on to speak of "the ridiculous state of affairs whereby the U.K. cotton industry is the only industry in any developed country of the world to have zero protection against a major supplier."

While recognizing that the "market disruption" in the British textile industry has been far greater than in other developed countries, one cannot fail to detect in this account a double standard frequently characteristic of attitudes in developed countries toward trade with the less developed countries: Free trade in textiles within the Commonwealth seemed logical and desirable as long as the flow was from the United Kingdom outward, but ceased to be so when the flow reversed (though the initial impact of British factory-produced textiles on the Indian handicraft industry in the nineteenth century had been no less disruptive than that more recently experienced in the United Kingdom when the tide turned).

bilateral agreements aimed at limiting the further growth of the trade. The United States, after a rapid rise in imports from some of these countries and from Japan, took the lead in negotiating in 1961 a short-term and then, in 1962, a long-term international cotton textile "arrangement," under which it has made numerous bilateral agreements for "voluntary restraints" by the exporters. Continental European countries were happy to join in the arrangement, with the blessing it confers on avoidance of "market disruption," but for the greater part have continued to prove willing and able to apply their own import restraints.

These restraints are sometimes more than meet the eye. The director-general of GATT, in opening the "major review" called for in the arrangement at the end of the third year, noted that "all trade restrictions on cotton textiles are not fully notified by participating governments" and urged them to "help lift the haze which still rests over this subject." [10]

Despite these open and hidden restrictions, imports of cotton textiles by the developed countries from "Group II" countries (i.e., developing exporting countries") have increased relatively fast. Those of Western Continental European countries doubled from about $50 million in 1961 to something over $100 million in 1964. At that level, however, they still fell short of imports from "Group II" countries by the United Kingdom (around $170 million) and by the United States ($126 million), both of which had risen substantially as well.[11]

Apart from the United Kingdom, these increases have all been from extremely low levels compared with home consumption—so low in several of the Western Continental European countries that, according to Gardner Patterson, even their commitment to large percentage increases under the five-year arrangement was regarded by some of the exporting countries "as bordering on fraud." [12] In his remarks quoted above open-

[10] Press release GATT/946, December 8, 1965.

[11] These estimates (derived from *Study on Cotton Textiles,* GATT, Geneva, June 1966, Table VI) relate only to textiles, clothing, and other products of cotton and, in some cases, are adjusted to exclude textiles of other fibers. In addition, the figures for the United Kingdom and Western Continental European countries are adjusted to an approximate f.o.b. basis. "Group II" in the text includes Spain, Portugal, and Turkey in addition to various of the less developed countries as defined here. As noted earlier in this chapter, the United Kingdom tightened restraints in the latter part of 1964, resulting in a decline in its imports of cotton textiles from the less developed countries, but those of the United States and Western Continental Europe have continued to rise.

[12] Gardner Patterson, *Discrimination in International Trade: The Policy Issues, 1945–1965,* Princeton, 1966, p. 311. Patterson gives in Chapter VI an illuminating account of the background and working of the international cotton textile arrangement.

ing the "major review" of the arrangement, the director-general of GATT expressed the hope that it had brought "some semblance of order" into the trade through restraint actions, and that the parties to the arrangement could begin to give effect to its "long-term and positive aims," including in particular expanded access to markets for the less developed countries.

It remains to see how much emphasis will be given to these long-run objectives during the further three-year period, starting October 1, 1967, for which the cotton textile arrangement has been extended. At least as far as the United States is concerned, government officials reporting to business groups on the renewal of the arrangement have stressed rather the objective of avoiding "market disruption," the expectation that the rapid growth of U.S. imports of cotton textiles would be greatly slowed down, the intention of acting to regulate imports from new suppliers, and continued close cooperation with the industry through the Management-Labor Textile Advisory Committee.[13] In connection with the extension of the arrangement, stress has also been placed on the limited extent of the tariff cuts on textiles made by the United States and other developed countries in the Kennedy Round.[14]

Jute, Leather, and Wood Products

Among the other product groups covered by Table 17, the market prospects for products of jute and other coarse fibers appear none too favorable at best because of the inroads of synthetic fibers and new methods of materials handling and packaging. Similar influences may bear adversely on leather and leather products. Perhaps for these very reasons one might expect growth-minded governments in the developed countries to be willing to accord a larger place to manufactures of

[13] See especially the address by Stanley Nehmer, Deputy Assistant Secretary of Commerce for Resources, before the Underwear Institute in Atlantic City on May 9, 1967. The "close industry-government relationship" was sharply criticized as "a dangerously intimate industry role in the administration of this major international program" in the report of August 29, 1966, by Congressman Curtis already cited in Chapter 3. He raised the "troublesome question . . . whether it is the policy of the U.S. cotton textile industry that the U.S. government has for the last five years been implementing, rather than a policy representative of the national interest."

[14] "Because of the import sensitivity of textiles in general here and abroad, the cuts made by the U.S. and other major importing countries average less than 25 per cent and much less than that on the more sensitive product areas such as woolen and man-made textiles. Many textile products were excluded altogether" (Quoted from address by the then Acting Secretary of Commerce, Alexander B. Trowbridge, at the Alabama International Business Forum, Tuscaloosa, May 17, 1967).

these products by India and Pakistan, which are the main suppliers, giving them an opportunity to increase their export earnings over the amounts now received for the crude or semimanufactured materials. Lower prices for the finished products might also be expected to help strengthen the competitive position of these materials and to contribute in this way also toward improving the export earnings of the suppliers.

Wood and wood products are of interest for rather the opposite reasons. First, many of the less developed countries in Asia, Africa, and Latin America are large actual or potential exporters of tropical hardwoods, which are the type principally involved in the trade at present, and some of them are also capable of becoming mass producers of coniferous wood for pulp and paper and other uses. Second, Western Europe and Japan appear slated to become increasingly heavy importers of tropical hardwoods. A study by the FAO for UNCTAD in 1964 [15] placed their hardwood imports from less developed countries in 1959–61 at an annual average of about $250 million, f.o.b., consisting overwhelmingly of unprocessed timber. It projected an increase of approximately $1 billion, at 1959–61 prices, in these imports from the less developed countries by 1975, if all of Western Europe's additional takings and "a reasonable proportion" of Japan's were fully processed in the form of sawn wood, veneers, and plywood. But the increase would be less than half that amount if, as at present, the imports were predominantly in the form of logs. The study stressed that these hardwood imports would have to come from the less developed countries. It also foresaw that Western Europe and Japan would have a growing deficit in softwood, which could be met by the less developed countries to the extent of $100 million in 1975 and in increasing amounts thereafter.[16]

A companion analysis underlying these projections found that there were "good reasons to expect the production both of quality hardwood plywood and veneer, and of the mass produced paper and paperboard grades based essentially on long-fibre woodpulp, to become concentrated near their source of material." Among the reasons developed

[15] See "Prospects for Expanding Forest Products Exports from Developing Countries," in *Proceedings of the United Nations Conference on Trade and Development,* Vol. III, *Commodity Trade,* United Nations, 1964.

[16] In addition, the FAO study projected that imports of tropical sawn wood and plywood (SITC nos. 243 and 631) by the United States and Canada from the less developed countries would rise from $50 million annually in 1959–61 to $150 million in 1975 (a figure which now seems low by comparison with their actual imports of $114 million in 1965); and that Australia, New Zealand, and South Africa would import some $130 million, and the Soviet Union and Eastern Europe $40 million, of hardwood from the less developed countries in 1975.

for this view were the following: "The 'creaming' of the forests of West Africa to sustain an export trade in high-quality veneer logs of a limited range of species is a much more costly and inefficient way of drawing on these forests than to use them as a base for a balanced range of forest industries designed for integral utilization, located in that region. Quite apart from this, the shipping of wood products rather than logs reduces the incidence of freight. Also, the extra stages of drying, shipping and 're-slushing' of wood pulp can add 10 to 15 per cent to the final cost of papers with a high wood-fibre content." The study added, however, that "The earlier pattern of supply developed around a series of tariffs which generally encouraged the import of roundwood rather than wood products," and that "A freer flow of plywood and veneer and of paper and paperboard would require a change in tariff structures to remove this discrimination." [17] The infinitesimal amount of plywood and other wood manufactures imported by Western Continental Europe from less developed countries (Table 17) suggests, however, that nontariff barriers may also be important.

In brief, the developed countries would seem to have it within their power, by reducing the tariff and other barriers to imports of finished manufactures, to influence greatly the export earnings of the less developed countries and therewith their possibilities of economic growth.

The Problem of Increased Access to Markets

The Issue of Preferences

The first condition for a continued rapid growth of exports of manufactures by the less developed countries to the advanced countries would seem to be greater accessibility to these markets. Greater accessibility would mean the scaling down of the tariff rates of developed countries, particularly the "effective rates," on goods of which the less developed countries are actual or potential suppliers; the progressive loosening of quantitative restrictions, both those imposed by the importing countries and the "voluntary restraints" exercised by the exporting countries; and the identification and removal of other, less obvious impediments to imports. More broadly, greater accessibility would mean recognition that international specialization has a place for the products in which the less developed countries have a comparative advantage, and that this place will widen and deepen as the rise in produc-

[17] *European Timber Trends and Prospects: A New Appraisal, 1950–1975,* Food and Agriculture Organization of the United Nations, New York, 1964, p. 212.

tivity and wages in the developed countries produces divergent effects on unit wage costs in different industries.

The great debate in recent years on commercial policies affecting the less developed countries, reaching a crescendo at the U.N. Conference on Trade and Development in 1964 and still continuing, has turned increasingly on the issue of tariff preferences; that is, whether the enlargement of market opportunities for the less developed countries should be sought within the most-favored-nation framework embodied in the GATT, whereby the concessions made would be generalized and extended also to developed countries, or whether the less developed countries should be accorded preferential treatment in recognition of their difficulties in competing with the developed countries.[18] Rightly or wrongly, the less developed countries seem to have become convinced that only a system of preferences would meet their needs, though they differ among themselves, as well as with the developed countries, as to what the terms of the preferences should be. The United States, adhering to the principle of nondiscrimination, has been in the invidious position of leading the opposition to these demands, sometimes to the point of seeming to be the only voice in opposition.[19]

After the vast exceptions to the most-favored-nation principle constituted by the European Economic Community and the European Free Trade Area, the idea of tariff preferences to favor the less developed countries may appear to be a modest objective. It seems to accord ill, however, with the realities of the present trading situation in which, as the director-general of GATT has observed, "the tendency is, in the sectors where the less developed countries are already competitive, for the developed countries to discriminate against the export products of these countries." [20] Unless the developed countries are ready to forgo those features of their commercial policies which seem to fall with particular severity on exports of the less developed countries, what expectation can there be of shifting all the way over to discrimination in their favor?

The heart of the difficulty, as far as exports of labor-intensive manu-

---

[18] For a much fuller account of the history of this issue, see Patterson, *Discrimination in International Trade,* especially Chapter VII.

[19] Harry G. Johnson, though severely critical of the negative stance of the United States and of its failure to develop a more positive and imaginative policy, suggests that, to an important extent, the United States served as a scapegoat for other countries, especially the European Common Market countries, which avoided commitment by abstaining from voting while the United States carried the burden of resistance. (*Economic Policies Toward Less Developed Countries,* Washington, 1967, especially p. 39.)

[20] Address in Bad Godesberg, Germany, October 27, 1966.

factures by the less developed countries are concerned, is that these products tend to compete with those sectors in the developed countries which are frequently the least prosperous and the most successful in obtaining protection against imports. The problem is illustrated by one of the provisions of the U.S. Trade Expansion Act of 1962, namely, that authorizing the President to negotiate tariffs down to zero on groups of industrial products of which the United States and the European Common Market together accounted for 80 per cent or more of world exports. This formula reflected an erroneous expectation that the United Kingdom was about to become a member of the Common Market (without which the 80 per cent level would be realized only exceptionally). But it also had the important effect of excluding products, notably textiles, of which Japan and the less developed countries were significant exporters. In other words, the United States was prepared to consider reducing tariffs by as much as 100 per cent on products which, as President Kennedy said, "can be produced here or in Europe more efficiently than anywhere else in the world," [21] but only by half as much in principle (perhaps a good deal less in practice) on products in which Japan and the less developed countries were most competitive. This, however, is only a specific illustration of the general tendency of U.S. tariffs to bear more heavily on labor-intensive manufactures than on other goods.[22] It raises the question whether, even if the most-favored-nation rule is rigorously respected, unequal tariff treatment of different products may not be tantamount to unequal treatment of different countries.

The Prebisch Proposals

Awareness of these difficulties led Raúl Prebisch, in his advance message as secretary-general to UNCTAD in 1964, to envisage something less than a fully generalized system of preferences.[23] As he saw it, developed countries could not be expected to give preferential treatment to those industries in the less developed countries that were already fully competitive in world markets, and each country granting preferences might therefore establish a reserve list of such products to be excluded from preferences (but not, he stressed, from most-favored-na-

---

[21] See *Department of State Bulletin*, February 12, 1962, p. 236.

[22] See Beatrice N. Vaccara, *Employment and Output in Protected Manufacturing Industries*, Washington, 1960, pp. 55–66, and David Stafford Ball, "United States Effective Tariffs and Labor's Share," *Journal of Political Economy*, April 1967, pp. 183–187.

[23] *Proceedings of the United Nations Conference on Trade and Development*, Vol. II, *Policy Statements*, 1964, pp. 35–40.

tion treatment under GATT). Prebisch's case for preferences was, as he said, "a logical extension of the infant industry argument" [24] aimed at enabling the less developed countries to become competitive in manufactures that they could not now export. Both the duration of the preferences (a minimum of ten years was suggested) and the margin of preference should be great enough to provide adequate incentive for the establishment of new export industries.

Prebisch considered it desirable, but not indispensable, that all developed countries participate in granting preferences. He hoped that they would avoid the crippling complexities of a highly selective country-by-product approach, but recognized that they might insist on an over-all quota, and possibly quotas on particular categories, governing the amount of goods to be imported preferentially.

As to the preference-receiving countries, Prebisch recognized that it would not be easy to set any kind of cutoff point above which countries would not be eligible. Among those which were eligible, he felt it necessary to distinguish between the "more advanced" and the "less developed" among them, suggesting for the latter wider margins of preference. This might be reinforced by a special grant of quotas in their behalf and perhaps even by preferential tariff treatment on items which the developed countries had reserved from general preferences.

Australian Preference System

Despite vigorous efforts by the less developed countries at UNCTAD for a declaration of principle in favor of preferences, all that emerged in the final act of the 1964 conference was a decision to set up a committee to consider the best method of implementing such a system and to discuss differences of views on the question of principle.[25] The topic seems destined to figure even more prominently in the debates of

[24] Johnson (*Economic Policies Toward Less Developed Countries*, pp. 181–184) notes various differences between the infant-industry argument and the tariff-preference argument, among them being that the first envisages a social investment paid for by the consumers of the country in which the protected industry is located, whereas the second envisages that the cost is borne by consumers in developed countries for the benefit of less developed countries. Johnson further suggests (p. 198) that many of the objections to preferences growing out of adherence to foreign trade principles would disappear, if preferences were looked upon as "essentially additional foreign aid." The key word here is *additional*, and the argument loses force to the extent that, if the case for preferences were presented on this basis, cuts might be made in appropriations for aid in other forms.

[25] *Proceedings of the United Nations Conference on Trade and Development,* Vol. I, *Final Act and Report,* 1964, p. 13.

the second conference scheduled for 1968. Meanwhile, the only specific action by way of preferences favoring imports from the less developed countries is that taken by Australia under a waiver from the most-favored-nation rule approved by GATT in March 1966.[26] Though staunchly defended by Australia as a manifestation of its willingness to help overcome the trade problems of the less developed countries and as a lead to other developed countries wishing to apply similar methods, the Australian preferential system may also be taken as indicative of the limitations and problems in this approach. Its main features may be summed up as follows from materials made public at the time of requesting the waiver from GATT: [27]

1. Preferential duties, zero in some cases, were to be introduced in favor of the less developed countries, comprehensively defined, on some sixty items.
2. Each such concession was, however, subject to a quota limit, above which regular duties would apply to imports from less developed countries.
3. These quotas added up to a total of £A6,680,000, or about $15,000,000, representing in principle the amount of goods that might enter in a year's time on a preferential basis.
4. More than 40 per cent of this total was made up of items which, it would seem, were unlikely to provide the basis for any new export industries in less developed countries, at least in the near future. These included, in particular, newsprint, £A2,000,000; machine-made paper £A500,000; rubber thread, vulcanized, £A100,000; household washing machines, £A150,000; machine tools, £A150,000.
5. Other, generally more likely, items thus added up to £A3,780,000, or about $8,500,000 in terms of amounts eligible for preferential treatment, made up chiefly of consumer manufactures.[28]
6. More generally, it was indicated that the list was drawn up so as to omit "products in which less developed countries are already competitive in world markets," and that "the preferential rates should be subject to modification as producers in less developed countries become competitive."

[26] According to the GATT press release of March 30, 1966 (GATT/953), the contracting parties approved the request "by a substantial majority." Newspaper reports at the time indicated that the United States cast the only dissenting vote.

[27] From statement and accompanying exhibits submitted by the Rt. Hon. J. McEwen, Deputy Prime Minister and Minister for Trade and Industry, to the Australian House of Representatives on May 19, 1965.

[28] Actual imports of these goods from less developed countries in 1963–64 had amounted to £A1,300,000, or $2,900,000, some of which had entered under Commonwealth preferential duties, leaving the effective net amount of additional preferential imports presumably somewhat smaller than $8,500,000.

7. On the other hand, it was also indicated that the items specified constituted an "initial list" and that other products might be added from time to time.[29]

Unless the Australian list were to be significantly expanded, it could scarcely be said to open up major new export possibilities for the less developed countries or to provide a challenging example for other developed countries to follow. Indeed, the positive effect of Australia's action was at least partially offset by another step taken at the same time whereby it informed GATT that, in accepting the new Part IV on Trade and Development, it would not consider itself bound by the provisions under which the developed countries undertook "to accord high priority to the reduction and elimination of tariff and non-tariff barriers to products of actual or potential export interest to less developed countries" and "to refrain from increasing tariff and non-tariff barriers against such products." [30]

The "Brasseur Plan"

Except for the exclusion of Hong Kong from the benefits on certain items, the Australian preferences are available to all less developed countries, broadly defined. In this respect the Australian system appears to be more generous than the "Brasseur Plan," with which it has been compared, would be. This plan, named after the Belgian Minister of Foreign Trade and Technical Assistance who made the proposals to GATT in 1963, would entail negotiations with individual less developed countries to determine in each case the products to be covered, the margin and duration of preference, and the quantities eligible to benefit. If the plan were seriously looked upon as applying to most bilateral relationships between developed and less developed countries and to

[29] The list of goods specified in the annex accompanying the waiver voted by GATT on March 28, 1966, included two additional groups called "various" which were to be free of duty without quota limit. These appear to be mainly, if not entirely, handicraft items. See the Fourteenth Supplement to the *Basic Instruments and Selected Documents,* issued by the Contracting Parties to the General Agreement on Tariffs and Trade, Geneva, July 1966, pp. 23–31 and 162–177. On the other hand, one item on the original list was omitted from the final version, i.e., "matt-woven fabrics of jute, weighing more than 12 ozs. per sq. yd.," for which a duty-free quota of £A20,000 had been proposed, but with the notation that India and Pakistan (the principal exporters of jute manufactures) were to be excluded from the preference.

[30] From Mr. McEwen's statement of May 19, 1965. Mr. McEwen denounced these provisions as a "blank check" and said that their effect would be "to severely curtail our right to increase, or even to maintain, tariffs on any products that might be designated—now or in the future—as being of actual or potential export interest to the less developed countries."

most items of interest in the trade, the amount of negotiation and specification required would be astronomical. Patterson suggests, however, that "this approach had the great virtue to some members of the European Economic Community that it would facilitate their safeguarding the value of the existing preferences to each other and, more important, to the Associated States." [31] It is not clear how valuable these latter preferences are, in fact, to the Associated States—i.e., the former African dependencies of France and Belgium—in view of the extremely low level of their exports of manufactures to the former mother countries or other members of the European Economic Community.

Diverse Policies and Common Objectives

The effectiveness of tariff preferences in opening new markets for the less developed countries cannot be judged in the abstract, but depends on the terms of the preferences in each case. The measures adopted in Australia and those contemplated under the Brasseur Plan are not reassuring, however, if taken as a foretaste of the kind of preferential concessions to be expected. Rather, they give point to Prebisch's warning that "it would not be worth facing all the political and other difficulties entailed in a new departure from the most-favored-nation principle simply for the sake of token margins of preference on a few selected products for a very limited period, amounting to little more in toto than a gesture in the face of the immense problems of the trade gap." [32] He might have added that, the more selective preferences are by beneficiaries, the more fragmented is the bargaining power of the less developed countries and the greater their economic dependence becomes on particular developed countries.

It is equally true that the gains to be achieved by the less developed countries through the most-favored-nation approach cannot be judged in the abstract. In principle, their bargaining position for obtaining meaningful concessions from the developed countries is strengthened by three considerations. First, the developed countries have, as noted, pledged themselves in GATT as well as at UNCTAD to give "high priority" to the reduction of both tariff and nontariff barriers to the exports of the less developed countries. Second, the need of the less developed countries to increase exports to cover their growing import requirements is widely recognized. Third, the gains from trade between

[31] *Discrimination in International Trade*, p. 361.

[32] *Proceedings of the United Nations Conference on Trade and Development*, Vol. II, *Policy Statements*, p. 38.

countries with wide differences in factor endowments should be particularly large to both sides.

In fact, however, the Kennedy Round of GATT negotiations seems to have been regarded by the developed countries as primarily concerned with trade relations among themselves,[33] and it is by no means clear what will follow to give effect to their commitments to the less developed countries. As far as the United States is concerned, the tariff-cutting authority vested in the executive branch by the Trade Expansion Act of 1962 does not extend beyond mid-1967, and proposals for a new trade program remain to be formulated and approved. In the European Economic Community there seems to be an increasing tendency to look on the common external tariff as a condition for internal unification, while the United Kingdom appears to be mainly concerned with joining the EEC and perhaps more inclined to restrain than to stimulate its imports from less developed countries, to judge by the uneven incidence noted in Chapter 4 of the restrictions imposed in 1964 to bolster its balance of payments.

Under these conditions, it may be difficult to develop and carry out a common program of action by developed countries to remove barriers to imports of manufactures from less developed countries, whether by the preferential route or by the most-favored-nation approach. The United States and other countries wishing to provide enlarged trade opportunities to the less developed countries may therefore be faced with the difficult choice, noted by Harry Johnson,[34] between (1) unilaterally reducing tariffs on items of interest to these countries without insisting on reciprocal concessions by developed countries benefiting under the most-favored-nation principle, or (2) abandoning that principle and granting concessions to the less developed countries only, or to some of them, on a preferential basis compared with the tariff treatment accorded imports from developed countries. The United

---

[33] Gains for the less developed countries were particularly limited in textiles and clothing, as noted above, both as the result of the adamant insistence of the developed countries on renewal of the Long-Term Cotton Textile Arrangement, with its provision for "voluntary restraints" by the exporting countries, and as the result of a last-minute decision, demanded by the EEC, to cut sharply the extent of the tariff reductions made on textiles (a feature which could become more consequential when the long-term cotton arrangement expires). It is an open question, however, to what degree the less developed countries themselves were responsible for their failure to get more out of the Kennedy Round, possibly because of inadequate representation during the long and many-sided negotiations and possibly also because of a widespread tendency to think that only preferential duty reductions would meet their needs.

[34] *Economic Policies Toward Less Developed Countries*, pp. 41 and 239.

States would thus have to abandon one of two basic principles—either that of reciprocity or that of nondiscrimination.

Whatever the answer to this last question,[35] it seems likely that, viewed as a whole, the trade policies of the developed countries vis-à-vis the less developed countries will continue to be a mixed bag—equal treatment in some sectors and areas and unequal treatment in others, measures to expand trade along with restraints, declarations of good intentions followed by good, bad, and indifferent results. One of the weaknesses of the selective preferential approach in particular is that it lends itself to illusions, by both preference-giving and preference-receiving countries, as to how much has been accomplished. A great amount of paper work may yield very little trade.

In the face of this prospective diversity and uncertainty, the question arises whether it would be useful to try to make sure that the policies pursued by the developed countries, whatever their form in each case, were consistent with the results aimed at, which would involve quantifying these aims with regard to the levels and rates of increase contemplated for the trade. It may be recalled that Prebisch broached such an idea in his advance report to the United Nations Conference on Trade and Development in 1964, though it was only briefly considered, with little support, at that meeting [36]—that is, that targets be set for

[35] An indication that the United States was willing to consider some modification of its position against trade preferences was given in President Johnson's statement at Punta del Este in April 1967: "We are ready to explore with other industrialized countries—and with our own people—the possibility of temporary preferential tariff advantages for all developing countries in the markets of all the industrialized countries." (See *Department of State Bulletin,* May 8, 1967, p. 709.) The key word in this formulation is no doubt *all* as applied to both beneficiaries and givers of preferences.

The possibility of a more specific and immediate step, though a modest one, was indicated in the statement issued on May 15, 1967, by the director-general of GATT in summing up the results of the Kennedy Round. Noting that the tariff reductions agreed on in the negotiations would, in general, be phased over a period of years, he said that the participants had, however, "recognized that, for the developing countries, the immediate implementation of such tariff cuts would be of great value in maximizing the benefits to them of these negotiations." He further stated that efforts to achieve the advance application of the cuts to imports from the developing countries would continue, and that a decision on this point was expected to be reached by the time that the agreement embodying the results of the Kennedy Round was ready for signature. GATT press release, May 17, 1967 (GATT/990). No such decision was announced at the time, however, and subsequent Congressional testimony by U.S. officials has indicated that the issue was left for later consideration and that the United States had not taken a firm position (*The New York Times,* July 13, 1967, p. 51).

[36] For Prebisch's suggestions on this point, see pp. 38 and 60 of Vol. II of the conference proceedings. In the form considered at the conference, this idea (the first of thirteen "special principles" following fifteen "general principles")

developed countries, collectively and individually, with respect to their imports of manufactures from less developed countries.

Possible disadvantages of such a course are immediately obvious. If the targets were set too low in relation to the potentialities of the trade, they would be more of a hindrance than a help to its development. If they were set too high, achievement of the targets could present embarrassment to private-enterprise economies.

Such problems may, however, be more theoretical than real in the present instance. Reasons have been given in Chapter 4 for believing that the forces underlying the rapid growth of the trade from the early 1950's to the mid-1960's may become progressively stronger. If that view is correct, it would probably not be too much to suggest that, by 1975, the trade will again have grown fourfold or more to something like $10 billion (at present prices). Higher figures could be envisaged if the enlargement of market opportunities extended to all of the developed countries, including those that so far have lagged behind in imports of manufactures from less developed countries.

Fulfillment of targets by the developed countries in these conditions would not be a matter of creating artificial inducements but of removing artificial impediments to the trade. Some developed countries might elect to do so by reducing import barriers over the whole range of products of interest to less developed countries and to do so on a most-favored-nation basis. Some others might choose to proceed much more selectively with respect to both the products and the countries benefiting by the concessions. Whatever the method, a set of agreed targets should help to give a common purpose and meaningful content to their actions.

It would doubtless require a good deal of study and negotiation to obtain agreement on a global target for imports of manufactures from the less developed countries that would be both consistent with their growing foreign exchange needs and acceptable to the developed countries. Arriving at an agreed basis for distributing a global target among individual importing countries could well prove even more difficult.[37]

was that "Developed countries should cooperate with developing countries in setting targets for the expansion of trade of the latter and in periodically reviewing measures for their achievement." The United States and Canada voted against the proposal, and the United Kingdom, Germany, and seven other developed countries elected to abstain. Interestingly, France, Italy, and Belgium—all with relatively small imports from the less-developed countries—voted in favor of the proposal.

[37] Prebisch suggested that the total might be divided up (1) according to each importing country's consumption of manufactures or (2) according to its share in total imports of manufactures from all sources. The first criterion,

A more modest and perhaps more realistic alternative would be for each developed country simply to provide a quantitative analysis and projection, by main groups of manufactures, of the expected evolution of its imports from less developed countries, taking account of market trends and its own commercial policies. Such an undertaking should at least serve to direct thinking about commercial policies affecting less developed countries toward results as well as methods and to make it more difficult to generate schemes lacking in effective content.

It would no doubt be more difficult—but also more questionable—to divide up a global import target, or even a set of projections, among individual exporting countries. Too much depends on their own economic situations and policies in each case. The Prebisch proposal on preferences calling for gradation of preferential margins among the less developed countries implies that the ability to export manufactures is positively correlated with their stage of economic development. This must be true in some sense, if one thinks of potential exports. But the analysis offered here has also revealed that, typically, the "more advanced" of the less developed countries, including some that have had preferential access to certain developed countries' markets, have not done well as exporters of manufactures to developed countries. If, as this experience suggests, the basic difficulty lies in their own economic situations and policies, it would be of little advantage to them, and an unnecessary limitation on other less developed countries' possibilities, to reserve for them specified shares in a global import target. Even in such cases, however, a more receptive attitude by developed countries toward imports from less developed countries, along with quantitative assessments and projections of these imports, would help to clarify the issues and to encourage policies in the less developed countries conducive to the growth of their exports.

however, would tend to overstate, and the second to understate, import objectives for large countries with diversified economies and less dependent on imports than small countries with more specialized economies. Prebisch concluded that a combination of the two criteria might yield a formula acceptable to all developed countries (p. 38 of Vol. II of the conference proceedings).

VALUE ADDED BY MANUFACTURE AND RELATED VARIABLES

Wages and Human Capital

The variables plotted in Chart 2 are reproduced, along with the names of the industries, in Table A-1. The basic source is Helen Waehrer's study "Inter-Industry Skill Differences, Labor Earnings, and United States Foreign Trade, 1960" (unpublished Ph.D. dissertation, Department of Economics, Columbia University, 1966), supplemented by data supplied directly by her on twenty-four industries not treated as "export industries" or "import-competing industries" in her study. Her "occupational index" and "educational index," derived from *Census of Population* data, are briefly described in Chapter 2, above (footnote 22), and various qualifications and limitations of the data are also noted. Her series on average annual earnings is derived from the *Annual Survey of Manufactures, 1960* (total payroll divided by employment) and involved fitting the Standard Industrial Classification [1] used in the latter into the more summary industrial classification used in the *Census of Population*. The conversion system employed by Mrs. Waehrer for this purpose is as follows, the *Census of Population* code being given first (for names of industries, see Table A-1) followed by SIC numbers in parentheses: 206 (241), 207 (242,3), 208 (244,9), 209 (25), 216 (321-3), 217 (324,7), 218 (325), 219 (326), 236 (328,9), 237 (3312,3), 238 (3315-7, 332, 3391,9), 239 (333-6, 3392-9), 246 (342), 247 (344), 248 (341,3, 5-9), 256 (352), 257 (357), 258 (351, 3-6, 8,9), 259 (36), 267 (371), 268 (372), 269 (373), 276 (374,5,9), 286 (194,[2] 381-5), 287 (386), 289 (387), 296 (39), 306 (201), 307 (202), 308 (203), 309 (0713,[2] 204), 316 (205), 317 (207), 318 (208), 319 (206,9), 329 (21), 346 (225),

---

[1] See *Standard Industrial Classification Manual*, Executive Office of the President, Bureau of the Budget, 1957, and *Supplement*, 1963.

[2] Item excluded from computation of average annual earnings.

347 (226), 348 (227), 349 (221-4, 8), 356 (229), 359 (231-8), 367 (239), 386 (261-3,6), 387 (265), 389 (264), 396 (271), 398 (272-9), 406 (2823,4), 407 (283), 408 (285), 409 (281,2,4,6-9), 416 (291), 419 (295,9), 426 (301,3,6), 429 (307), 436 (311), 437 (313,4), 438 (312,5-7,9).

The variables plotted in Chart 3 are also reproduced in Table A-1. The sources and methods employed in deriving these variables are described briefly in Chapter 2 of this study and more fully in *Differentials in Hourly Earnings by Region and City Size 1959*, Occasional Paper 101, New York, 1967, by Victor R. Fuchs of the National Bureau. It may be noted that, unlike the earnings figures in Waehrer's study, the actual hourly and annual earnings figures in Fuchs's study are obtained from the same *Census of Population* sample as that used in computing his "expected" hourly earnings series.

Nonwage Value Added and Physical Capital

The variables for the United States plotted in Chart 4 are given in Table A-2. The basic sources of the data are as follows: (1) depreciable and depletable assets, end of 1957, from the *Census of Manufactures, 1958,* Vol. I, *Summary Statistics,* Section 9, Table 1; [3] (2) nonwage value added, as well as employment, in 1957 from the *Annual Survey of Manufactures, 1957,* Chapter II, Table 1, and inventories at end of 1957, same source, pp. 130–144 (all series being on the Standard Industrial Classification prior to the 1957 revision). Both Chart 4 and Table A-2 give the variables at the three-digit level of the SIC. The computations have also been done at the four-digit level (276 items), as reported in Chapter 2, and have been drawn on in Table 4.

The variables for India plotted in Chart 5 are given in Table A-3. Both series are derived from the *Annual Survey of Industries, 1961* (Calcutta, Central Statistical Organization). The same industries have been used as in the U.S.-Indian comparison in Chart 13 (see Table B-3) subject to deletion of two industries, as explained in Chapter 2.

A test of linearity and Bartlett's test of homoscedasticity were applied to the data on physical capital and nonwage value added for both the United States and India in an effort to determine whether the arithmetic or logarithmic form of correlation was appropriate. For both countries (and, in the U.S. case, at both the three- and four-digit levels) these tests indicated that the logarithmic transformations of the data yielded variables that were linearly related and satisfied the assumptions of

[3] See Chapter 2, footnote 29, of this study for the combinations of items used in computing net and gross assets.

correlation analysis. As shown in Table A-4, these data were not linearly related in the arithmetic form but were linearly related when the variables were transformed into logarithms; all results were significant at the 1 per cent level of confidence.

The variances of the observations were not homogeneous for the arithmetic form of the variables, but were homogeneous for the logarithmic form; all the results were significant at the 1 per cent level of confidence. In making this test, the observations were ranked in ascending order of the independent variable; those for the United States were divided into eight groups of approximately thirty-five observations each at the four-digit level and into six groups of approximately twenty observations each at the three-digit level, and those for India into six groups of approximately nineteen observations each.

The regression equations obtained from the data and used in computing the figures in the middle column of each of Tables A-2 and A-3 are given below, X being in each case the log of physical assets per employee and Y the log of nonwage value added per employee:

United States (122 three-digit industries, net assets)

$$Y = -.050 + .822X$$

India (115 industries, "productive assets")

$$Y = -.031 + .839X$$

TABLE A-1

Variables Used in Analysis of Wages and Skills in U.S. Manufacturing Industry

Code No. (Census of Population)	Name of Industry	Derived from H. Waehrer's Study (Data for 1960)		Derived from NBER Study of the Service Industries (Data for 1959)		
		Average Annual Earnings (dollars)	Percentage of Labor Force Classed as Skilled by H. Waehrer	Average Annual Earnings (dollars)	Average Hourly Earnings (dollars)	Expected Hourly Earnings (dollars)
206	Logging	3,386	14.8	3,075	2.05	2.29
207	Sawmills, planing mills, and millwork	3,683	29.8	3,513	1.94	2.31
208	Miscellaneous wood products	3,519	35.0	3,986	2.09	2.35
209	Furniture and fixtures	4,191	44.2	4,208	2.17	2.32
216	Glass and glass products	5,343	38.7	5,189	2.76	2.47
217	Cement, and concrete, gypsum, and plaster products	5,092	43.4	5,674	2.72	2.58
218	Structural clay products	4,389	31.9	5,050	2.54	2.47
219	Pottery and related products	4,467	30.9	4,644	2.35	2.45
236	Misc. nonmetallic mineral and stone products	5,324	50.7	5,230	2.71	2.51
237	Blast furnaces, steel works, and rolling and finishing mills	6,592	53.6	5,614	3.39	2.57
238	Other primary iron and steel industries	5,633	50.4	5,331	2.80	2.45
239	Primary nonferrous industries	5,799	51.4	5,668	2.98	2.63

(continued)

TABLE A-1 (continued)

Code No. (Census of Population)	Name of Industry	Derived from H. Waehrer's Study (Data for 1960)		Derived from NBER Study of the Service Industries (Data for 1959)		
		Average Annual Earnings (dollars)	Percentage of Labor Force Classed as Skilled by H. Waehrer	Average Annual Earnings (dollars)	Average Hourly Earnings (dollars)	Expected Hourly Earnings (dollars)
246	Cutlery, hand tools, and other hardware	5,275	47.9	4,900	2.48	2.39
247	Fabricated structural metal products	5,562	57.8	5,719	2.93	2.59
248	Miscellaneous fabricated metal products	5,378	57.5	5,522	2.80	2.52
256	Farm machinery and equipment	5,451	55.0	5,449	2.80	2.72
257	Office, computing, and accounting machines	6,316	64.5	6,036	3.05	2.65
258	Miscellaneous machinery	5,943	61.8	5,757	2.85	2.67
259	Electrical machinery, equipment, and supplies	5,404	54.6	5,326	2.80	2.49
267	Motor vehicles and motor vehicle equipment	6,486	47.3	5,838	3.05	2.56
268	Aircraft and parts	6,842	71.5	6,095	3.01	2.74
269	Ship and boat building and repairing	5,842	72.1	5,154	2.73	2.61
276	Railroad and misc. transportation equipment	5,352	52.2	4,214	2.43	2.39
286	Professional equipment and supplies	5,818	64.4	5,837	2.96	2.63
287	Photographic equipment and supplies	6,735	62.1	6,530	3.32	2.64
289	Watches, clocks, and clockwork-operated devices	4,959	46.4	5,114	2.83	2.14
296	Miscellaneous manufacturing industries	4,276	46.4	4,628	2.45	2.27
306	Meat products	5,077	31.9	4,852	2.42	2.33

(continued)

TABLE A-1 (continued)

Code No. (Census of Population)	Name of Industry	Derived from H. Waehrer's Study (Data for 1960)		Derived from NBER Study of the Service Industries (Data for 1959)		
		Average Annual Earnings (dollars)	Percentage of Labor Force Classed as Skilled by H. Waehrer	Average Annual Earnings (dollars)	Average Hourly Earnings (dollars)	Expected Hourly Earnings (dollars)
307	Dairy products	5,017	40.0	5,141	2.32	2.64
308	Canning and preserved fruits, vegetables, and sea foods	3,602	38.5	3,887	2.20	2.33
309	Grain-mill products	5,188	52.6	5,159	2.42	2.44
316	Bakery products	4,799	55.6	4,895	2.35	2.39
317	Confectionery and related products	4,099	40.5	3,607	2.16	1.87
318	Beverage industries	5,391	47.7	5,529	2.78	2.55
319	Misc. food preparations and kindred products	4,915	49.0	4,999	2.54	2.42
329	Tobacco manufactures	3,871	34.1	3,900	2.18	2.00
346	Knitting mills	3,232	22.8	2,959	1.67	1.96
347	Dyeing and finishing textiles, exc. wool and knit goods	4,287	32.8	3,521	1.83	2.29
348	Floor coverings, exc. hard surface	3,810	36.4	5,185	2.67	2.56
349	Yarn, thread, and fabric mills	3,493	27.6	3,485	1.82	2.11
356	Miscellaneous textile mill products	4,314	38.1	5,144	2.77	2.39
359	Apparel and accessories	3,056	20.0	3,587	2.17	1.89
367	Miscellaneous fabricated textile products	3,460	32.1	3,858	2.10	2.15

(continued)

TABLE A-1 (concluded)

Code No. (Census of Population)	Name of Industry	Derived from H. Waehrer's Study (Data for 1960)		Derived from NBER Study of the Service Industries (Data for 1959)		
		Average Annual Earnings (dollars)	Percentage of Labor Force Classed as Skilled by H. Waehrer	Average Annual Earnings (dollars)	Average Hourly Earnings (dollars)	Expected Hourly Earnings (dollars)
386	Pulp, paper, and paperboard mills	5,959	43.1	5,652	2.72	2.58
387	Paperboard containers and boxes	4,946	41.1	4,906	2.55	2.40
389	Miscellaneous paper and pulp products	5,037	46.3	4,446	2.30	2.24
396	Newspaper publishing and printing	5,445	93.5	3,998	3.02	2.69
398	Other printing and publishing	5,643	80.5	5,134	2.76	2.46
406	Synthetic fibers	5,535	47.4	5,848	2.84	2.80
407	Drugs and medicines	6,108	73.0	5,998	2.93	2.99
408	Paints, varnishes, and related products	6,022	62.4	6,104	3.01	2.59
409	Miscellaneous chemicals and allied products	6,189	63.6	6,121	3.12	2.76
416	Petroleum refining	7,087	67.8	6,902	3.41	2.90
419	Miscellaneous petroleum and coal products	5,698	59.0	5,922	2.93	2.81
426	Rubber products	5,737	42.1	5,507	2.88	2.48
429	Miscellaneous plastic products	4,682	43.0	5,421	2.77	2.51
436	Leather, tanned, curried, and finished	4,744	28.7	4,423	2.40	2.23
437	Footwear, exc. rubber	3,278	21.9	3,345	1.97	1.98
438	Leather products, exc. footwear	3,851	29.0	3,345	1.93	2.08

TABLE A-2

Variables Used in Analysis of Nonwage Value Added and
Physical Assets per Employee in 122 (Three-digit)
U.S. Manufacturing Industries, 1957
(dollars)

| SIC Code No. (pre-1958) | Name of Industry | Nonwage Value Added per Employee | | Physical Assets, Net per Employee (3) |
		Actual (1)	Estimated by Regressing 1 on 3 (2)	
201	Meat products	3,419	3,319	4,958
202	Dairy products	4,756	3,679	5,620
203	Canned and frozen foods	4,160	5,477	9,118
204	Grain-mill products	8,847	6,236	10,677
205	Bakery products	3,895	2,275	3,131
206	Sugar	8,122	8,790	16,214
207	Candy and related products	5,464	4,096	6,402
208	Beverages	8,105	6,782	11,827
209	Miscellaneous foods	9,752	5,768	9,712
211	Cigarettes	24,158	10,001	18,971
212	Cigars	3,191	2,133	2,895
213	Chewing and smoking tobacco	9,385	5,243	8,646
221	Woolen and worsted manufacturers	2,028	4,155	6,515
222	Yarn and thread mills	2,034	3,471	5,234
223	Broad-woven fabrics	1,712	3,628	5,524
224	Narrow-fabric mills	2,044	2,707	3,869
225	Knitting mills	1,935	2,615	3,708
226	Finishing textiles, except wool	1,954	3,390	5,087
227	Carpet and rugs	3,677	5,540	9,247
228	Hats, except cloth and millinery	0,844	2,434	3,399
229	Miscellaneous textile goods	3,299	4,021	6,261
231	Men's and boys' suits and coats	1,491	1,793	2,343
232	Men's and boys' furnishings	1,522	1,694	2,186
233	Women's and misses' outerwear	2,130	1,527	1,927
234	Women's undergarments	2,292	1,885	2,490

(continued)

TABLE A-2 (continued)

SIC Code No. (pre-1958)	Name of Industry	Nonwage Value Added per Employee Actual (1)	Estimated by Regressing 1 on 3 (2)	Physical Assets, Net per Employee (3)
235	Millinery	2,339	1,434	1,786
236	Children's outerwear	1,493	1,606	2,049
238	Miscellaneous apparel	1,920	1,802	2,358
239	Fabricated textiles, n.e.c.	2,148	2,500	3,511
241	Logging camps and contractors	2,450	3,016	4,413
242	Lumber and basic products	1,506	3,158	4,666
243	Millwork and related products	2,100	3,107	4,575
244	Wooden containers	1,739	2,335	3,232
249	Miscellaneous wood products	2,140	2,667	3,799
251	Household furniture	2,463	2,650	3,769
252	Office furniture	5,047	3,491	5,272
253	Public and professional furniture	3,341	3,470	5,232
254	Partitions and fixtures	3,403	2,898	4,202
261	Pulp, paper, and board	6,973	8,676	15,959
264	Paper coating and glazing	6,358	5,133	8,426
266	Paper bags	4,164	4,457	7,097
267	Paperboard containers	3,104	3,995	6,212
269	Pulp, paper, and products, n.e.c.	5,325	4,592	7,359
275	Commercial printing	3,384	3,026	4,430
276	Lithographing	3,640	3,401	5,106
278	Bookbinding and related industries	2,404	2,532	3,566
279	Printing trade services	2,543	2,114	2,864
281	Inorganic chemicals	9,889	7,890	14,217
282	Organic chemicals	10,640	8,903	16,466
283	Drugs and medicines	15,444	6,412	11,045
284	Soap and related products	16,787	6,816	11,898
285	Paints and allied products	8,574	5,850	9,878
287	Fertilizers	5,049	7,142	12,595
288	Vegetable and animal oils	6,698	10,511	20,154
289	Chemical products, n.e.c.	11,899	5,949	10,083
291	Petroleum refining	12,272	17,363	37,118

(continued)

TABLE A-2 (continued)

SIC Code No. (pre-1958)	Name of Industry	Nonwage Value Added per Employee		Physical Assets, Net per Employee (3)
		Actual (1)	Estimated by Regressing 1 on 3 (2)	
295	Paving and roofing materials	6,916	5,807	9,791
299	Petroleum and coal products, n.e.c.	6,129	6,032	10,255
301	Tires and inner tubes	5,791	5,182	8,525
302	Rubber footwear	3,132	2,812	4,051
303	Reclaimed rubber	4,065	5,587	9,341
309	Rubber industries, n.e.c.	3,689	3,530	5,344
311	Leather tanning and finishing	2,963	3,768	5,785
313	Footwear cut stock	1,895	1,999	2,675
314	Footwear, except rubber	1,816	1,629	2,086
316	Luggage	2,681	2,297	3,168
317	Purses and small leather goods	1,958	1,459	1,823
321	Flat glass	5,842	5,955	10,096
322	Pressed and blown glassware	4,144	3,433	5,166
323	Products of purchased glass	6,341	3,580	5,436
324	Cement, hydraulic	10,703	12,047	23,792
325	Structural clay products	2,618	3,378	5,065
326	Pottery and related products	2,248	2,667	3,799
327	Concrete and plaster products	6,100	4,844	7,853
328	Cut-stone and stone products	2,666	2,481	3,480
329	Nonmetallic mineral products, n.e.c.	5,569	4,845	7,854
331	Blast furnaces and steel mills	5,827	7,537	13,447
332	Iron and steel foundries	2,590	2,951	4,297
333	Primary nonferrous metals	9,378	10,432	19,969
334	Secondary nonferrous metals	3,169	5,807	9,791

(continued)

TABLE A-2 (continued)

| SIC Code No. (pre-1958) | Name of Industry | Nonwage Value Added per Employee | | Physical Assets, Net per Employee (3) |
		Actual (1)	Estimated by Regressing 1 on 3 (2)	
335	Nonferrous rolling and drawing	5,009	6,464	11,155
336	Nonferrous foundries	2,524	2,798	4,027
339	Primary metal industries, n.e.c.	4,587	5,384	8,930
341	Tin cans and other tinware	6,530	7,441	13,238
342	Cutlery, tools, and hardware	3,766	3,689	5,637
343	Heating and plumbing equipment	3,131	4,396	6,978
344	Structural metal products	3,857	4,120	6,449
346	Metal stamping and coating	2,984	3,189	4,721
347	Lighting fixtures	3,283	3,404	5,111
348	Fabricated wire products, n.e.c.	3,468	3,450	5,195
349	Metal products, n.e.c.	4,101	4,475	7,131
351	Engines and turbines	5,019	4,877	7,917
352	Tractors and farm machinery	4,106	4,937	8,036
353	Construction and mining machinery	4,899	5,262	8,685
354	Metalworking machinery	3,601	4,061	6,337
355	Special-industry machinery, n.e.c.	3,474	4,498	7,175
356	General industrial machinery	4,353	4,311	6,814
357	Office and store machines	3,801	5,352	8,866
358	Service and household machines	4,378	4,550	7,276
359	Miscellaneous machinery parts	3,793	3,546	5,373
361	Electrical industrial apparatus	4,589	3,743	5,738
362	Electrical appliances	5,208	3,600	5,472
364	Engine electrical equipment	3,929	2,763	3,966
365	Electric lamps (bulbs)	7,898	3,204	4,749

(continued)

TABLE A-2 (concluded)

SIC Code No. (pre-1958)	Name of Industry	Nonwage Value Added per Employee		Physical Assets, Net per Employee (3)
		Actual (1)	Estimated by Regressing 1 on 3 (2)	
366	Communication equipment	3,410	3,451	5,198
369	Electrical products, n.e.c.	5,101	4,041	6,298
371	Motor vehicles and equipment	6,329	4,691	7,552
372	Aircraft and parts	2,783	3,964	6,154
373	Ships and boats	2,375	3,389	5,085
374	Railroad equipment	5,111	4,720	7,608
381	Scientific instruments	2,813	3,621	5,511
382	Mechanical measuring instruments	4,071	3,811	5,864
384	Medical equipment and supplies	5,010	3,585	5,445
386	Photographic Equipment	6,240	4,745	7,658
387	Watches and clocks	2,861	3,378	5,066
391	Jewelry and silverware	3,043	3,079	4,524
393	Musical instruments and parts	2,813	2,948	4,291
394	Toys and sporting goods	2,702	2,611	3,703
395	Office supplies	3,591	3,409	5,122
396	Costume jewelry and notions	2,233	2,456	3,437
397	Plastics products, n.e.c.	2,970	3,239	4,813
398	Miscellaneous manufacturers	3,171	2,832	4,086

Note: n.e.c. = not elsewhere classified.

TABLE A-3

Variables Used in Analysis of Nonwage Value Added and Productive Assets in Indian Manufacturing Industry, 1961
(dollars)

		Nonwage Value Added per Employee		Productive Assets per Employee, Net (3)
Indian Industrial Classification			Estimated by Regressing	
Code No.	Name of Industry	Actual (1)	1 on 3 (2)	
2021,2	Manufacture of milk foods and other dairy products	664	1,063	4,409
203	Canning and preserving of fruits and vegetables	223	263	835
204	Canning and preserving of fish and other seafoods	692	203	613
2052	Rice mills	191	202	609
2051,3	Flour mills	484	523	1,894
206	Manufacture of bakery products	685	408	1,411
2071	Sugar	575	628	2,354
208	Manufacture of cocoa, chocolate, and sugar confectionery	553	444	1,560
2093	Hydrogenated oil	1,207	745	2,890
2099	Salt	206	215	656
211,2	Spirits and wine	433	561	2,059
213	Breweries and manufacture of malt	3,042	751	2,914
214	Soft drinks and carbonated water industries	936	693	2,649
2202,3	Cigars and cigarettes	1,210	748	2,900
2311	Cotton textiles	268	245	770
2313	Woolen textiles	515	443	1,555
2314,5	Silk and artificial silk	326	318	1,047
2316	Webbing, narrow fabrics embroidery and lace manufacturing	219	391	1,342
2317	Textiles dyeing, bleaching, finishing, and processing, etc.	294	287	927
2318	Thread and threadball making	588	711	2,730
232	Knitting mills	297	225	694
233	Cordage, rope, and twine industries	245	258	816

(continued)

TABLE A-3 (continued)

| Indian Industrial Classification | | Nonwage Value Added per Employee | | Productive Assets per Employee, Net (3) |
Code No.	Name of Industry	Actual (1)	Estimated by Regressing 1 on 3 (2)	
2395,6	Coated fabric and linoleum	894	640	2,409
2398	Tarpaulins, tents, sails, and other made-up canvas goods	245	217	666
2431,3	Clothing and tailoring	160	183	544
2432	Umbrella manufacture	172	323	1,067
241	Manufacture of footwear	301	135	377
2511	Sawmilling	163	185	551
2512	Plywood	275	356	1,196
252	Wooden and cane containers and cane small ware	142	174	509
2602,3	Furniture and fixtures, metal	296	406	1,401
2711-3	Pulp and paper mills	640	818	3,228
2714,6	Paperboard	616	701	2,686
2715,7	Paper and paper products	858	346	1,157
2801,2	Printing and bookbinding	265	315	1,036
291	Tannery and leather finishing plants	192	351	1,179
293	Manufacture of leather prod. exc. footwear and other wearing apparel	137	484	1,727
3001	Tires and tubes	3,705	1,204	5,118
3002,4	Surgical and medical products	517	347	1,164
3003	Rubber footwear	200	168	489
31111,3	Fertilizers	833	1,683	7,628
31121	Heavy chemicals, inorganic	874	1,134	4,762
3113,5	Synthetic resins and man-made fibers	2,165	1,818	8,361
3116	Explosives including gunpowder and safety fuses	652	1,079	4,488
3117	Dyestuffs	4,040	1,987	9,297
3118	Turpentine and rosin	1,638	689	2,633
313	Manufacture of paints, varnishes, and lacquers	751	603	2,246
3196	Soaps and glycerine	2,323	953	3,872

(continued)

TABLE A-3 (continued)

| Indian Industrial Classification | | Nonwage Value Added per Employee | | Productive Assets per Employee, Net (3) |
Code No.	Name of Industry	Actual (1)	Estimated by Regressing 1 on 3 (2)	
3195	Drugs and pharmaceuticals	1,468	846	3,362
3197	Perfumes, cosmetics, and other toilet preparations	430	360	1,216
3198	Matches	403	217	663
3192	Insecticides, fungicides, and weedicides	1,368	1,123	4,709
31910	Glue and gelatine	126	525	1,902
3311-3	Fire bricks and refractories	246	346	1,160
3314	Tiles	142	148	421
3321,4-6	Pressed and blown glassware	168	178	526
3322	Sheet and plate glass	268	642	2,418
3331	Chinaware and pottery	105	253	800
3332	Sanitaryware and whiteware	161	286	922
334	Manufacture of cement	989	1,111	4,649
3391	Asbestos cement	725	409	1,412
3392	Hume pipes and other cement and concrete products	313	349	1,172
3395, 39916 }	Stone and slate products	148	192	574
3411	Iron and steel (metal)	852	1,199	5,089
3396	Grinding wheels and abrasives	1,160	813	3,204
3412	Ferro-alloys	1,667	2,082	9,827
3413	Iron and steel castings and forgings	106	213	649
3414	Iron and steel structurals	270	429	1,495
3415	Iron and steel pipes	808	698	2,670
342	Nonferrous basic metal industries	1,113	1,393	6,090
3501	Metal containers & steel trunks	606	551	2,017
3502	Cutlery, locks, etc.	334	204	616
3503	Bolts, nuts, nails, screws, springs, chains, etc.	391	629	2,359

(continued)

TABLE A-3 (continued)

Indian Industrial Classification		Nonwage Value Added per Employee		Productive Assets per Employee, Net (3)
		Actual (1)	Estimated by Regressing 1 on 3 (2)	
Code No.	Name of Industry			
36061	Ball, roller, and tapered bearings	680	515	1,859
3504	Enameling, japanning and lacquering, galvanizing, plating, etc.	307	371	1,260
3507	Safes and vaults	139	141	396
35010	Hand tools and small tools	483	438	1,533
35012	Sanitary and plumbing fixtures and fittings of metal	134	220	675
360111,2	Typewriters and office machines	1,150	712	2,738
3607	Machine tools	413	791	3,100
36012	Weighing machines	510	326	1,079
3603	Internal combustion engines	594	468	1,658
360411	Paper machinery	261	704	2,699
36041	Textile machinery, etc.	271	374	1,271
36044, 360414	Food products machinery	380	442	1,550
36049	Chemical machinery	357	282	908
360513	Refrigeration plants for industrial use	843	302	987
36081,2	Farm machinery and equipment	322	325	1,073
360511	Power driven pumps-reciprocating, centrifugal, etc.	439	423	1,471
360512	Air and gas compressors and vacuum pumps	907	518	1,874
360113	Air conditioners and refrigerators	516	366	1,237
360115	Sewing and knitting machines	204	284	915
36052	Conveying equipment-bucket elevators, skip hoists, etc.	366	481	1,714
37011	Equipment for generation, transmission and distribution of electricity	479	416	1,442

(continued)

TABLE A-3 (concluded)

Indian Industrial Classification		Nonwage Value Added per Employee		Productive Assets per Employee, Net (3)
		Actual (1)	Estimated by Regressing 1 on 3 (2)	
Code No.	Name of Industry			
37012	Electric motors	578	488	1,745
37013	Electric fans	511	279	896
37014	Electric lamps	506	604	2,248
37016	Electric cables and wires	1,345	1,115	4,667
37019	Household appliances, such as electric irons, heaters, etc.	323	315	1,037
370110	Storage batteries	869	799	3,138
370111	Dry cells	646	509	1,836
37021,2	Telephone and telegraph apparatus	279	490	1,753
37023,4	Radio communication apparatus and receivers	675	621	2,326
3812	Boatbuilding	236	498	1,786
383	Manufacture of motor vehicles	734	689	2,630
385	Manufacture of motor cycles and bicycles	422	493	1,766
3911,3,4 39121	Scientific, medical, optical, measuring, and drawing instruments	419	429	1,495
3924	Manufacture of photographic and optical goods-others	155	195	586
393	Manufacture of watches and clocks	104	403	1,387
3941	Jewelry	213	239	745
3993,4	Pens and pencils	370	275	883
3995	Button making	675	497	1,781
3997	Plastic molded goods	378	388	1,328
39910	Brooms and brushes	353	252	793
39911,2	Toys, games, and sport goods	109	106	284

TABLE A-4

Linearity and Bartlett Tests for Comparisons of Nonwage Value Added and Net Physical Capital per Employee in the United States and India

Test	Number of Industries	Arithmetic Form	Logarithmic Form
Linearity			
United States			
Four-digit level	276	2.87*	.58
		(18,256)	(13,261)
Three-digit level	122	4.68*	.40
		(3,117)	(3,117)
India	115	3.96*	.47
		(18,95)	(15,98)
Bartlett			
United States			
Four-digit level	276	200.82**	14.72
		(7)	(7)
Three-digit level	122	102.04**	3.64
		(5)	(5)
India	115	125.95**	2.44
		(5)	(5)

Note: Linearity test is derived from W. J. Dixon and F. J. Massey, Jr., *Introduction to Statistical Analysis,* New York, 1957, p. 197. Bartlett's test is derived from G. W. Snedecor, *Statistical Methods,* Ames, Iowa, 1947, pp. 250-251. Numbers in parentheses indicate degrees of freedom for each statistic.

*Variables not linearly related at 1 per cent level of confidence.

**Variances significantly different from one another at 1 per cent level of confidence.

BILATERAL COMPARISONS
OF VALUE ADDED PER EMPLOYEE

Tables B-1, B-2, and B-3 give the variables plotted in Charts 11, 12, and 13, respectively. The United States data are derived from the *1958 Census of Manufactures* (used in the comparison with the United Kingdom), the *1962 Annual Survey of Manufactures* (used in the comparison with Japan), and the *1963 Census of Manufactures* (used in the comparison with India), all of which are publications of the Bureau of the Census, U.S. Department of Commerce. The sources of the data for the other three countries are as follows: United Kingdom: *Reports on the Census of Production, 1958,* London, Board of Trade, 1962; Japan: *Census of Manufactures, 1962,* Ministry of International Trade and Industry, Research and Statistics Division, Tokyo, 1964; India: *Annual Survey of Industries, 1961,* Central Statistical Organization, Calcutta, 1965.

To make these bilateral comparisons, it has been necessary to establish a conversion between the industrial classification used by the United States and that used in each of the other three countries. The conversions developed for this purpose are indicated in Tables B-1, B-2, and B-3.

The British classification, a very summary one of only 109 items (at the three-digit and four-digit levels, free of duplication), has been maintained almost intact, only a few combinations of items from the British schedule being necessary in the interest of comparability. This yields 103 items for comparison with the United States.

The Japanese classification is far more detailed, comprising 501 items at the four-digit level. In many cases, however, it has seemed preferable to establish the conversion at the three-digit level for Japan, and in other cases it has been deemed necessary to combine two or more four-digit items and, more exceptionally, some three-digit ones.

In addition, the following numbers from the Japanese classification have been omitted altogether because of inability to identify a corresponding item in the United States classification: 1841, 1845, 1891, 1892, 1893, 1895, 1896, 1897, 1898, 1899, 201, 2025, 2026, 2027, 2034, 2039, 2092, 2093, 2094, 2097, 2099, 2141, 215, 2191, 2192, 2199, 2241, 2321, 2425, 2426, 2427, 2439, 244, 249, 251, 2521, 2692, 2699, 2731, 2741, 2759, 2762, 2763, 2769, 3031, 3044, 3121, 3122, 3123, 319, 3212, 3215, 3216, 3217, 3219, 329, 3482, 3491, 3631, 3641, 3653, 3659, 369, 3811, 3971, 3981, 3982, 3983, 3984, 3986, 3987, 3988, 3989, 399. The net effect of these combinations and deletions has been to provide 178 items for which there seemed to be a reasonably close correspondence between the Japanese and the U.S. industries.

The Indian classification, comprising 194 items (some three-digit and others four- or five-digit), has also been subjected to some combinations in the search for comparability with the United States. More important, a considerable number of items have had to be deleted altogether. One reason, as in the case of Japan, has been the lack of reasonably similar items identifiable in the statistics for the United States, the Indian code numbers so deleted being as follows: [1] 2072, (2091, 20910), 2094, 2095, 2097, 2201, (2204, 2205), 2206, 2312, 2391, 2394, (2397, 2399), 2591, 2592, (3119, 31110), 31122, 3121, 3191, (3193, 3194), 31912, 3199, 329, 3333, 3397, 3398, 3505, (3508, 35014), 3509, 35013, (3609, 36010), 36042, 36045, (36047, 360410), 360412, 360413, 36051, (36054, 36056, 36062), 360514, (37015, 3704), 39915, (395, 3998, 39913, 39917).

A second reason for deletion of items from the Indian schedule is that, according to the details contained in the source, some industries are engaged mainly or largely in repair or service work as distinguished from manufacturing proper. The code numbers omitted for this reason are as follows: 2096, 2098, 2392, 2393, 3506, 36013, 36046, 3811, 3821, 3822, 3823, 384, 386, 3942, 39914. Finally, two items have been deleted from the Indian schedule because (according to details published for individual Indian states) the industries concerned employ sizable numbers of unpaid prison labor at nominal wages, the items deleted for this reason being Nos. 2092 and 2601.

The net effect of the combinations and deletions noted above is to give 117 items from the Indian side for comparison with the United States. As reported in Chapter 3, additional computations have been

---

[1] Indian numbers here grouped in parentheses are combined in the source.

made, excluding (1) Indian industries with total employment of less than 1,000 each and (2) others with total employment of less than 2,000 each. The items in question are as follows:

(1) 204, 208, 213, 214, 293, 3118, 31910, 3507, 36049, 360411, 360513, 37019, 3812, 393, 3995, 39910, (39911, 39912).

(2) 203, 2318, 232, (2395, 2396), 2398, 241, 3192, 3396, 3412, 35012, (360111, 360112), 36012, 360512, 36052, 36061, 3924, 3941.

A test of linearity and Bartlett's test for homoscedasticity were applied to the data in an effort to determine whether the arithmetic or logarithmic form of correlation was appropriate. The results of these tests are given in Table B-4. For both the United States–Japan and the United States–India comparisons the linearity test showed that the variables were not linearly related in the arithmetic form but were so related in the logarithmic form; the results were significant at the 1 per cent level of confidence. However, for both functional forms, Bartlett's test showed that the variances of the observations (the data were arranged in ascending order of the independent variable and divided into groups of approximately twenty observations) were not homogeneous for the complete sets of industries; the results were significant at the 1 per cent level of confidence. For the more limited number of observations, as specified in each case in Table 6, the variances were homogeneous in the logarithmic form but not in the arithmetic form. In brief, on statistical grounds alone, the logarithmic form seems more appropriate than the arithmetic form for both the U.S.–Japan and U.S.–India correlations, as shown in the accompanying table.

For the U.S.–U.K. comparison, the variables are shown to be linearly related in both the arithmetic and logarithmic forms, according to the linearity test. Bartlett's test shows, however, that the variances of the observations (the data were arranged in ascending order of the independent variable and divided into four groups) were homogeneous in the logarithmic form but not in the arithmetic form. That is, only the logarithmic form passes both of these tests. On the basis of these tests, all of the bilateral comparisons were computed with the variables transformed into logarithms.

The regression equations obtained from the bilateral comparisons and used in deriving the middle column of figures in each of Tables B-1, B-2, and B-3 are given below, X being in each case the log of value added by manufacture per employee in the United States and Y the log of value added by manufacture per employee in the foreign country concerned:

United States–United Kingdom (103 industries)

$$Y = -.317 + .795X$$

United States–Japan (178 industries)

$$Y = -.608 + .966X$$

United States–India (117 industries)

$$Y = -1.053 + .917X$$

TABLE B-1

Variables Used in Comparison of Value Added per Employee in the United Kingdom and the United States, 1958

(dollars)

U.K. Industrial Classification		Matched with U.S. SIC No.	Value Added per Employee		
			U.K. Actual (1)	U.K. Estimated by Regressing 1 on 3 (2)	U.S. Actual (3)
Code No.	Name of Industry				
211,9	Grain-mill products	204 (less 2046)	5,199	4,209	15,269
212	Bread and related products	2051	2,296	2,572	8,217
213	Biscuits and crackers	2052	2,192	3,428	11,795
214	Meat and fish products	201, 2031, 6	2,634	2,467	7,796
215	Dairy products	202	4,033	2,949	9,758
216	Sugar	206	2,532	3,436	11,828
217	Candy and related products	207	2,645	2,854	9,364
218	Fruit and vegetable products	203, 2087 (less 2031, 6)	2,584	2,969	9,842
2292	Starch and misc. foods	2046, 2098, 9	4,341	4,282	15,604
231	Brewing and malting	2082, 3	5,533	4,331	15,828
2391	Spirit distilling and compounding	2085	8,285	5,565	21,698
2392, 3	Wines and soft drinks	2084, 6	3,858	2,858	9,383
240	Tobacco products	21	5,354	4,525	16,728
262	Petroleum refining	2911	5,014	4,043	14,516

(continued)

TABLE B-1 (continued)

| U.K. Industrial Classification | | Matched with U.S. SIC No. | Value Added per Employee | | |
Code No.	Name of Industry		U.K. Actual (1)	U.K. Estimated by Regressing 1 on 3 (2)	U.S. Actual (3)
263	Lubricating oils and greases	2992	7,268	3,831	13,566
2711	Dyestuffs	2815, 2861	3,971	3,858	13,684
2712	Agricultural chemicals	287	4,361	3,177	10,718
2713	Industrial chemicals and chemical products	281 (less 2815) 289	3,778	4,822	18,118
2721	Pharmaceutical preparations	283	4,368	5,597	21,858
2722	Toilet preparations	2844	5,161	5,958	23,644
273	Explosives	2892	2,828	2,710	8,773
274	Paint and printing ink	2851, 2893	4,029	3,867	13,725
2291, 2751	Vegetable and animal oils and fats	209 (less 2095, 7-9	4,777	3,837	13,590
2752	Soap, detergents, and candles	2841, 3984	5,263	6,672	27,268
276	Synthetic resins and plastic materials	2821, 2	4,500	4,605	17,098
2771	Polishes, etc.	2842	4,947	4,802	18,024
2772	Glue and gelatin	2891	3,304	3,810	13,468
311	Iron and steel forging and rolling	331, 3391 (less 3315, 7)	3,772	3,408	11,709
312	Pipes, tubes, and fittings	3494, 9, 3317	3,667	3,038	10,130
321	Light metals	3334, 3352, 3361	2,767	3,512	12,159
322	Copper, brass, and other base metals	33ª, 3461	3,238	2,799	9,139

(continued)

TABLE B-1 (continued)

| U.K. Industrial Classification | | Matched with U.S. SIC No. | Value Added per Employee | | |
Code No.	Name of Industry		U.K. Actual (1)	U.K. Estimated by Regressing 1 on 3 (2)	U.S. Actual (3)
331	Farm machinery and equipment	3522	3,208	3,011	10,017
332, 3	Metalworking machinery and tools	354, 3623 (less 35481, 2)	2,906	2,712	8,780
3341	Internal combustion engines	3519	2,373	2,994	9,946
335	Textile machinery	3552	2,452	2,068	6,245
336	Construction machinery and equipment	3531	2,861	3,181	10,732
337	Mechanical handling equipment	3534-6	3,041	3,084	10,326
338	Office machinery	3571-2, 3579	2,746	2,499	7,923
339	Miscellaneous machinery	3532, 3548, 355-9b	3,081	2,775	9,040
341	Fabricated structural metal products	344 (less 3442)	3,336	2,721	8,819
3491	Ball and roller bearings	3562	2,984	2,713	8,787
351	Scientific, surgical, and photographic instruments	38 (less 387)	2,813	3,023	10,066
352	Watches and clocks	387	1,985	2,267	7,008
361	Electrical machinery	35111, 361, 2 (less 3623, 4)	2,918	2,975	9,865
363	Telephone and telegraph apparatus	3661	2,200	2,683	8,666
364	Radio and other electronic apparatus	365-7, 3693 (less 3661)	2,389	2,655	8,551

(continued)

TABLE B-1 (continued)

| U.K. Industrial Classification | | Matched with U.S. SIC No. | Value Added per Employee | | |
Code No.	Name of Industry		U.K. Actual (1)	U.K. Estimated by Regressing 1 on 3 (2)	U.S. Actual (3)
365	Domestic electric appliances	363 (less 3632)	2,915	3,241	10,989
369	Miscellaneous electrical goods	364, 9 (less 3693)	2,582	2,858	9,381
3701	Shipbuilding and ship repairing	373	2,261	2,371	7,417
3342, 3702	Steam engines	3511 (less 35111)	2,755	3,128	10,509
381	Motor vehicle manufacturing	3537, 371, 3791	3,371	3,350	11,456
382	Motorcycles, bicycles, and parts	3751	2,234	2,227	6,855
383	Aircraft and parts	372	2,901	2,776	9,046
385	Railroad and street cars	3742	2,166	2,238	6,897
389	Perambulators, hand trucks, etc.	3943, 3799	2,193	2,356	7,358
391	Metal tools and implements	3423, 5	2,400	2,757	8,967
392	Cutlery	3421	4,039	3,174	10,703
393	Bolts, nuts, screws, rivets, etc.	3451, 2	2,558	2,733	8,868
362, 394	Wire and wire manufactures	3315, 3357, 3481	2,994	2,810	9,185
395	Metal cans and boxes	3411	2,365	3,553	12,339
396	Jewelry, silverware, and plated ware	391	2,441	2,447	7,716
399	Miscellaneous fabricated metal products	25, 3442, 349[c]	2,560	2,581	8,250

(continued)

TABLE B-1 (continued)

| U.K. Industrial Classification | | Matched with U.S. SIC No. | Value Added per Employee | | |
| | | | U.K. Actual (1) | U.K. Estimated by Regressing 1 on 3 (2) | U.S. Actual (3) |
Code No.	Name of Industry				
411	Production of man-made fibers	2823-4	3,757	3,825	13,538
412	Spinning and doubling of cotton, flax, silk, and man-made fibers	228 (less 2283)	1,532	1,637	4,651
413	Broad-woven fabric mills, cotton, man-made fibers, and silk	2211, 2221	1,711	1,667	4,759
414	Woolen and worsted manufactures	2231, 2283, 2291, 7	2,080	2,042	6,146
416	Rope, cordage, and twine	2296, 8	2,095	2,053	6,188
417	Knitting mills	225	2,037	1,778	5,164
418	Lace goods	2292	2,050	1,762	5,105
419	Carpets, rugs, and mats	227	2,721	2,451	7,730
421	Narrow fabrics	2241	1,976	1,950	5,797
422	Made-up textiles	239	1,792	1,917	5,676
423	Dyeing and finishing textiles	226	2,133	2,064	6,228
431	Leather tanning and finishing	311	2,511	2,376	7,434
432	Leather goods	312, 315-7, 319	1,773	1,903	5,624
433	Fur	2371, 3992	2,260	2,977	9,876
441	Raincoats and other weatherproof outerwear	2385	1,546	1,880	5,538
442	Men's and boys' suits, coats, and overcoats	231	1,465	1,804	5,258

(continued)

TABLE B-1 (continued)

U.K. Industrial Classification		Matched with U.S. SIC No.	Value Added per Employee		
Code No.	Name of Industry		U.K. Actual (1)	U.K. Estimated by Regressing 1 on 3 (2)	U.S. Actual (3)
443	Women's and girls' outerwear	233	1,811	1,820	5,316
444	Men's and boys' furnishings	232	1,327	1,501	4,172
445	Dresses, lingerie, infants' wear, etc.	232, 6 2384	1,499	1,761	5,101
446	Millinery, hats, and caps	235	1,750	1,909	5,645
449	Miscellaneous apparel and umbrellas	2381, 7, 9, 3995	1,805	1,677	4,797
450	Nonrubber footwear	313, 4	1,958	1,756	5,083
461	Structural clay products	325	2,433	2,259	6,976
462	Pottery and related products	326	1,756	2,115	6,423
463	Glass	321-3	3,027	2,970	9,845
464	Cement	324	5,666	4,719	17,635
469	Abrasives and misc. building material	327-9	2,984	3,069	10,261
471	Sawmilling and related products	243	2,421	2,228	6,857
472	Wooden furniture	251-4 d	2,338	2,002	5,993
475	Wooden containers	244	2,103	1,632	4,634
479	Misc. wood products	249	2,132	1,981	5,915
481	Paper and paperboard mills	261-3, 266	3,602	3,592	12,507
482	Paperboard containers and boxes	265	2,396	2,590	8,287
483	Converted paper and paperboard products	264	2,656	2,852	9,357

(continued)

TABLE B-1 (concluded)

U.K. Industrial Classification		Matched with U.S. SIC No.	Value Added per Employee		
Code No.	Name of Industry		U. K. Actual (1)	U.K. Estimated by Regressing 1 on 3 (2)	U.S. Actual (3)
4911	Tires and tubes	3011	2,904	3,749	13,199
4912	Rubber footwear and other products	302-3, 306	2,561	2,571	8,212
492	Linoleum and other coated fabrics	2295, 3982	3,086	3,157	10,632
493	Brooms and brushes	3981	2,283	2,529	8,041
494	Toys and sporting goods	394 (less 3942)	2,260	2,325	7,235
495	Office supplies	395	2,737	2,554	8,144
496	Plastic molding and fabricating	3079	2,290	2,515	7,988

[a]Less 331, 2, 3334, 3352, 7, 3361, 3391, 9.
[b]Less 35483-5, 3552, 3562, 5, 6, 7, 3571, 2, 9, 3581, 2, 9.
[c]Less 2511, 2, 9, 2521, 253, 2541, 259, 3494, 8, 9.
[d]Less 2514, 5, 2522, 2542.

TABLE B-2

Variables Used in Comparison of Value Added per Employee in Japan and the United States, 1962

(dollars)

U.S. Standard Industrial Classification		Matched with Japanese Code No.	Value Added per Employee		
Code No.	Name of Industry		Japan Actual (1)	Japan Estimated by Regressing 1 on 3 (2)	U.S. Actual (3)
201	Meat products	1811	2,154	2,176	9,528
202	Dairy products	1812	2,472	2,711	11,960
2031, 6	Canned and frozen seafoods	182	1,552	1,825	7,941
2033	Canned fruits and vegetables	183	1,305	2,133	9,330
2035	Pickles and sauces	1842, 3, 4, 9	2,939	2,579	11,359
2044	Rice milling	1851	2,464	3,345	14,868
2041	Flour and meal	1852, 3, 1894	3,962	3,844	17,169
2042	Prepared animal feeds	1854	3,529	3,522	15,681
206	Sugar	186	7,846	3,504	15,600
205, 207	Bakery, candy, and related products	187	2,144	2,331	10,229
208	Beverages	188	3,563	3,677	16,395
2092, 3, 5, 6	Edible oil	2651	5,301	4,506	20,237
2094	Grease and tallow	2652	2,065	2,830	12,506
2211	Weaving mills, cotton	2031	1,034	1,396	6,020
222	Weaving mills, synthetics	2032	1,178	1,773	7,707
223	Weaving, finishing mills, wool	2033, 2056, 9	1,856	1,821	7,925

(continued)

TABLE B-2 (continued)

| U.S. Standard Industrial Classification | | Matched with Japanese Code No. | Value Added per Employee | | |
Code No.	Name of Industry		Japan Actual (1)	Japan Estimated by Regressing 1 on 3 (2)	U.S. Actual (3)
224	Narrow-fabric mills	2071	1,101	1,734	7,530
225	Knitting mills	204	1,534	1,392	6,001
226	Textile finishing, except wool	205 (less 2056, 9)	2,113	1,872	8,154
227 (less 2272)	Carpets and rugs	2096	1,298	1,932	8,422
2281, 2	Yarn mills, except wool	2021, 2, 4	1,899	1,402	6,044
2283	Wool yarn mills	2023	1,832	1,408	6,073
2284	Thread mills	2028	1,122	1,548	6,696
2298	Cordage and twine	206, 2074	1,349	1,624	7,040
2291	Felt goods, n.e.c.	2095	1,815	2,666	11,755
2292	Lace goods	2072, 3	2,175	1,511	6,533
2297	Scouring and combing plants	2091	1,654	1,830	7,963
231, 233, 236a	Men's, women's, and children's outerwear	211	1,101	1,365	5,882
2321, 2, 234	Shirts, nightwear, and underwear	212	1,150	1,229	5,273
235	Millinery, hats, and caps	213	1,569	1,363	5,870
2393	Textile bags	2194	2,240	1,786	7,764
2394	Canvas products	2193	1,706	1,435	6,194

(continued)

TABLE B-2 (continued)

U.S. Standard Industrial Classification		Matched with Japanese Code No.	Value Added per Employee		
Code No.	Name of Industry		Japan Actual (1)	Japan Estimated by Regressing 1 on 3 (2)	U.S. Actual (3)
241, 242	Logging and sawmills	221	1,430	1,446	6,243
243	Millwork and related products	222, 233	1,768	1,706	7,404
244	Wooden containers	223	1,351	1,320	5,678
249	Miscellaneous wood products	229, 3985	1,407	1,563	6,767
2511, 2	Household wood furniture	2311	1,507	1,571	6,802
2514	Metal household furniture	2312	2,208	1,769	7,690
2515	Mattresses and bedsprings	2313	1,304	1,921	8,375
252, 253, 254, 259	Office and public bldg. furniture and fixtures	239	1,726	2,138	9,357
261	Pulp mills	241	4,461	3,158	14,006
262	Paper mills, except building	2421, 2	4,366	3,242	14,393
263, 266	Building paper and paperboard mills	2423, 4	3,835	3,527	15,705
2641	Paper coating and glazing	2431	2,483	3,405	15,141
2643	Bags, except textile bags	2451	1,768	2,141	9,370
2644	Wallpaper	2433	1,612	2,004	8,750
2645	Die-cut paper and board	2432	3,512	2,369	10,405
265	Paperboard containers and boxes	2452-5	1,820	2,184	9,564
274, 2751	Commercial letterpress printing	253	1,917	2,118	9,266
2732	Book printing	254	1,598	2,128	9,308
2752, 3	Commercial lithographic printing and engraving	259	1,782	2,277	9,987

(continued)

TABLE B-2 (continued)

U.S. Standard Industrial Classification		Matched with Japanese Code No.	Value Added per Employee		
Code No.	Name of Industry		Japan Actual (1)	Japan Estimated by Regressing 1 on 3 (2)	U.S. Actual (3)
2871, 2	Fertilizers	261	4,445	2,645	11,658
2812, 3, 6, 9, 2895	Inorganic chemicals	262	3,847	4,803	21,620
2814, 5, 8	Organic chemicals	263	5,811	6,018	27,301
282 (less 2822)	Fibers and plastic materials	264	4,550	4,139	18,532
283	Drugs	268	5,405	5,491	24,831
2844	Toilet preparations	2694, 5	6,134	6,639	30,223
2841-3, 2894	Cleaning agents and fatty acids	2661-3, 2666	4,424	6,371	28,961
286	Gum and wood chemicals	267	2,155	3,618	16,125
285	Paints and varnishes	2664	4,060	3,682	16,420
2873, 9	Agricultural chemicals	2693	5,393	3,774	16,845
2891	Glue and gelatin	2696	2,921	3,446	15,332
2892	Explosives	2691	3,048	2,418	10,624
2893	Printing ink	2665	3,080	3,403	15,133
2911	Petroleum refining	271	12,168	5,339	24,120
2992	Lubricating oils and greases	272	3,560	3,783	16,888
3011	Tires and inner tubes	281	4,442	3,332	14,806

(continued)

TABLE B-2 (continued)

U.S. Standard Industrial Classification		Matched with Japanese Code No.	Value Added per Employee		
			Japan Actual (1)	Japan Estimated by Regressing 1 on 3 (2)	U.S. Actual (3)
Code No.	Name of Industry				
3021	Rubber footwear	282	1,294	1,815	7,896
3031	Reclaimed rubber	283, 284			
		285	2,052	2,895	12,802
3069	Fabricated rubber products, n.e.c.	286, 289	2,407	2,353	10,329
3079	Plastics products, n.e.c.	396	1,940	2,178	9,536
3111	Leather tanning and finishing	291	2,439	1,910	8,326
3121	Industrial leather belting	292	2,013	3,104	13,761
3131, 3141, 2	Footwear, except rubber	293, 294	1,743	1,322	5,690
3151	Leather gloves	295	1,793	972	4,138
3161	Luggage	296	1,669	1,582	6,849
3171	Handbags and purses	297	2,003	1,298	5,582
3172, 3199	Small leather goods	299	1,890	1,513	6,542
3211	Flat glass	3011	10,244	3,176	14,092
3221, 9	Pressed and blown glassware	2013-6, 7, 9	2,563	2,519	11,084
3231	Products of purchased glass	3018	2,024	2,474	10,879
3241	Cement, hydraulic	302	9,423	4,753	21,386
3251	Brick and structural tile	3032	1,128	1,657	7,188
3253	Ceramic wall and floor tile	3045, 6	1,456	2,076	9,073

(continued)

TABLE B-2 (continued)

U.S. Standard Industrial Classification		Matched with Japanese Code No.	Value Added per Employee		
			Japan Actual (1)	Japan Estimated by Regressing 1 on 3 (2)	U.S. Actual (3)
Code No.	Name of Industry				
3255	Clay refractories	305	1,709	2,147	9,397
3259	Structural clay products, n.e.c.	3033, 9	1,347	1,966	8,577
3261	Vitreous plumbing fixtures	3041	1,944	2,279	9,992
3262, 3	China and earthenware food utensils	3042	1,214	1,351	5,817
3264	Porcelain electrical supplies	3043	2,119	1,899	8,276
3269	Pottery products, n.e.c.	3047, 9	1,235	1,415	6,102
327	Concrete and plaster products	308	2,252	2,657	11,713
329 (less 3291)	Nonmetallic minerals, n.e.c.	309	2,020	2,817	12,444
3291	Abrasive products	307	2,753	3,151	13,977
3312	Blast furnaces and steel mills	2761, 311, 3125, 315	3,658	2,978	13,183
3313	Electrometallurgical products	3133	3,107	3,306	14,688
3315, 6, 7	Steel pipe, tubes, and wire	313, 314 (less 3133)	3,268	2,903	12,837
332, 3391	Iron and steel foundries and forging	316, 317	2,101	2,168	9,491
3331	Primary copper	3211	3,131	3,627	16,167
3333	Primary zinc	3213	3,574	2,066	9,030
3334	Primary aluminum	3214	7,418	6,040	27,407
334	Secondary nonferrous metals	322	2,598	2,723	12,014

(continued)

TABLE B-2 (continued)

U.S. Standard Industrial Classification		Matched with Japanese Code No.	Value Added per Employee		
Code No.	Name of Industry		Japan Actual (1)	Japan Estimated by Regressing 1 on 3 (2)	U.S. Actual (3)
3351	Copper rolling and drawing	3231	2,756	2,624	11,564
3352	Aluminum rolling and drawing	3233	3,183	2,551	11,229
3356	Rolling and drawing, n.e.c.	3232, 9	3,314	2,644	11,655
3357	Nonferrous wire drawing, etc.	325	3,323	2,715	11,979
336, 3392	Nonferrous foundries and forgings	324	2,131	2,153	9,425
341	Metal cans	331	2,542	3,277	14,554
3421	Cutlery	3321, 3	1,937	2,062	9,010
3423	Edge tools	3322	2,339	2,417	10,621
3425	Hand saws and saw blades	3326	2,084	2,780	12,277
3429	Hardware, n.e.c.	3324, 5, 7, 9	2,041	2,445	10,750
343	Plumbing and nonelectric heating	333	2,080	2,597	11,438
3441, 9	Fabricated structural steel	3341	2,512	2,122	9,281
3442	Metal doors, sash, and trim	3342	2,858	2,087	9,123
3443, 4, 3491	Boiler shop products, metal drums, barrels, etc.	3343, 3411	2,316	2,167	9,485
345	Screw machine products and bolts	337	1,785	2,342	10,282
346, 347	Metal stampings	335	1,784	2,125	9,298
3492, 3, 6, 7, 9	Misc. fabricated metal products	339 (less 3396)	2,030	2,406	10,570

(continued)

TABLE B-2 (continued)

U.S. Standard Industrial Classification		Matched with Japanese Code No.	Value Added per Employee		
Code No.	Name of Industry		Japan Actual (1)	Japan Estimated by Regressing 1 on 3 (2)	U.S. Actual (3)
3481	Fabricated wire products, n.e.c.	336	2,441	2,126	9,300
3511	Steam engines and turbines	3412	9,375	2,791	12,325
3519	Internal combustion engines	3413, 4, 9	2,118	2,607	11,484
352	Farm machinery and equipment	342	2,664	2,578	11,352
3531, 2	Mining and construction machinery	3431	2,163	2,592	11,420
3534, 5	Elevators and conveyors	3473, 4	3,356	3,262	14,487
3537	Industrial trucks and tractors	3432	3,319	2,423	10,648
354	Metalworking machinery	344	2,796	2,576	11,345
3551	Food products machinery	3461	2,339	2,595	11,431
3552	Textile machinery	345	2,109	2,053	8,970
3553	Woodworking machinery	3462	2,219	2,602	11,461
3554	Paper industries machinery	3463	3,176	2,316	10,163
3555	Printing trades machinery	3464	2,293	2,764	12,201
3559	Special industry machinery, n.e.c.	3465, 9 3478	2,954	2,452	10,782
3561, 4	Pumps, compressors, blowers, fans, etc.	3471, 2	3,317	2,532	11,143
3566	Power transmission equipment	3475	2,753	2,575	11,340
3567	Industrial furnaces and ovens	3476	2,224	2,414	10,607
3569	General industry machinery, n.e.c.	3477, 9	2,633	1,973	8,609
3571, 2	Typewriters and office machines	3481	3,817	2,372	10,415

(continued)

TABLE B-2 (continued)

U.S. Standard Industrial Classification		Matched with Japanese Code No.	Value Added per Employee		
			Japan Actual (1)	Japan Estimated by Regressing 1 on 3 (2)	U.S. Actual (3)
Code No.	Name of Industry				
3579, 3589	Office and service industry machines, n.e.c.	3489	2,347	3,020	13,376
3585	Refrigeration machinery, n.e.c.	3483	2,366	2,460	10,819
3494	Valves and pipe fittings	3492	2,667	2,606	11,481
3498	Fabricated pipe and fittings	3493	1,718	2,451	10,774
3562	Ball and roller bearings	3494	3,304	2,649	11,676
3599	Machine shops	3495, 9	2,101	2,208	9,672
3611	Electric measuring instruments	357	2,631	2,256	9,892
3612, 3, 3643	Electric distribution products	3512-4	2,651	2,422	10,644
3621	Motors and generators	3511	2,784	2,363	10,375
3624	Carbon and graphite products	306	2,748	2,988	13,229
3623	Welding apparatus	3516	3,561	3,032	13,431
3629	Electric industrial goods, n.e.c.	3519	2,321	1,777	7,724
363 (less 3636)	Electric household appliances[b]	352	3,925	2,984	13,210
3641	Electric lamps	353	1,523	3,647	16,256
3642	Lighting fixtures	3515	2,521	2,406	10,569
3651	Radios and TV receiving sets	3543, 4	4,947	2,385	10,475

(continued)

TABLE B-2 (continued)

			Value Added per Employee		
U.S. Standard Industrial Classification		Matched with Japanese Code No.	Japan Actual (1)	Japan Estimated by Regressing 1 on 3 (2)	U.S. Actual (3)
Code No.	Name of Industry				
3661, 2	Communications equipment	3541, 2, 5, 6, 9	1,962	2,439	10,723
367	Electronic components	355, 3569	3,160	1,987	8,670
3693	X-ray and therapeutic apparatus	3561	2,339	2,767	12,216
3691	Storage batteries	3591	4,187	2,933	12,976
3692	Primary batteries, dry and wet	3592	2,116	2,964	13,119
3694	Engine electrical equipment	3517	1,914	2,638	11,628
3699	Electrical products, n.e.c.	3599	1,659	1,862	8,110
3713, 7	Motor vehicles and parts	361	3,952	3,939	17,607
3721	Aircraft	3651	2,827	2,349	10,313
3722	Aircraft engines and parts	3652	2,936	2,524	11,106
3732	Boat building and repairing	3642, 3	1,379	1,511	6,533
374	Railroad equipment	362	2,612	2,728	12,037
3811	Scientific instruments	374	2,691	2,605	11,477
382	Mechanical measuring devices	371, 372	2,064	2,448	10,761
3831, 3851	Optical instruments and ophthalmic goods	3012, 375, 376[c]	1,705	1,903	8,292
384	Medical instruments and supplies	2098, 373	1,978	2,722	12,013

(continued)

TABLE B-2 (concluded)

U.S. Standard Industrial Classification		Matched with Japanese Code No.	Value Added per Employee		
Code No.	Name of Industry		Japan Actual (1)	Japan Estimated by Regressing 1 on 3 (2)	U.S. Actual (3)
3861 (less 38615, 6, 7)	Photographic equipment	3752, 3	1,773	3,202	14,212
38615, 6, 7	Sensitized photographic materials	2697	4,004	4,997	22,525
387	Watches and clocks	377	2,121	2,187	9,579
391	Jewelry and silverware	391	2,376	2,090	9,137
392	Musical instruments and parts	392	1,959	1,747	7,588
393	Toys and sporting goods	393	1,365	2,016	8,802
394	Office supplies	394	2,395	2,288	10,033
395	Costume jewelry and notions	395	1,734	1,678	7,281
3984	Candles	2667	1,338	1,734	7,530

Note: n.e.c. = not elsewhere classified.

[a] Plus 2328 and 2385.

[b] Except sewing machines.

[c] Less 3752 and 3753.

TABLE B-3

Variables Used in Comparison of Value Added Per Employee in India (1961) and the United States (1963)

(dollars)

| Code No. | Indian Industrial Classification Name of Industry | Matched with U.S. SIC Code | Value Added per Employee | | |
			India Actual (1)	India Estimated by Regressing 1 on 3 (2)	U.S. Actual (3)
2021,2	Manufacture of milk foods and other dairy products	202	1,066	891	12,400
203	Canning and preserving of fruits and vegetables	2033,4,5,7	438	776	10,666
204	Canning and preserving of fish and other seafoods	2031,6	922	585	7,849
2052	Rice mills	2044	308	1,312	18,916
2051,3	Flour mills	2041	793	1,167	16,652
206	Manufacture of bakery products	205	1,087	786	10,818
2071	Sugar	206	899	1,283	18,460
208	Manufacture of cocoa, chocolate, and sugar confectionery	2071,2	774	820	11,330
2093	Hydrogenated oil	2096	1,664	1,354	19,576
2099	Salt	28991	451	1,340	19,363
211,2	Spirits and wine	2084,5	741	2,098	31,551
213	Breweries and manufacture of malt	2082,3	3,376	1,419	20,598

(*continued*)

TABLE B-3 (continued)

Indian Industrial Classification		Matched with U.S. SIC Code	Value Added per Employee		
Code No.	Name of Industry		India Actual (1)	India Estimated by Regressing 1 on 3 (2)	U.S. Actual (3)
214	Soft drinks and carbonated water industries	2086,7	1,216	1,001	14,092
2202,3	Cigars and cigarettes	2111,2121	1,908	1,800	26,702
2311	Cotton textiles	2211, 22811,2	676	452	5,924
2313	Woolen textiles	2231,2283	835	583	7,812
2314,5	Silk and artificial silk	2221	663	562	7,504
2316	Webbing, narrow fabrics embroidery and lace manufacturing	2241,2292	467	545	7,267
2317	Textiles dyeing, bleaching, etc.	226	640	611	8,221
2318	Thread and threadball making	2284	984	564	7,539
2319	Carpet weaving	2271,9	267	635	8,581
232	Knitting mills	225	517	481	6,331
233	Cordage, rope, and twine industries	2298	485	489	6,459
2395,6	Coated fabric and linoleum	2295,3982	1,202	1,064	15,057
2398	Tarpaulins, tents, sails, and other made-up canvas goods	2394	524	498	6,583
2431,3	Clothing and tailoring	22 (less 239)	302	457	5,999
2432	Umbrella manufacture	3995	482	470	6,183

(continued)

TABLE B-3 (continued)

Code No.	Indian Industrial Classification Name of Industry	Matched with U.S. SIC Code	Value Added per Employee		
			India Actual (1)	India Estimated by Regressing 1 on 3 (2)	U.S. Actual (3)
241	Manufacture of footwear	313,314	781	460	6,032
2511	Sawmilling	242	325	491	6,480
2512	Plywood	2432	523	627	8,453
252	Wooden and cane containers and cane small ware	244	488	431	5,630
2711-3	Pulp and paper mills	2611,2621	1,065	1,051	14,851
2714,6	Paperboard	2631,2661	950	1,240	17,793
2715,7	Paper and paper products	264,265	1,211	772	10,613
2801,2	Printing and bookbinding	275,276, 277,2789	696	725	9,909
291	Tannery and leather finishing plants	3111	504	643	8,692
293	Manufacture of leather products, except footwear and other wearing apparel	312,316, 317,319	553	498	6,586
3001	Tires and tubes	301	4,715	1,093	15,502
3002,4	Surgical and medical products of rubber	30697	837	793	10,924
3003	Rubber footwear	3021	788	557	7,443
31111,3	Fertilizers	2871,2	1,238	956	13,393
31121	Heavy chemicals—inorganic	2812,9	1,351	1,535	22,450

(continued)

TABLE B-3 (continued)

Indian Industrial Classification		Matched with U.S. SIC Code	Value Added per Employee		
			India Actual (1)	India Estimated by Regressing 1 on 3 (2)	U.S. Actual (3)
Code No.	Name of Industry				
3113,5	Synthetic resins and man-made fibers	282	2,844	1,368	19,800
3116	Explosives including gunpowder and safety fuses	2892	920	810	11,187
3117	Dyestuffs	28152,3 2816	4,654	1,431	20,799
3118	Turpentine and rosin	28611	1,893	1,195	17,080
313	Manufacture of paints, varnishes, and lacquers	285	1,248	1,263	18,144
3196	Soaps and glycerine	2841	3,003	2,424	36,936
3195	Drugs and pharmaceuticals	283	1,982	1,902	28,356
3197	Perfumes, cosmetics, and other toilet preparations	2844	781	2,362	35,904
3198	Matches	3983	795	618	8,320
3192	Insecticides, fungicides, and weedicides	2879	1,821	1,343	19,398
31910	Glue and gelatin	2891	592	1,206	17,252
321	Petroleum refineries	2911,2992	9,798	1,764	26,122
3311–3	Fire bricks and refractories	3255,9	505	704	9,597
3314	Tiles	3251,3	341	589	7,898
3321,4–6	Pressed and blown glassware	322,323	390	822	11,370

(continued)

TABLE B-3 (continued)

Code No.	Indian Industrial Classification Name of Industry	Matched with U.S. SIC Code	Value Added per Employee		
			India Actual (1)	India Estimated by Regressing 1 on 3 (2)	U.S. Actual (3)
3322	Sheet and plate glass	3211	625	1,124	15,974
3331	Chinaware and pottery	326	332	486	6,403
3332	Sanitaryware and whiteware	3261	373	794	10,937
334	Manufacture of cement	3241	1,466	1,541	22,536
3391	Asbestos cement	32924	1,166	954	13,362
3392	Hume pipes and other cement and concrete products	3272	563	753	10,325
3395, 39916	Stone and slate products	3281	310	539	7,168
3411	Iron and steel (metal)	3312	1,488	1,060	14,996
3396	Grinding wheels and abrasives	3291	1,621	1,046	14,782
3412	Ferro-alloys	3313	2,013	992	13,941
3413	Iron and steel castings and forgings	332,3391	393	730	9,981
3414	Iron and steel structurals	344	643	724	9,892
3415	Iron and steel pipes	3317	1,347	924	12,902
342	Nonferrous basic metal industries	333	1,666	1,428	20,754
2602,3	Furniture and fixtures, metal	2514,5, 2522,2542	811	717	9,788
3501	Metal containers and steel trunks	341,3491	1,103	1,054	14,903

(continued)

TABLE B-3 (continued)

Code No.	Indian Industrial Classification — Name of Industry	Matched with U.S. SIC Code	Value Added per Employee		
			India Actual (1)	India Estimated by Regressing 1 on 3 (2)	U.S. Actual (3)
3502	Cutlery, locks, etc.	3421 (less 34212),34294	580	746	10,229
3503	Bolts, nuts, nails, screws, springs, chains, etc.	345,348, 3493	817	774	10,635
36061	Ball, roller, and tapered bearings	3562	1,116	864	11,998
3504	Enameling, japanning and lacquering, galvanizing, plating, etc.	347	591	626	8,452
3507	Safes and vaults	3492	370	1,177	16,803
35010	Hand tools and small tools	3423,5	998	848	11,753
35012	Sanitary and plumbing fixtures and fittings of metal	3431,2	425	816	11,270
360111,2	Typewriters and office machines	3571,2	1,722	848	11,754
3607	Machine tools	354	869	846	11,728
36012	Weighing machines	3576	972	809	11,164
3603	Internal combustion engines	3519	1,035	941	13,174
360411	Paper machinery	3554	592	844	11,689
36041	Textile machinery, etc.	3552	648	645	8,726

(continued)

TABLE B-3 (continued)

| Indian Industrial Classification | | Matched with U.S. SIC Code | Value Added per Employee | | |
| | | | India Actual (1) | India Estimated by Regressing 1 on 3 (2) | U.S. Actual (3) |
Code No.	Name of Industry				
36044, 360414	Food products machinery	3551	762	865	12,006
36049	Chemical machinery	35591	725	830	11,479
360513	Refrigeration plants for industrial use	3585	1,301	887	12,341
36081,2	Farm machinery and equipment	3522	667	851	11,795
360511	Power-driven pumps—reciprocating, centrifugal, etc.	35611	842	896	12,477
360512	Air and gas compressors and vacuum pumps	35614,6	1,279	841	11,656
360113	Household air conditioners and refrigerators	3632	1,150	1,038	14,658
360115	Sewing and knitting machines	3636	940	921	12,860
36052	Conveying equipment—bucket elevators, skip hoists, etc.	3535,6	747	904	12,607
37011	Equipment for generation, transmission, and distribution of electricity	3612,3 35111	845	834	11,542
37012	Electrical motors	3621	1,025	768	10,547
37013	Electrical fans	36341	1,110	842	11,670
37014	Electrical lamps	3641	953	1,091	15,477
37016	Electrical cables and wires	3357,33151	1,826	865.	12,014

(continued)

TABLE B-3 (continued)

Code No.	Indian Industrial Classification — Name of Industry	Matched with U.S. SIC Code	Value Added per Employee		
			India Actual (1)	India Estimated by Regressing 1 on 3 (2)	U.S. Actual (3)
37019	Household appliances, such as electric irons, heaters, etc.	36343, 3635,9	673	949	13,295
370110	Storage batteries	3691	1,434	992	13,942
370111	Dry cells	3692	1,344	958	13,421
37021,2	Telephone and Telegraph apparatus	3661	727	820	11,331
37023,4	Radio communication apparatus and receivers	36511,3 3662,3671	1,120	795	10,963
3812	Boatbuilding	3732	663	552	7,363
383	Manufacture of motor vehicles	3717	1,272	1,317	18,995
385	Manufacture of motorcycles and bicycles	3751	868	631	8,512
3911,3,4 39121	Scientific and medical instruments	381,382,384	849	850	11,789
3924	Manufacture of photographic and optical goods—others	3831,3851, 38611,3	424	765	10,512
393	Manufacture of watches and clocks	387	448	753	10,327

(continued)

TABLE B-3 (concluded)

| Code No. | Indian Industrial Classification
Name of Industry | Matched
with U.S.
SIC Code | Value Added per Employee | | |
			India Actual (1)	India Estimated by Regressing 1 on 3 (2)	U.S. Actual (3)
3941	Jewelry	391	628	706	9,634
3993,4	Pens and pencils	3951,2	630	729	9,972
3995	Buttonmaking	3963	1,073	583	7,814
3997	Plastic molded goods	30793	700	888	12,368
39910	Brooms and brushes	3981	606	737	10,089
39911,2	Toys, games, and sport goods	394	349	640	8,649

TABLE B-4

Linearity and Bartlett Tests for Bilateral Comparisons of Value Added per Employee

Test	Number of Industries	Arithmetic Form	Logarithmic Form
Linearity			
U.S.–U.K.	103	1.16	.08
		(8,93)	(8,93)
U.S.–Japan	178	3.67*	1.10
		(5,171)	(8,168)
U.S.–India	117	5.21*	1.85
		(9,106)	(18,97)
Bartlett			
U.S.–U.K.	103	67.18**	12.54
		(4)	(4)
U.S.–Japan	178	143.88**	25.57**
		(7)	(7)
	169	56.06**	9.28
		(5)	(5)
U.S.–India	117	169.38**	26.29**
		(5)	(5)
	76	29.75**	.85
		(3)	(3)

Note: See Table A-4 for sources of tests used. Numbers in parentheses indicate degrees of freedom for each statistic.

*Variables not linearly related at 1 per cent level of confidence.

**Variances significantly different from one another at 1 per cent level of confidence.

APPENDIX C

THE SELECTION OF
LABOR-INTENSIVE MANUFACTURES

The manufactures selected as labor-intensive on the basis of the value-added criterion developed in Chapters 2 and 3 are given in detail in Table C-1, the items being specified according to the U.S. Standard Industrial Classification (SIC) and the Standard International Trade Classification (SITC) and combined into four main groups and twenty-four subgroups.[1] The methods employed and problems encountered in applying this approach are indicated in the first section of Chapter 4, and only a few supplementary observations need be made here.

In principle, the criterion of value added per employee has been applied on the basis of U.S. manufacturing statistics at the four-digit level of the SIC. In some cases, as may be seen in Table C-1, the selection has been made at the three-digit level when a high degree of homogeneity with respect to value added per employee is found among the four-digit components. In some other cases, however, even the four-digit items prove to be very mixed in this regard (e.g., film is included in No. 3861, photographic equipment, and is much higher than the cameras and other components of this item in value added per employee) or are unduly broad compared with the corresponding items figuring in imports from less developed countries. In such cases, the selection is made at the five-digit level of the SIC (necessitating resort to the *1963 Census of Manufactures,* as explained in the notes to Table C-1, since the annual *Survey of Manufactures* does not go below the four-digit level).

The selection of items indicated by value added per employee in the United States has been supplemented by detailed examination of manu-

[1] *Standard Industrial Classification Manual,* Executive Office of the President, Bureau of the Budget, 1957, and *Supplement* to the foregoing, 1963; *Standard International Trade Classification, Revised,* Statistical Papers, Series M, No. 34, United Nations, 1961. Names of items are sometimes abbreviated or consolidated in Table C-1.

factures actually imported by developed from less developed countries to see if any additional items needed to be taken into account. On this basis several items have, in fact, been added to the list (as mentioned in the footnotes to Table C-1) on the basis of value added per employee in other countries where (a) this average was lower (in relation to the corresponding national average in each case) than in the United States, or (b) the item was not separately shown in the U.S. statistics (examples: (a) electric lamps, (b) essential oils).

As will be clear upon examination of Table C-1, a precise matching of output statistics (SIC) and import statistics (SITC) is impossible. The difficulty is particularly great in the case of the numerous residual items ("n.e.c.," "n.e.s.," "other," "miscellaneous," etc.), which may be rather differently constituted in the two classification systems, but various other problems as well are encountered. It seems unlikely, however, that uncertainties in matching the two sets of data have caused any significantly large items in the trade to be erroneously included in, or excluded from, the statistics underlying the trade analysis in Chapter 4. As noted there, the most serious omission is probably cut diamonds and another of some interest is pleasure boats and other small craft; these omissions are attributable chiefly to inadequate specification of the items in the SITC.

Table C-1 was prepared prior to and independently of the publication of information relating to a concordance between the SIC and the SITC in *U.S. Exports of Domestic Merchandise, SIC-Based Products and Area*, FT610, for the year 1965, U.S. Bureau of the Census, April 1967. Comparison of Tables 2 and 3 in that source with Table C-1 below will reveal minor discrepancies in matching the two classification codes.[2]

---

[2] The tables mentioned in the Census publication give concordances between SIC-based product codes and Schedule B (the latter being a seven-digit export commodity code, the first five digits of which are based on the SITC).

TABLE C-1

Selection of Labor-Intensive Manufactures Figuring in Imports of Developed from Less Developed Countries
(V.A.E. = value added per employee; V.A.M. = value added by manufacture; V.S. = value of shipments)

U.S. Standard Industrial Classification		V.A.M. Production, 1965			Standard International Trade Classification		Value of Imports, 1965 ($ million)			
							U.S. (f.o.b.)		Other Developed Countries (c.i.f.)[a]	
Code	Industry	V.A.E. (all U.S. mfg.=100)	V.A.M. ($ million)	V.S. ($ million)	Code	Product	Total	From LDC's	Total	From LDC's
	All items listed below, total	75.0	72,593	140,841			5,696.6	1,009.8	27,558.9	1,571.8
	1. Textiles, clothing, and accessories									
	a. Yarn and thread	53.7	14,758	33,945			1,052.9	286.3	5,316.5	534.0
		60.0	865	2,405			63.6	5.9	1,035.1	31.1
228	Yarn and thread mills	60.0	865	2,405	651b	Textile yarn and thread	63.6	5.9	1,035.1	21.1
	b. Cotton fabrics, woven	61.2	1,967	4,219			134.5	61.5	642.0	122.2
2211	Broad-woven fabric mills, cotton	60.1	1,624	3,350	652	Cotton fabrics, woven	134.5	61.5	642.0	122.2
2261	Finishing of broad-woven cotton fabrics	66.7	343	869						
	c. Other woven fabrics, excl. jute fabrics	71.9	1,866	4,862			236.0	9.2	1,244.8	12.4
2231	Broad-woven fabric mills, wool	70.6	409	1,096	6532	Woolen fabrics, woven	106.5	4.2	423.8	2.2

(continued)

TABLE C-1 (continued)

| U.S. Standard Industrial Classification | | U.S. Manufacturing Production, 1965 | | | Standard International Trade Classification | | Value of Imports, 1965 ($ million) | | | |
| | | | | | | | U.S. (f.o.b.) | | Other Developed Countries (c.i.f.)[a] | |
Code	Industry	V.A.E. (all U.S. mfg.=100)	V.A.M. ($ million)	V.S. ($ million)	Code	Product	Total	From LDC's	Total	From LDC's
2221	Broad-woven fabric mills, man-made fiber and silk	66.6	827	2,116	6531	Silk fabrics, woven	29.7	2.3	45.5	2.5
2262	Finishing of broad-woven fabrics of man-made fiber and silk	74.5	216	441	6535	Fabrics, woven of synthetic fibers	28.1	.6	239.0	1.6
					6536	Fabrics, woven of regenerated fibers	25.0	.7	334.7	2.5
2256	Knit-fabric mills	86.8	329	1,022	6533	Linen, ramie, hemp, etc.	—c	—c	16.0	.2
					6537	Knitted or crocheted fabrics not elastic or rubberized				
2299	Textile goods, n.e.c.	81.0	85	187	6539	Fabrics, woven, n.e.s.	9.4	.1	169.2	3.2
	d. Textile small wares and specialties	63.2	1,772	4,363			37.4	1.5	16.4	.2
							67.3	12.9	563.7	35.8

(continued)

TABLE C-1 (continued)

Value of Imports, 1965 ($ million)

U.S. Standard Industrial Classification		V.A.E. (all U.S. mfg.=100)	V.A.M. ($ million)	V.S. ($ million)	Standard International Trade Classification		U.S. (f.o.b.)		Other Developed Countries (c.i.f.)a	
Code	Industry				Code	Product	Total	From LDC's	Total	From LDC's
2241	Narrow fabrics and other small wares mills	62.1	193	385	654	Tulle, lace, embroidery, ribbons, trimmings, etc.	16.5	2.2	153.1	2.6
2292	Lace goods	57.1	33	55						
2293	Padding and upholstery filling	85.3	78	176	655d	Special textile fabrics and related products	15.9	4.3	212.5	1.3
2295	Artificial leather, oilcloth, etc.	103.2	223	537	656e	Made-up articles, wholly or chiefly of textile materials, n.e.s.				
2296	Tire cord and fabric	72.6	95	465						
239f	Misc. textile products	57.6	1,150	2,745			34.8	6.5	198.3	31.8
	e. *Carpets and other floor coverings*	74.4	133	331			54.3	15.7	415.1	120.7
2271	Woven carpets and rugs	78.1	109	283	657	Floor coverings, tapestries, etc.				
2279	Carpets, rugs and mats, n.e.c.	60.0	24	48			54.3	15.7	415.1	120.7
	f. *Clothing and accessories excl. goods of leather and rubber*	47.4	8,155	17,765			497.1	181.1	1,415.8	211.7

(continued)

TABLE C-1 (continued)

| U.S. Standard Industrial Classification | | U.S. Manufacturing Production, 1965 | | | Standard International Trade Classification | | Value of Imports, 1965 ($ million) | | | |
| | | | | | | | U.S. (f.o.b.) | | Other Developed Countries (c.i.f.)[a] | |
U.S. Code	Industry	V.A.E. (all U.S. mfg.=100)	V.A.M. ($ million)	V.S. ($ million)	Code	Product	Total	From LDC's	Total	From LDC's
225g	Knitting mills	49.4	1,315	2,894						
2311	Men's and boys' suits and coats	55.9	942	1,757						
232	Men's and boys' furnishings	42.4	1,811	4,162	8411	Clothing of textile fabric, not knitted or crocheted	214.2	100.5	611.3	104.7
233	Women's and misses outerwear	47.6	2,546	5,568	8412	Clothing accessories of textile fabrics not knitted or crocheted				
234	Women's and children's underwear	49.6	741	1,651						
235	Millinery, hats, and caps	43.6	138	272	8414	Clothing and accessories, knitted or crocheted	48.4	15.5	127.9	11.5
236	Children's outerwear	46.8	504	1,092	8415	Headgear	221.5	64.2	631.0	94.7
2381	Fabric dress and work gloves	43.5	85	182			13.0	.9	45.6	.9
2384	Robes and dressing gowns	45.8	73	187						
	2. *Other light manufactures except food*	86.0	48,424	86,076			3,281.8	269.4	16,845.6	250.9

(continued)

TABLE C-1 (continued)

U.S. Standard Industrial Classification		V.A.E. (all U.S. mfg.=100)	V.A.M. ($ million)	V.S. ($ million)	Standard International Trade Classification		U.S. (f.o.b.)		Other Developed Countries (c.i.f.)a	
		U.S. Manufacturing Production, 1965					Value of Imports, 1965 ($ million)			
Code	Industry				Code	Product	Total	From LDC's	Total	From LDC's
	a. Footwear and other products of leather, rubber and plastic	57.6	3,169	5,813			337.2	54.2	913.7	43.5
3131	Boot and shoe, cut stock and findings	54.7	95	242						
3199	Leather goods, n.e.c.	50.1	37	76	612	Manufactures of leather or of artificial or reconstituted leather, n.e.s.	10.2	1.7	45.8	2.4
3161	Luggage	57.2	137	259						
3171	Handbags and purses	45.7	138	275	831	Travel goods, handbags, and similar articles	50.0	18.6	91.4	5.9
3172	Small leather goods	52.1	95	169						
2386	Leather and sheep-lined clothing	66.8	34	77						
*23871	Leather belts	65.9	33	61	8413	Apparel and clothing accessories of leather	43.9	9.2	35.1	1.7
3151	Leather gloves	39.2	37	81						
3141	Shoes, except rubber	49.9	1,351	2,466	851	Footwear	159.9	10.6	367.9	26.6
3142	House slippers	46.4	70	137						
3021	Footwear, rubber	62.6	247	398						
2371	Fur goods	97.1	113	344	842	Clothing and other articles of fur	2.0	.2	28.7	.3

(continued)

TABLE C-1 (continued)

Value of Imports, 1965 ($ million)

U.S. Standard Industrial Classification		V.A.E. (all U.S. mfg.=100)	V.A.M. ($ million)	V.S. ($ million)	Standard International Trade Classification		U.S. (f.o.b.)		Other Developed Countries (c.i.f.)[a]	
Code	Industry				Code	Product	Total	From LDC's	Total	From LDC's
*30696	Rubber heels and soles	76.2	69	.139	6299	Articles of rubber, n.e.s.	_h	_h	81.0	1.3
*30697	Druggist and medical sundries	92.7	61	94	8416	Apparel and clothing accessories of rubber	_h	_h	9.9	.1
*30698	Other rubber goods, n.e.c.	96.1	224	464						
*30797	Plastic dinnerware, etc.	90.7	80	146	893	Articles of artificial plastic materials, n.e.s.	71.0	13.9	253.9	5.2
*30798	Consumer and commercial plastic products, n.e.c.	73.6	214	387						
		81.4 / 84.0	1,307 / 680	1,962 / 1,092			111.7	3.1	324.6	2.0
	b. Glassware, china, pottery, and misc. nonmetallic mineral products									
3221	Glass containers	97.3	208	268	665	Glassware	36.2	2.2	192.9	.5
*32291	Table, kitchen, art, and novelty glassware									
326	Pottery and related products	68.7	376	546	666	Pottery	75.5	1.0	131.8	1.4

(continued)

TABLE C-1 (continued)

		U.S. Manufacturing Production, 1965			Standard International Trade Classification		Value of Imports, 1965 ($ million)			
							U.S. (f.o.b.)		Other Developed Countries (c.i.f.)[a]	
U.S. Standard Industrial Classification		V.A.E. (all U.S. mfg.=100)	V.A.M. ($ million)	V.S. ($ million)			Total	From LDC's	Total	From LDC's
Code	Industry				Code	Product				
	c. *Furniture*	64.3	3,051	5,923			59.9	6.8	338.1	4.1
251	Household furniture	62.5	2,400	4,697						
2521	Wood office furniture	69.5	66	121						
2531	Public building furniture	70.4	166	313						
2541	Wood partitions and fixtures	71.3	232	422	821	Furniture	59.9	6.8	338.1	4.1
259	Furniture and fixtures, n.e.c.	73.8	187	370						
	d. *Books and other printed matter*	78.5	3,954	6,569			58.5	4.2	436.8	2.7
2771	Greeting card manufacturing	78.4	254	404						
2732	Book printing	80.7	396	611						
2751	Printing, except lithographic	73.5	1,723	2,882	892[i]	Printed matter	58.5	4.2	436.8	2.7
2752	Printing, lithographic	84.6	1,456	2,506						
2753	Engraving and plate printing	79.2	125	166						

(continued)

TABLE C-1 (continued)

| U.S. Standard Industrial Classification | | V.A.E. (all U.S. mfg.=100) | V.A.M. ($ million) | V.S. ($ million) | Standard International Trade Classification | | U.S. (f.o.b.) | | Other Developed Countries (c.i.f.)a | |
Code	Industry				Code	Product	Total	From LDC's	Total	From LDC's
	e. *Games, toys, sporting goods, and musical instruments*	77.6	1,563	2,941			368.5	25.8	650.3	40.9
3751	Motorcycles, bicycles, and parts	72.5	107	247	7329	Motorcycles, motorized cycles, and their parts	141.0	—	77.6	—
					7331	Bicycles and other cycles, not motorized, and their parts				
3652	Phonograph records	106.8	137	195	891j	Musical instruments, sound recorders and reproducers and parts	30.9	.3	42.7	.1
3931	Musical instruments and parts	74.3	231	403						
3941	Games and toys	69.8	559	1,064	894k	Perambulators, toys, games, and sporting goods	56.0	1.9	166.3	.7
3942	Dolls	54.7	90	161						
3943	Children's vehicles	62.6	46	101						
3949	Sporting and athletic goods	73.5	393	770			140.6	23.6	363.6	40.1

(continued)

TABLE C-1 (continued)

| U.S. Standard Industrial Classification | | U.S. Manufacturing Production, 1965 | | | Standard International Trade Classification | | Value of Imports, 1965 ($ million) | | | |
| | | | | | | | U.S. (f.o.b.) | | Other Developed Countries (c.i.f.)[a] | |
Code	Industry	V.A.E. (all U.S. mfg.=100)	V.A.M. ($ million)	V.S. ($ million)	Code	Product	Total	From LDC's	Total	From LDC's
	f. *Jewelry and silverware*	81.6	500	971	667[l]	Pearls, precious and semi-precious stones, unworked or worked	61.8	17.6	233.0	42.2
3911	Jewelry, precious metal	84.4	312	613						
3912	Jewelers' findings and material	55.1	38	88	8971	Jewelry of gold, silver, and platinum and goldsmith's or silversmith's ware	46.0	16.4	117.2	38.4
3914	Silverware and plated ware	86.6	150	270			15.8	1.1	115.8	3.8
	g. *Misc. manufactures, including costume jewelry, stationery, and notions*	79.3	4,966	10,597			242.6	90.3	783.2	60.7
	Not separately shown[m]				551	Essential oils, perfume, and flavor materials	45.6	18.8	164.8	33.7

(continued)

TABLE C-1 (continued)

U.S. Standard Industrial Classification		U.S. Manufacturing Production, 1965			Standard International Trade Classification		Value of Imports, 1965 ($ million)			
							U.S. (f.o.b.)		Other Developed Countries (c.i.f.)[a]	
Code	Industry	V.A.E. (all U.S. mfg.=100)	V.A.M. ($ million)	V.S. ($ million)	Code	Product	Total	From LDC's	Total	From LDC's
2642	Envelopes	73.3	207	397						
2643	Bags, except textile bags	83.8	482	1,206						
2649	Converted paper products, n.e.c.	88.3	370	719	642[n]	Articles made of paper pulp, of paper, or of paperboard	16.8	.4	209.1	.7
265	Paperboard containers and boxes	77.8	2,136	5,175						
3964	Needles, pins, and fasteners	80.0	231	398	6985	Pins and needles of iron or steel, etc.	7.7	1.4	34.8	.3
3951	Pens, pen points, and fountain pens	81.3	132	202	8952	Pens, pencils, and fountain pens	7.9	.4	63.4	.5
3952	Lead pencils, crayons	71.9	73	145						
3961	Costume jewelry and costume novelties	62.0	172	311	8972	Imitation jewelry	17.5	5.0	32.4	3.5
3981	Brooms and brushes	85.4	193	371	8992	Basketwork, brooms, brushes, etc.	24.1	5.0	53.9	3.6
3983	Matches	70.5	40	66	8993	Candles, matches, lighters	19.2	.8	60.0	2.0
3984	Candles	58.6	27	50						
3995	Umbrellas, parasols, and canes	71.6	17	35	8994	Umbrellas, parasols, walking sticks, etc.	7.6	1.3	17.5	1.1

(continued)

TABLE C-1 (continued)

U.S. Manufacturing Production, 1965					Standard International Trade Classification		Value of Imports, 1965 ($ million)			
U.S. Standard Industrial Classification		V.A.E. (all U.S. mfg.=100)	V.A.M. ($ million)	V.S. ($ million)			U.S. (f.o.b.)		Other Developed Countries (c.i.f.)a	
Code	Industry				Code	Product	Total	From LDC's	Total	From LDC's
3842	Surgical appliances and supplies	102.3	412	670	8996	Orthopedic appliances, etc.	3.1	.3	26.4	.4
3843	Dental equipment and supplies	98.6	118	194	8991	Articles and manufactures of carving or moulding material	2.6	.8	12.7	1.2
3963	Buttons	61.6	39	66	8995	Small-wares and toilet articles, n.e.s.	8.7	.7	57.2	2.1
3962	Artificial flowers	66.7	36	73						
3999	Misc. products, n.e.c.	67.3	281	519	8999	Other manufactured articles, n.e.s.	81.7	55.8	50.9	11.7
h. Optical goods, cameras, watches, and instruments		92.9	1,289	2,062			200.9	3.0	658.9	5.8
3851	Ophthalmic goods	73.4	215	317	8612	Spectacles and frames	17.0	.2	41.6	.3
3831	Optical instruments and lenses	96.4	199	292	8613	Binoculars, microscopes, and other optical instruments	28.8	.6	54.8	1.4

(continued)

TABLE C-1 (continued)

| U.S. Manufacturing Production, 1965 | | | | Value of Imports, 1965 ($ million) | | | | | |
| U.S. Standard Industrial Classification | | V.A.E. (all U.S. mfg.=100) | V.A.M. ($ million) | V.S. ($ million) | Standard International Trade Classification | | U.S. (f.o.b.) | | Other Developed Countries (c.i.f.)a | |
Code	Industry				Code	Product	Total	From LDC's	Total	From LDC's
*38611	Still picture equipment	108.0	227	351	8614	Photographic cameras and flash-light apparatus	37.4	1.1	101.7	1.6
					8616	Photographic and cinematographic apparatus and equipment, n.e.s.	4.3	–	119.8	.6
3841	Surgical and medical instruments	94.6	189	294	8617	Medical instruments, n.e.s.	13.2	.2	89.2	.8
3871	Watches and clocks	89.4	340	624	8641	Watches, watch movements and cases	79.3	.8	141.0	.7
3872	Watchcases	63.1	29	45	8642	Clocks, clock movements and parts	20.9	–	110.7	.4
	i. *Cutlery, tools, hardware, and other metal products*	91.3	3,507	6,341			340.4	14.1	1,466.3	12.1
3498	Fabricated pipe and fittings	91.5	184	397	6785	Tube and pipe fittings of iron or steel	8.9	.3	103.5	.1
3481	Fabricated wire products, n.e.c.	81.8	631	1,167	693	Wire products and fencing grills	44.5	.4	90.7	.1

(continued)

TABLE C-1 (continued)

U.S. Standard Industrial Classification		V.A.E. (all U.S. mfg.=100)	V.A.M. ($ million)	V.S. ($ million)	Standard International Trade Classification		U.S. (f.o.b.)		Other Developed Countries (c.i.f.)[a]	
Code	Industry				Code	Product	Total	From LDC's	Total	From LDC's
*34521	Bolts, nuts, and other standard industrial fasteners	100.7	510	901	694	Nails, screws, nuts, etc. of iron, steel or of copper	100.8	1.0	165.7	1.1
3423	Hand and edge tools	98.3	456	714	695	Tools for use in the hand or in machines	39.7	.6	356.6	1.2
*34211	Cutlery, scissors, shears, etc.	72.7	63	95	696	Cutlery	43.1	1.5	110.3	3.2
*34611	Vitreous enameled products	85.5	58	100						
*34614	Stamped and spun utensils, aluminum	98.5	75	163	697	Household equipment of base metals	33.2	4.8	175.7	3.4
*34615	Stamped and spun utensils, other	99.1	82	157						
*34618	Other stamped metal products	81.7	138	262						
*34294	Builder's hardware	90.4	313	506	6981	Locksmiths' wares	14.8	1.0	128.6	.8
3449	Misc. metal work	102.2	364	856	6983	Chains and parts thereof of iron or steel	10.2	.2	56.6	.3

(continued)

TABLE C-1 (continued)

U.S. Standard Industrial Classification Code	Industry	V.A.E. (all U.S. mfg.=100)	V.A.M. ($ million)	V.S. ($ million)	Standard International Trade Classification Code	Product	U.S. (f.o.b.) Total	U.S. From LDC's	Other Developed Countries (c.i.f.)[a] Total	Other Developed Countries From LDC's
3499	Fabricated metal products, n.e.c.	91.0	366	701	6988	Miscellaneous articles of base metal	3.9	1.1	72.4	.3
					6989	Articles of base metals, n.e.c.	41.4	3.3	206.3	1.6
	j. *Electrical apparatus and appliances*	91.5	14,666	24,100			703.5	46.3	3,600.1	27.0
3636	Sewing machines	99.1	90	130	7173	Sewing machines	71.2	.1	133.7	.6
3612	Transformers	107.1	521	912	722	Electric power machinery and switchgear	67.2	.9	1,029.2	2.6
3613	Switchgear and switchboards	104.2	785	1,292						
3621	Motors and generators	88.7	1,214	2,089	7294	Automotive electrical equipment	9.1	–	142.0	.7
3629	Electric industrial goods, n.e.c.	72.2	156	290	7299	Electrical machinery and apparatus, n.e.s.	56.9	2.6	351.0	1.0
*32294	Other pressed and blown glassware	104.3	49	61	7232	Electrical insulating equipment	5.2	–	44.9	.1
3264	Porcelain electrical supplies	80.8	114	164						

(continued)

TABLE C-1 (continued)

U.S. Standard Industrial Classification		V.A.E. (all U.S. mfg.=100)	V.A.M. ($ million)	V.S. ($ million)	Standard International Trade Classification		Value of Imports, 1965 ($ million)			
U.S. Manufacturing Production, 1965							U.S. (f.o.b.)		Other Developed Countries (c.i.f.)[a]	
Code	Industry				Code	Product	Total	From LDC's	Total	From LDC's
36511	Household and automobile radios	97.8	201	452	7242	Radio broadcast receivers	149.0	19.8	201.3	8.2
3661	Telephone, telegraph apparatus	101.6	1,362	2,263	7249	Telecommunications equipment, n.e.s.	105.2	5.9	631.4	2.1
3662	Radio, TV communications equipment	95.0	4,388	6,864						
3631	Electric household cooking equipment	97.6	268	556	72503	Electro-mechanical domestic appliances, n.e.s.	8.0	.1	86.5	.1
3634	Electric housewares and fans	100.7	542	966	72505	Electric space heating equipment, etc.	7.3	.1	84.1	—
3692	Primary batteries[o]	121.2	141	233	7291	Batteries and accumulators	13.7	1.9	67.3	1.4
3641	Electric lamps[o]	130.4	442	673	7292	Electric lamps	14.1	.7	133.7	1.1
367	Electronic components	79.5	3,321	5,041	7293	Thermionic, etc., valves and tubes, photocells, transistors, etc.	63.2	9.2	375.2	.8
3642	Lighting fixtures	90.4	740	1,429	8124	Lighting fixtures and fittings, etc.	33.0	4.8	108.1	8.0

(continued)

TABLE C-1 (continued)

Value of Imports, 1965 ($ million)

U.S. Standard Industrial Classification Code	Industry	V.A.E. (all U.S. mfg.=100)	V.A.M. ($ million)	V.S. ($ million)	SITC Code	Product	U.S. (f.o.b.) Total	U.S. From LDC's	Other Developed Countries (c.i.f.)[a] Total	Other From LDC's
*36513	Recorders, audio-amplifiers, phonographs, tuners, etc.	71.6	192	393	8911	Phonographs, tape and other sound recorders and reproducers	100.6	—	211.6	.2
	k. *Nonelectrical machinery and equipment*	102.0	10,452	18,797			796.8	3.9	7,440.8	9.9
3522	Farm machinery and equipment	100.1	1,621	3,464	712p	Agricultural machinery and implements	194.5	.5	935.7	.1
*35712	Computing and accounting machinery including cash registers	88.5	611	1,096	7142	Calculating machines, accounting machines, etc.	53.7	.2	347.1	.1
					7143	Statistical machines	4.2	—	264.0	4.0
					7149	Office machines, n.e.s.	31.2	1.1	360.1	.3
3541	Metal-cutting machinery tools	104.9	978	1,518	7151	Machine-tools for working metals	56.1	.3	684.1	.5
3542	Metal-forming machinery tools	104.4	350	581	7152	Metalworking machinery other than machine tools	7.4	—	145.2	.1
3544	Special dies and tools	96.7	1,317	1,792						

(continued)

TABLE C-1 (continued)

| | U.S. Manufacturing Production, 1965 | | | | | | Value of Imports, 1965 ($ million) | | | |
| | U.S. Standard Industrial Classification | V.A.E. (all U.S. mfg.=100) | V.A.M. ($ million) | V.S. ($ million) | Standard International Trade Classification | | U.S. (f.o.b.) | | Other Developed Countries (c.i.f.)[a] | |
Code	Industry				Code	Product	Total	From LDC's	Total	From LDC's
3552	Textile machinery	76.0	412	708	7171	Textile machinery	81.4	–	547.5	.3
3554	Paper industries machinery	88.6	233	482	7181	Paper mill and pulp mill machinery	22.4	–	173.9	.1
3551	Food products machinery	104.9	460	749	7183	Food-processing machines	14.7	.1	90.0	.2
3561	Pumps and compressors	108.0	1,050	1,868	7192	Pumps and centrifuges	34.7	.2	643.8	.9
					7195	Powered-tools, n.e.s.	34.3	.1	261.8	.2
3564	Blowers and fans	100.1	221	393	7196	Other nonelectrical machines	17.9	.1	307.9	.5
3565	Industrial patterns	101.1	158	198						
3566	Power transmission equipment	102.8	707	1,145	7198	Machinery and mechanical appliances, n.e.s.	55.6	.3	447.0	.4
3569	General industrial machines	97.4	484	799	71991	Moulding boxes for metal foundry	11.6	.1	38.9	.2
3581	Automatic vending machinery	89.0	140	257	71992	Taps, cocks, valves and similar appliances, n.e.s.	12.2	.2	309.1	.5
3742	Railroad and street cars	100.5	539	1,588	731	Railway vehicles	7.4	–	114.5	.2

(continued)

TABLE C-1 (continued)

U.S. Standard Industrial Classification — Code	Industry	V.A.E. (all U.S. mfg.=100)	V.A.M. ($ million)	V.S. ($ million)	SITC Code	Product	U.S. (f.o.b.) Total	U.S. (f.o.b.) From LDC's	Other Developed Countries (c.i.f.)a Total	Other Developed Countries (c.i.f.)a From LDC's
*37176	Motor vehicle parts and accessories	102.9	439	834	7328	Bodies, chassis, frames and other parts of motor vehicles	157.6	.7	1,770.0	1.0
	3. Labor-intensive food manufactures and cigars	89.7	2,748	6,674			268.3	112.4	1,773.2	380.0
	a. Fish and fish products	95.5	221	574			124.4	44.6	705.5	193.4
2031	Canned and cured seafoods	92.5	191	481	032	Fish in airtight containers	83.6	20.0	304.6	36.6
*20943	Animal and marine oil products	101.5	24	72	0814	Meat meal and fish meal	34.9	23.9	267.8	127.9
					4111	Oils of fish and marine mammals	6.0	.7	133.1	28.9
	b. Fruits and vegetables	90.5	1,303	3,332			117.4	65.3	884.5	175.0
2033	Canned fruits and vegetables	89.5	1,174	2,975	052	Dried fruit	4.6	3.6	165.8	11.9
					053	Fruit, preserved, and fruit preparations	67.4	38.5	480.1	110.5

Value of Imports, 1965 ($ million)

U.S. Manufacturing Production, 1965

(continued)

TABLE C-1 (continued)

U.S. Manufacturing Production, 1965					Standard International Trade Classification		Value of Imports, 1965 ($ million)			
U.S. Standard Industrial Classification		V.A.E. (all U.S. mfg.=100)	V.A.M. ($ million)	V.S. ($ million)			U.S. (f.o.b.)		Other Developed Countries (c.i.f.)[a]	
Code	Industry				Code	Product	Total	From LDC's	Total	From LDC's
2034	Dried and dehydrated fruits and vegetables	99.9	129	357	055	Vegetables, roots and tubers, preserved or prepared, n.e.s.	45.3	23.1	238.6	52.6
	c. *Misc. food products and cigars*									
2071	Confectionery products	87.8	1,224	2,768	062	Sugar confectionery	26.5	2.5	183.2	11.5
2035	Pickles, sauces, salad dressings	84.3	723	1,582	099	Food preparations, n.e.s.	16.6	.4	58.3	1.3
		108.1	281	784			7.8	1.2	88.6	5.3
2121	Cigars	80.1	220	402	1221	Cigars and cheroots	2.1	1.0	36.3	4.9
	4. *Labor intensive industrial materials*	66.4	6,663	14,146			1,093.6	341.7	3,623.6	406.9
	a. *Products of jute and other coarse fibres*	58.5	140	403	6519	Yarn of textile fibers, n.e.s.q	238.2	194.6	228.2	122.0
*22992	Jute goods and other textile goods, n.e.c.	63.4	19	45	6534	Jute fabrics, woven	2.0	1.2	35.5	13.2
							186.7	174.0	76.5	55.9

(continued)

TABLE C-1 (continued)

| U.S. Standard Industrial Classification | | U.S. Manufacturing Production, 1965 | | | Standard International Trade Classification | | Value of Imports, 1965 ($ million) | | | |
| | | | | | | | U.S. (f.o.b.) | | Other Developed Countries (c.i.f.)[a] | |
Code	Industry	V.A.E. (all U.S. mfg.=100)	V.A.M. ($ million)	V.S. ($ million)	Code	Product	Total	From LDC's	Total	From LDC's
2298	Cordage and twine	62.9	75	167	6556	Cordage, cables, ropes, twines	48.7	19.0	42.1	2.5
2393	Textile bags	53.0	46	191	6561	Bags and sacks of textile materials	.7	.4	74.2	50.4
	b. Leather and tanned or dressed furs	80.6	363	892			78.7	20.5	539.0	77.7
3111	Leather tanning and finishing	79.9	333	850	611	Leather	67.5	20.4	313.9	73.6
3992[r]	Furs dressed and dyed	99.6	30	42	613	Fur skins, tanned or dressed	11.2	.1	105.5	1.8
	Not separately shown				621	Materials of rubber	—	—	119.6	2.3
	c. Lumber, plywood, veneers, crates, and other simple wood products	58.3	3,802	8,948	243	Wood, shaped or simply worked	648.8	115.8	2,019.9	204.4
2421	Sawmills and planing mills	53.4	1,415	3,351						
2426	Hardwood dimension and flooring	44.4	175	392			375.2	25.3	1,466.0	162.7

(continued)

TABLE C-1 (continued)

U.S. Manufacturing Production, 1965					Standard International Trade Classification		Value of Imports, 1965 ($ million)			
							U.S. (f.o.b.)		Other Developed Countries (c.i.f.)[a]	
U.S. Standard Industrial Classification		V.A.E. (all U.S. mfg.=100)	V.A.M. ($ million)	V.S. ($ million)						
Code	Industry				Code	Product	Total	From LDC's	Total	From LDC's
2429	Special product sawmills, n.e.c.	46.7	44	108	6318	Wood, simply shaped or worked, n.e.s.	20.7	8.6	18.5	.3
2431	Millwork plants	64.8	549	1,359						
2432	Veneer and plywood plants	67.7	638	1,588	6311	Veneer sheets	45.8	16.6	101.8	6.3
					6312	Plywood (incl. veneered panels)	124.9	56.0	191.4	27.7
2433	Prefabricated wood products	80.1	177	467	6314	"Improved" wood	.8	.1	53.5	.6
244	Wooden containers	48.4	206	472	632	Wood manufactures, n.e.s.	77.4	9.1	144.7	4.4
2491	Wood preserving	70.3	104	280	633	Cork manufactures	3.9	.1	43.9	2.4
2499	Wood products, n.e.c.	61.7	494	931						
	d. *Building materials of clay, stone, etc.*	83.8	2,356	3,900	6613	Building and monumental stone, worked	128.0	10.8	836.4	2.9
3281	Cut stone and stone products	57.3	133	218			15.1	.4	42.9	.7

(continued)

TABLE C-1 (concluded)

U.S. Standard Industrial Classification Code	Industry	V.A.E. (all U.S. mfg.=100)	V.A.M. ($ million)	V.S. ($ million)	SITC Code	Product	U.S. (f.o.b.) Total	U.S. (f.o.b.) From LDC's	Other Developed Countries (c.i.f.)a Total	Other Developed Countries (c.i.f.)a From LDC's
3271	Concrete block and brick	86.0	276	566	6618	Building materials of asbestos-cement and fiber-cement				
3272	Other concrete products	83.7	621	1,055			5.8	1.0	46.0	.8
325	Structural clay products	71.4	628	968	662	Clay construction materials				
3293	Gaskets and insulations	74.8	168	303			33.8	3.0	228.2	.1
3299	Nonmetallic minerals, n.e.c.	81.7	67	114	663	Mineral manufactures, n.e.s.	16.6	3.9	240.9	.9
3211	Flat glass	139.2	463	676	664	Glass	56.6	2.4	278.4	.4

U.S. Manufacturing Production, 1965

Value of Imports, 1965 ($ million)

Source: U.S. Bureau of the Census, Annual Survey of Manufactures: 1965, *General Statistics for Industry Groups and Industries,* M65(AS)-1, supplemented by *1963 Census of Manufactures* for data on five-digit product classes.

Note: n.e.c. = not elsewhere classified; n.e.s. = not elsewhere specified.

*All five-digit items are for 1963. Index of value added per employee is on basis of national average in that year. In adding to 1965 totals for the groups and subgroups used in this study, value added and value of shipments (third and fourth columns) of each such five-digit item are raised in same proportion as shown by their parent four-digit group from 1963 to 1965. Employment (not shown) is treated in the same way, and value added per employee for groups and subgroups in 1965 is derived from the totals so adjusted.

aExcept Canada and Australia, which are on f.o.b. basis.

bLess SITC 6519, yarn of textile fibers, n.e.s. (mostly jute yarn).

cU.S. import data are included in SITC 6537 and 6539.

dLess 6551, felt and felt articles, n.e.s., and 6555, elastic fabrics and trimmings of elastic.

eLess SITC 6561, bags and sacks of textile materials.

fLess SIC 2393, textile bags.

gLess 2256.

hU.S. import data are included in SITC 893.

iLess SITC 8922, newspapers and periodicals.

jLess SITC 8911, phonographs, tape recorders, and other sound recorders and reproducers.

kLess SITC 8943, nonmilitary arms, and 8945, fairground amusements, etc.

lLess SITC 6672, diamonds not set or strung.

mIncluded on basis of relative position with respect to value added per employee in India. See Chapter 3.

nImport data given here include SITC 6417, handmade papers.

oIncluded on basis of relative position with respect to value added per employee in Japan. See Chapter 3.

pExcluding SITC 7123, milking machines, cream separators, etc.

qConsists mainly of jute yarn imported from India and Pakistan.

r1963 data used because of qualifications expressed in 1965 *Survey* regarding accuracy of reported data for this item.

STATISTICS OF IMPORTS OF LABOR-INTENSIVE MANUFACTURES BY DEVELOPED COUNTRIES, 1964 AND 1965

Tables D-1, D-2, D-3, and D-4 show additional details, beyond those given in Chapter 4, of imports of labor-intensive manufactures by developed from less developed countries in 1964 and 1965. The data have been especially compiled for this study by the United Nations Statistical Office on the basis of the import statistics submitted by individual developed countries. The figures received from the U.N. Statistical Office have been adjusted in some cases, as noted below, to delete elements which, at least for purposes of a study such as the present one, must be deemed irrelevant and inaccurate. The c.i.f./f.o.b. adjustment (see Appendix E) has not been attempted in this detail, however, and the figures are therefore a mixture of the f.o.b. values reported by the United States, Canada, and Australia with the c.i.f. values reported by all other developed countries.

These four main tables and the subgroups into which they are divided correspond to the main groups and subgroups distinguished in Table C-1, and their composition in terms of the Standard International Trade Classification is specified in that table.

The sixteen countries here treated as "developed" correspond to those included in "Economic Class I" in the trade statistics publications of the United Nations, except that the Union of South Africa and Portugal have been omitted (Portugal being excluded also from the subgroup EFTA and, instead, included with Southern Europe under "other low-wage countries" among the sources of imports specified in the tables). All sixteen countries are shown separately in each of the tables.

The composition of the "less developed countries" in these tables corresponds to that of "Economic Class II" in the trade statistics publications of the United Nations. Generally speaking, the country subgroups are also the same as in the U.N. publications. The principal exception is that the U.N.'s group "other countries, n.e.s." (which, as far as the trade examined here is concerned, is chiefly accounted for by the islands of the Caribbean) is combined with Latin America and called "Western Hemisphere" in the present tables. Only the most important countries of origin are individually shown in each table, and those chosen vary from one table to another depending on the products covered. This has the consequence that the residual regional country groups ("Other Far East," etc.) vary in composition from one table to another depending on which countries are individually specified. Similarly, the final residual group "Other less developed countries" varies according to the individual countries and country groups separately listed.

The tables also show imports from "other low-wage countries," comprising Japan and Southern Europe other than Italy (i.e., Portugal, Spain, Yugoslavia, Greece, and Turkey).

Adjustments to Delete Irrelevant Elements

The statistics in several of the tables in this appendix have had to be adjusted in an effort to eliminate elements which seem to represent merchandise returned to the importing country or, in any event, are clearly not the product of the less developed country listed as the source of the imports. An example of this kind of statistic is the United Kingdom's reported imports of aircraft (SITC 734) and aircraft engines (SITC 7114), totaling $25.2 million in 1965 from a long list of less developed countries. It may be safely assumed that these are items of British origin brought back for repair. The United Kingdom and, to a smaller extent, various other developed countries appear to give the same kind of treatment to construction equipment and various other capital items brought back after use abroad. It is apparent from the origins indicated in the import returns that much of this equipment has been used in petroleum exploration and exploitation in the Middle East and other oil-producing areas. The aircraft, aircraft engines, and various other items are not of immediate concern here, being eliminated in any event from the statistics as capital-intensive. There are, however, a number of other items which are at least "marginally labor-intensive" (see Chapter 4) and which give rise to the same sort of doubt as that indicated. The method followed here, a second- or third-best solution, is to eliminate completely in such cases all imports shown as coming from the Middle East other than Israel, from "Other Africa," and from "other countries, n.e.s." but to give the benefit of the doubt to imports listed as coming from Israel, the Far East, and Latin America. The items so treated pertain to two of the subgroups in Table D-2 and consist of the following SITC numbers:

2(j)   Electrical apparatus and appliances: 722, 7249, 7294, 7299

2(k)   Nonelectrical machinery and equipment: 7121, 7122, 7125, 7129, 7142, 7143, 7149, 7171, 7183, 7192, 7196, 7198, 71991, 71992

Minor Discrepancies in the Tables

Summation of the U.N. tabulations for individual SITC items to obtain the product subgroups and main groups presented in the following tables has the consequence of accumulating minor discrepancies between (a) the sum of the figures for individual importing countries in a given column and (b) the subtotals for EFTA and the EEC as well as the grand totals for all developed countries shown in the same column. (These discrepancies arise because, in the detailed tabulations, amounts of less than $1,000 from any one source were omitted from the figures listed for individual importing countries but were retained for addition into the combined subtotals and totals.) The differences are positive (excess of b over a) in columns giving imports from individual less developed countries, but may be negative in columns for residual country groups (such as "Other Far East" and "Other less developed countries") where entries for the latter have been obtained by difference.

TABLE D-1
Textiles, Clothing, and Accessories, 1964
($ thousand)

Imports of	Total, All Sources	From Less Developed Countries								From Other Low-Wage Countries		
		Total	Hong Kong	India	Other Far East	Iran	Israel	Western Hemisphere	Other LDC's	Total	Japan	So. Europe excl. Italy
Developed countries, total	5,871,869	746,983	360,169	114,642	125,576	72,740	16,749	28,314	28,793	630,530	487,388	143,142
U.S.	864,800	213,657	104,816	20,544	57,071	6,451	4,127	16,739	3,909	301,408	277,813	23,595
Canada	339,539	26,383	10,834	6,316	5,707	180	1,770	1,452	124	47,264	43,070	4,194
EFTA, total	1,773,695	309,942	160,619	68,543	34,864	23,324	7,494	6,666	8,432	106,577	44,355	62,222
U.K.	655,689	244,748	131,027	65,025	29,165	7,754	3,300	6,103	2,374	39,858	12,763	27,095
Sweden	336,480	21,075	13,144	892	1,185	2,473	1,694	184	1,503	27,330	10,094	17,236
Denmark	211,398	14,349	5,874	1,693	772	2,773	1,046	279	1,912	15,715	8,952	6,763
Norway	146,973	6,895	4,663	487	333	399	346	15	652	6,250	2,862	3,388
Switz.	252,283	16,751	3,810	374	2,708	6,992	998	78	1,791	10,166	5,855	4,311
Austria	170,875	6,113	2,099	73	701	2,931	107	2	200	7,258	3,831	3,427
EEC, total	2,516,773	153,390	66,133	6,859	15,944	42,582	3,179	2,605	16,088	99,310	48,110	51,200
Germany	1,106,884	111,304	50,595	2,317	9,597	38,142	2,120	797	7,736	57,444	30,517	26,927
France	320,240	8,511	613	2,076	991	2,175	307	505	1,844	10,724	5,019	5,705
Italy	188,603	15,576	8,430	926	3,580	314	39	635	1,652	10,202	3,423	6,779
Neth.	575,870	9,785	5,392	293	1,113	909	688	180	1,210	11,049	5,735	5,314
Belg.-Lux.	325,178	8,207	1,101	1,245	662	1,040	25	488	3,646	9,889	3,416	6,473
Japan	57,974	4,214	1,087	104	2,459	25	5	517	17	79	—	79
Australia	219,845	24,782	12,048	7,959	3,871	176	171	334	223	59,865	58,013	1,852
N.Z.	99,250	14,604	4,629	4,315	5,660	—	—	—	—	16,028	16,028	—

TABLE D-1

Textiles, Clothing, and Accessories, 1965

($ thousand)

Imports of	Total, All Sources	From Less Developed Countries								From Other Low-Wage Countries		
		Total	Hong Kong	India	Other Far East	Iran	Israel	Western Hemisphere	Other LDC's	Total	Japan	So. Europe excl. Italy
Developed countries, total	6,369,363	820,326	407,498	105,616	140,460	87,925	16,992	34,886	26,949	726,747	574,438	152,309
U.S.	1,052,888	286,330	139,477	31,980	75,812	7,184	4,573	24,358	2,946	372,253	346,656	25,597
Canada	359,748	32,381	12,557	7,546	7,430	370	1,827	2,404	247	52,448	48,432	4,016
EFTA, total	1,722,776	267,446	144,401	48,234	28,619	25,557	7,209	5,311	8,115	108,236	48,784	59,452
U.K.	542,305	193,901	114,038	44,536	18,586	7,966	2,607	4,658	1,510	34,035	14,270	19,765
Sweden	366,413	27,745	13,789	1,010	5,347	3,269	2,514	222	1,594	30,413	11,210	19,203
Denmark	223,010	14,845	5,868	1,725	769	3,076	796	112	2,499	18,733	10,609	8,124
Norway	153,657	6,678	4,667	482	132	457	272	40	628	7,330	3,621	3,709
Switz.	253,505	17,721	3,638	368	2,969	8,055	892	170	1,629	9,531	4,992	4,539
Austria	183,884	6,540	2,398	112	816	2,731	125	103	255	8,189	4,079	4,110
EEC, total	2,860,674	184,904	82,753	6,710	19,916	54,613	3,223	2,314	15,375	116,165	54,734	61,431
Germany	1,384,474	142,048	66,403	3,729	11,216	46,971	2,338	869	10,522	77,215	38,274	38,941
France	319,557	8,560	481	1,224	1,440	3,034	164	215	2,002	9,560	4,447	5,113
Italy	174,641	15,290	8,296	663	3,325	1,745	12	547	702	7,087	2,474	4,613
Neth.	623,752	12,404	6,386	316	2,262	1,276	644	225	1,295	12,696	6,433	6,263
Belg.-Lux.	358,249	6,593	1,186	776	1,673	1,586	63	455	854	9,605	3,105	6,500
Japan	54,577	5,382	1,393	193	3,589	11	2	67	127	79	—	79
Australia	215,363	26,697	14,090	6,930	4,893	184	155	309	136	59,261	57,782	1,479
N.Z.	103,333	17,167	12,824	4,020	201	3	—	116	3	18,299	18,047	252

TABLE D-1a

Yarn and Thread, 1964

($ thousand)

Imports of	Total, All Sources	From Less Developed Countries								From Other Low-Wage Countries		
		Total	Hong Kong	India	Egypt	Israel	Brazil	Other Western Hemisphere	Other LDC's	Total	Japan	So. Europe excl. Italy
Developed countries, total	1,090,544	40,249	6,354	6,550	13,402	6,713	486	5,629	1,115	64,134	29,662	34,472
U.S.	51,621	3,319	134	9	115	881	410	1,755	15	12,916	8,300	4,616
Canada	44,590	2,292	117	79	70	1,016	–	976	34	5,103	3,042	2,061
EFTA, total	345,294	19,338	3,969	5,676	4,219	3,650	–	1,099	725	19,660	4,682	14,978
U.K.	80,996	12,975	3,944	5,624	655	1,361	–	737	654	4,984	122	4,862
Sweden	76,721	2,338	1	37	1,297	875	–	124	4	7,935	1,939	5,996
Denmark	55,189	2,707	17	1	1,629	839	–	216	5	3,100	1,256	1,844
Norway	30,479	815	4	–	534	266	–	5	6	1,188	457	731
Switz.	37,644	315	–	–	20	236	–	13	46	1,221	888	333
Austria	64,262	176	–	12	82	71	–	1	10	1,226	16	1,210
EEC, total	587,491	12,468	33	752	8,943	1,092	76	1,347	225	18,673	5,868	12,805
Germany	280,903	6,814	33	109	5,151	988	76	334	123	10,380	4,517	5,863
France	59,929	399	–	–	–	4	–	386	9	525	86	439
Italy	27,719	444	–	9	71	23	–	286	55	564	407	157
Neth.	131,322	400	–	7	261	67	–	62	3	2,861	722	2,139
Belg.-Lux.	87,616	4,406	–	627	3,459	8	–	277	35	4,339	134	4,205
Japan	5,894	490	7	–	–	–	–	449	34	10	–	10
Australia	39,479	632	443	1	54	71	–	–	63	6,575	6,574	1
N.Z.	16,172	1,698	1,648	31	–	–	–	–	19	1,194	1,194	–

TABLE D-1a

Yarn and Thread, 1965

($ thousand)

Imports of	Total, All Sources	From Less Developed Countries								From Other Low-Wage Countries		
		Total	Hong Kong	India	Egypt	Israel	Brazil	Other Western Hemisphere	Other LDC's	Total	Japan	So. Europe excl. Italy
Developed countries, total	1,098,738	37,073	6,152	3,665	11,469	6,454	2,443	5,764	1,126	65,804	35,967	29,837
U.S.	63,646	5,902	209	24	43	767	2,162	2,671	26	17,028	12,085	4,943
Canada	46,082	2,874	162	25	163	1,308	3	1,204	9	4,109	1,913	2,196
EFTA, total	333,350	15,963	3,800	2,959	4,412	2,951	110	1,132	599	20,853	7,336	13,517
U.K.	69,260	8,719	3,769	2,924	189	502	—	797	538	5,208	1,102	4,106
Sweden	75,425	2,744	1	5	1,189	1,408	—	123	18	7,697	2,678	5,019
Denmark	57,399	2,980	29	18	2,276	569	—	84	4	3,850	1,711	2,139
Norway	30,740	796	—	—	572	193	—	29	2	1,858	1,193	665
Switz.	38,458	376	—	—	45	190	19	93	29	637	474	163
Austria	62,066	334	—	10	138	86	91	1	8	1,598	176	1,422
EEC, total	611,041	9,930	3	512	6,790	1,397	166	755	307	17,540	8,360	9,180
Germany	314,789	8,384	3	188	6,210	1,320	162	271	230	11,625	7,075	4,550
France	53,956	76	—	7	—	4	—	62	3	425	141	284
Italy	25,115	111	—	—	28	—	4	22	57	375	164	211
Neth.	128,496	307	—	—	200	65	—	34	8	1,891	775	1,116
Belg.-Lux.	88,683	1,045	—	316	350	7	—	363	9	3,221	204	3,017
Japan	4,549	103	6	—	—	—	—	1	96	—	—	—
Australia	25,729	310	148	9	58	28	—	—	67	4,810	4,810	—
N.Z.	14,337	1,976	1,820	134	—	—	—	—	22	1,460	1,460	—

221

TABLE D-1b

Cotton, *Fabrics, Woven, 1964*

(\$ thousand)

Imports of	Total, All Sources	From Less Developed Countries								From Other Low-Wage Countries		
		Total	Hong Kong	India	Pakistan	Korea	Taiwan	Egypt	Other LDC's	Total	Japan	So. Europe excl. Italy
Developed countries, total	791,310	178,889	55,887	70,727	13,228	9,609	7,491	7,109	14,838	147,835	103,599	44,236
U.S.	104,997	42,561	16,402	11,210	2,929	2,841	3,489	3,369	2,321	37,272	31,251	6,021
Canada	69,195	7,784	2,302	3,229	1,684	49	84	–	436	9,508	8,693	815
EFTA, total	285,773	89,863	27,234	43,757	6,847	4,561	335	1,563	5,566	34,808	14,985	19,823
U.K.	180,009	86,161	25,804	42,477	6,592	4,544	308	1,071	5,365	16,783	5,188	11,595
Sweden	27,893	821	393	196	–	15	6	83	128	6,431	3,413	3,018
Denmark	23,378	1,322	82	738	251	–	–	208	43	3,673	1,577	2,096
Norway	13,097	357	10	290	1	1	–	52	3	1,394	678	716
Switz.	19,106	383	.213	35	2	–	–	107	26	2,064	1,311	753
Austria	22,288	808	729	19	–	–	20	39	1	4,459	2,815	1,644
EEC, total	213,443	11,388	2,079	3,080	1,473	1,224	708	2,073	751	22,523	6,480	16,043
Germany	68,915	2,270	791	765	95	324	19	188	88	8,364	3,005	5,359
France	28,386	2,412	13	1,715	375	59	2	172	76	4,501	1,555	2,946
Italy	30,025	3,601	903	235	683	155	555	945	125	6,257	572	5,685
Neth.	54,755	2,102	369	92	32	496	113	757	243	1,884	1,026	858
Belg.-Lux.	31,361	995	2	271	287	189	17	10	219	1,511	319	1,192
Japan	3,222	971	38	–	20	764	99	–	50	15	–	15
Australia	84,666	17,355	7,829	5,978	273	167	2,774	103	281	36,023	34,507	1,516
N.Z.	30,011	8,954	–	3,471	–	–	–	–	5,483	7,681	7,681	–

TABLE D-1b

Cotton Fabrics, Woven, 1965

($ thousand)

Imports of	Total, All Sources	From Less Developed Countries								From Other Low-Wage Countries		
		Total	Hong Kong	India	Pakistan	Korea	Taiwan	Egypt	Other LDC's	Total	Japan	So. Europe excl. Italy
Developed countries, total	776,454	183,730	70,797	63,331	14,176	8,124	8,765	4,933	13,604	146,844	110,752	36,092
U.S.	134,494	61,488	19,088	19,251	4,820	2,699	4,895	2,546	8,189	44,691	38,732	5,959
Canada	64,907	9,019	2,177	3,652	1,514	551	110	2	1,013	9,280	8,415	865
EFTA, total	243,752	72,359	30,843	29,572	6,566	1,007	227	843	3,301	28,915	14,149	14,766
U.K.	139,559	68,083	29,033	28,273	6,275	954	149	415	2,984	12,387	5,532	6,855
Sweden	28,229	1,248	492	310	–	30	6	229	181	4,816	2,194	2,622
Denmark	22,543	1,504	374	664	263	–	–	168	35	3,753	1,583	2,170
Norway	12,412	312	13	247	–	–	–	16	36	1,288	640	648
Switz.	17,531	298	213	23	3	1	–	8	50	2,068	1,380	688
Austria	23,475	906	716	53	23	22	72	5	15	4,598	2,817	1,781
EEC, total	213,680	10,759	2,078	2,486	800	2,598	655	1,502	640	20,213	6,949	13,264
Germany	81,699	3,774	1,441	1,378	277	291	39	199	149	7,929	3,494	4,435
France	29,150	1,284	41	710	185	107	–	138	103	4,309	1,404	2,905
Italy	22,290	1,952	225	75	273	668	238	316	157	3,781	381	3,400
Neth.	51,003	2,661	190	153	10	1,175	151	848	134	2,419	1,365	1,054
Belg.-Lux.	29,536	1,080	180	168	53	356	226	–	97	1,773	304	1,469
Japan	2,596	456	7	54	6	250	–	–	139	–	–	–
Australia	85,581	18,994	9,236	5,204	421	1,014	2,798	37	284	36,458	35,360	1,098
N.Z.	31,441	10,639	7,366	3,110	47	2	76	–	38	7,282	7,144	138

TABLE D-1c

Other Woven Fabrics, Excluding Jute, 1964

(\$ thousand)

Imports of	Total, All Sources	From Less Developed Countries								From Other Low-Wage Countries		
		Total	Hong Kong	India	Korea	Other Far East	Israel	Western Hemisphere	Other LDC's	Total	Japan	So. Europe excl. Italy
Developed countries, total	1,334,756	14,299	2,858	4,573	924	1,901	1,014	2,382	647	148,796	136,164	12,632
U.S.	177,855	5,715	206	1,786	653	839	206	2,001	24	86,113	85,667	446
Canada	90,664	1,077	54	815	13	52	74	68	1	13,389	13,265	124
EFTA, total	357,916	2,433	253	925	—	306	640	140	169	20,604	13,095	7,509
U.K.	106,002	1,527	188	370	—	121	617	68	163	4,587	2,451	2,136
Sweden	79,530	457	33	327	—	92	2	—	3	4,565	2,565	2,000
Denmark	52,652	250	9	175	—	17	2	46	1	5,141	3,681	1,460
Norway	26,416	13	2	2	—	9	—	—	—	1,325	884	441
Switz.	52,431	159	12	46	—	58	16	25	2	3,772	2,575	1,197
Austria	40,882	17	6	1	—	9	1	—	—	1,209	937	272
EEC, total	624,276	1,799	173	604	100	259	92	170	401	16,927	12,491	4,436
Germany	263,819	565	62	247	93	82	68	12	1	7,556	5,852	1,704
France	82,566	192	10	50	—	5	—	20	107	2,533	1,904	629
Italy	58,017	614	63	71	—	61	4	132	283	2,128	1,857	271
Neth.	132,620	241	30	87	7	88	20	1	8	2,458	1,176	1,282
Belg.-Lux.	87,254	179	6	147	—	23	—	1	2	2,250	1,701	549
Japan	33,494	410	14	55	156	176	—	—	9	24	—	24
Australia	19,702	968	433	244	—	248	—	—	43	5,436	5,344	92
N.Z.	30,850	1,884	1,722	141	—	21	—	—	—	6,299	6,299	—

TABLE D-1c

Other Woven Fabrics, Excluding Jute, 1965

($ thousand)

Imports of	Total, All Sources	From Less Developed Countries								From Other Low-Wage Countries		
		Total	Hong Kong	India	Korea	Other Far East	Israel	Western Hemisphere	Other LDC's	Total	Japan	So. Europe excl. Italy
Developed countries, total	1,480,766	21,633	4,212	5,053	4,781	2,738	1,673	2,545	631	189,995	173,959	16,036
U.S.	236,014	9,224	429	2,056	3,271	1,347	196	1,906	19	117,631	117,478	153
Canada	95,068	1,799	292	1,215	4	90	50	147	1	15,690	15,592	98
EFTA, total	355,491	3,715	563	986	82	641	1,289	34	120	24,546	15,538	9,008
U.K.	88,264	2,653	358	456	71	404	1,234	24	106	4,339	2,470	1,869
Sweden	84,825	627	140	321	10	132	17	–	7	6,348	3,719	2,629
Denmark	56,527	196	17	144	–	30	2	2	1	7,200	4,902	2,298
Norway	29,239	25	3	7	–	15	–	–	–	1,884	1,308	576
Switz.	51,656	185	36	52	–	55	33	5	4	3,385	2,148	1,237
Austria	44,976	24	5	3	–	11	1	2	2	1,384	988	396
EEC, total	704,928	2,082	143	456	235	220	134	455	439	19,460	12,977	6,483
Germany	320,263	718	111	277	46	103	92	76	13	9,339	6,976	2,363
France	83,493	388	5	57	–	9	2	26	289	2,118	1,448	670
Italy	55,132	565	15	15	68	23	–	344	100	1,859	1,551	308
Neth.	146,150	305	5	43	120	77	37	3	20	4,180	1,572	2,608
Belg.-Lux.	99,886	100	4	63	–	11	1	4	17	1,961	1,428	533
Japan	31,462	1,595	47	92	1,182	257	–	–	17	60	–	60
Australia	22,028	772	443	108	5	179	3	–	34	4,393	4,244	149
N.Z.	35,771	2,438	2,293	137	–	7	–	–	1	8,209	8,127	82

TABLE D-1d

Textile Small Wares and Specialties, 1964

($ thousand)

Imports of	Total, All Sources	From Less Developed Countries								From Other Low-Wage Countries		
		Total	Hong Kong	India	Taiwan	Other Far East	Mexico	Other Western Hemisphere	Other LDC's	Total	Japan	So. Europe excl. Italy
Developed countries, total	572,188	45,514	21,450	10,250	2,116	8,006	1,391	1,467	834	49,007	38,276	10,731
U.S.	61,733	11,666	3,095	2,574	1,406	2,316	1,323	860	92	20,648	18,519	2,129
Canada	52,462	1,424	796	434	57	17	33	18	69	4,560	4,190	370
EFTA, total	163,467	18,085	8,430	6,348	7	2,688	4	368	240	8,373	2,449	5,924
U.K.	55,043	16,499	7,430	6,016	–	2,575	2	340	136	4,440	959	3,481
Sweden	35,053	374	254	84	3	21	–	5	7	1,539	444	1,095
Denmark	22,405	686	426	150	–	76	–	–	34	1,488	943	545
Norway	18,260	252	169	75	–	–	–	–	8	670	50	620
Switz.	20,779	197	96	18	2	6	1	22	52	187	43	144
Austria	11,931	72	52	7	–	10	–	–	3	48	10	38
EEC, total	236,045	11,998	7,860	228	456	2,851	26	165	412	5,759	3,482	2,277
Germany	79,113	2,418	1,041	146	212	813	–	145	61	3,053	2,020	1,033
France	39,463	970	428	28	119	98	22	–	275	1,162	590	572
Italy	39,125	8,380	6,225	48	119	1,916	3	15	54	540	204	336
Neth.	48,407	99	72	7	4	7	–	4	5	701	494	207
Belg.-Lux.	29,938	122	92	–	1	17	–	1	11	299	173	126
Japan	5,237	418	92	3	167	98	–	54	4	–	–	–
Australia	39,043	801	539	199	19	24	3	–	17	8,813	8,783	30
N.Z.	14,205	1,108	635	461	–	12	–	–	–	854	854	–

TABLE D-1d

Textile Small Wares and Specialties, 1965
($ thousand)

Imports of	Total, All Sources	From Less Developed Countries								From Other Low-Wage Countries		
		Total	Hong Kong	India	Taiwan	Other Far East	Mexico	Other Western Hemisphere	Other LDC's	Total	Japan	So. Europe excl. Italy
Developed countries, total	631,010	48,745	24,796	10,203	2,074	7,979	1,409	1,640	644	56,575	46,062	10,513
U.S.	67,282	12,948	3,071	3,250	1,451	2,668	1,342	1,120	46	23,804	21,294	2,510
Canada	60,352	1,608	777	588	93	23	41	47	39	4,993	4,747	246
EFTA, total	174,063	17,645	10,364	5,126	24	1,664	3	231	233	9,149	3,472	5,677
U.K.	54,091	15,520	9,144	4,560	6	1,463	—	208	139	4,638	1,269	3,369
Sweden	39,288	537	337	84	9	92	1	—	14	2,009	783	1,226
Denmark	24,011	893	462	351	—	71	—	—	9	1,497	1,190	307
Norway	19,060	382	255	120	—	5	—	1	1	720	129	591
Switz.	22,818	230	124	4	7	15	1	18	61	200	69	131
Austria	14,792	76	40	4	—	22	—	1	9	79	30	49
EEC, total	267,415	13,734	9,024	542	378	3,291	8	172	319	7,041	5,000	2,041
Germany	103,833	3,593	1,362	465	134	1,436	—	140	56	4,403	3,290	1,113
France	40,773	856	234	29	137	239	7	18	192	926	551	375
Italy	37,458	8,531	6,845	27	106	1,509	—	9	35	471	148	323
Neth.	51,046	529	507	12	—	4	—	—	6	979	804	175
Belg.-Lux.	34,303	218	75	6	—	106	—	1	30	259	205	54
Japan	6,277	556	111	—	106	275	2	60	2	3	—	3
Australia	41,671	983	689	227	7	51	5	—	4	10,389	10,364	25
N.Z.	13,947	1,263	756	468	13	12	4	9	1	1,187	1,181	6

TABLE D-1e
Carpets and Other Floor Coverings, 1964
($ thousand)

Imports of	Total, All Sources	From Less Developed Countries								From Other Low-Wage Countries		
		Total	Hong Kong	India	Pakistan	Other Far East	Iran	Morocco, Algeria & Tunisia	Other LDC's	Total	Japan	So. Europe excl. Italy
Developed countries, total	411,784	119,323	2,903	19,798	4,285	13,998	72,620	4,034	1,685	36,490	30,964	5,526
U.S.	54,372	13,974	1,810	3,772	364	1,121	6,442	184	281	28,392	27,150	1,242
Canada	15,933	2,016	23	1,736	12	18	180	31	16	923	818	105
EFTA, total	127,102	46,206	580	10,579	3,045	6,857	23,246	1,386	513	2,756	850	1,906
U.K.	42,943	24,130	471	9,345	2,531	3,971	7,682	10	120	705	298	407
Sweden	22,638	3,201	41	229	96	260	2,473	69	33	593	364	229
Denmark	16,156	3,686	7	623	68	180	2,770	10	28	178	33	145
Norway	8,849	564	7	111	11	18	399	10	8	71	52	19
Switz.	25,911	10,935	39	240	292	1,817	6,989	1,260	298	947	65	882
Austria	10,601	3,679	12	30	44	611	2,931	25	26	257	35	222
EEC, total	187,424	54,136	426	1,926	805	5,131	42,550	2,431	867	3,283	1,102	2,181
Germany	120,257	46,690	250	991	677	4,919	38,130	1,288	435	2,032	449	1,583
France	18,731	3,916	85	237	113	102	2,167	930	282	470	232	238
Italy	6,364	906	23	411	5	10	314	74	69	225	140	85
Neth.	28,815	1,269	48	96	6	78	904	102	35	379	222	157
Belg.-Lux.	13,256	1,346	18	188	3	22	1,034	35	46	173	57	116
Japan	2,885	840	14	44	—	755	23	—	4	14	—	14
Australia	20,368	1,876	47	1,528	56	65	176	—	4	1,117	1,041	76
N.Z.	3,698	262	—	211	—	51	—	—	—	—	—	—

TABLE D-1e

Carpets and Other Floor Coverings, 1965
($ thousand)

Imports of	Total, All Sources	From Less Developed Countries								From Other Low-Wage Countries		
		Total	Hong Kong	India	Pakistan	Other Far East	Iran	Morocco, Algeria & Tunisia	Other LDC's	Total	Japan	So. Europe excl. Italy
Developed countries, total	469,460	136,385	3,489	18,494	4,598	14,508	87,845	5,519	1,932	36,141	29,644	6,497
U.S.	54,331	15,683	2,257	3,870	546	1,233	7,170	249	358	26,819	25,048	1,771
Canada	16,853	2,551	41	2,026	19	19	370	65	11	1,116	1,033	83
EFTA, total	136,776	46,467	480	8,540	2,900	7,134	25,522	1,328	563	2,977	954	2,023
U.K.	40,489	21,840	366	7,386	2,249	3,775	7,951	15	98	661	320	341
Sweden	28,552	4,288	43	237	128	464	3,268	88	60	911	401	510
Denmark	17,974	3,918	10	534	104	166	3,076	11	17	215	57	158
Norway	9,597	627	7	93	27	20	457	11	12	126	61	65
Switz.	27,981	12,273	46	252	306	2,135	8,043	1,144	347	852	86	766
Austria	12,180	3,508	5	36	83	574	2,724	57	29	209	27	182
EEC, total	233,512	68,613	592	2,473	1,081	5,015	54,586	3,874	992	3,783	1,255	2,528
Germany	150,599	57,225	390	1,353	866	4,480	46,963	2,629	544	2,379	537	1,842
France	23,441	5,102	122	328	130	168	3,028	1,030	296	498	257	241
Italy	7,280	2,593	30	473	69	226	1,745	22	28	246	88	158
Neth.	35,432	1,738	30	106	8	119	1,271	133	71	486	313	173
Belg.-Lux.	16,758	1,948	19	212	7	22	1,577	58	53	172	59	113
Japan	2,926	1,085	38	42	–	992	8	1	4	11	–	11
Australia	21,413	1,768	52	1,369	48	114	183	–	2	1,400	1,328	72
N.Z.	3,644	203	26	170	1	1	3	–	2	28	23	5

TABLE D-1f

Clothing and Accessories, Excluding Goods of Leather, Rubber and Fur, 1964

($ thousand)

Imports of	Total, All Sources	From Less Developed Countries								From Other Low-Wage Countries		
		Total	Hong Kong	Philippines	Korea	Other Far East	Israel	Jamaica	Other LDC's	Total	Japan	So. Europe excl. Italy
Developed countries, total	1,671,285	348,829	270,715	25,519	4,797	27,709	8,091	7,732	4,266	184,266	148,723	35,543
U.S.	414,219	136,420	83,167	25,418	3,283	13,572	3,006	6,235	1,739	116,062	106,923	9,139
Canada	66,694	11,789	7,539	22	116	3,575	441	32	64	13,777	13,061	716
EFTA, total	494,142	134,048	120,150	2	1,242	7,336	2,804	1,360	1,154	20,370	8,291	12,079
U.K.	190,693	103,454	93,187	-	110	6,716	1,108	1,353	980	8,354	3,743	4,611
Sweden	94,643	13,881	12,418	2	628	77	722	-	34	6,261	1,365	4,896
Denmark	41,615	5,695	5,330	-	-	172	169	-	24	2,130	1,459	671
Norway	49,869	4,890	4,467	-	-	303	73	-	47	1,595	737	858
Switz.	96,409	4,760	3,448	-	499	63	696	4	50	1,970	970	1,000
Austria	20,909	1,359	1,297	-	4	5	34	-	19	53	14	39
EEC, total	668,090	61,629	55,559	1	63	2,992	1,778	104	1,132	32,142	18,685	13,457
Germany	293,877	52,547	48,418	1	13	2,285	1,059	65	706	26,059	14,674	11,385
France	91,163	620	75	-	2	161	282	-	100	1,527	649	878
Italy	27,351	1,627	1,213	-	7	192	6	-	210	483	241	242
Neth.	179,949	5,671	4,871	-	40	241	418	21	80	2,760	2,092	668
Belg.-Lux.	75,749	1,157	979	-	-	113	12	17	36	1,309	1,027	282
Japan	7,240	1,083	920	23	90	39	-	-	11	14	-	14
Australia	16,583	3,148	2,753	50	-	121	58	-	166	1,896	1,761	135
N.Z.	4,314	698	624	-	-	74	-	-	-	-	-	-

TABLE D-1f

Clothing and Accessories, Excluding Goods of Leather, Rubber and Fur, 1965

($ thousand)

Imports of	Total, All Sources	From Less Developed Countries								From Other Low-Wage Countries		
		Total	Hong Kong	Philippines	Korea	Other Far East	Israel	Jamaica	Other LDC's	Total	Japan	So. Europe excl. Italy
Developed countries, total	1,912,932	392,838	298,050	21,983	17,062	34,797	8,020	7,218	5,727	231,247	178,054	53,193
U.S.	497,118	181,082	114,421	21,883	10,708	23,021	3,520	5,322	2,207	142,136	132,017	10,119
Canada	76,482	14,527	9,105	22	510	4,376	262	145	107	17,255	16,730	525
EFTA, total	479,342	111,320	98,349	15	4,766	2,285	2,628	1,571	1,706	21,790	7,332	14,458
U.K.	150,639	77,083	71,364	12	241	1,575	804	1,568	1,519	6,798	3,575	3,223
Sweden	110,091	18,298	12,774	1	4,106	413	939	–	65	8,626	1,432	7,194
Denmark	44,553	5,351	4,974	1	–	145	193	–	38	2,213	1,164	1,049
Norway	52,606	4,534	4,388	–	1	78	52	–	15	1,449	288	1,161
Switz.	95,057	4,356	3,216	–	417	64	604	2	53	2,382	832	1,550
Austria	26,392	1,690	1,630	–	–	10	34	–	16	316	39	277
EEC, total	830,096	79,811	70,910	9	755	4,914	1,563	173	1,487	48,120	20,189	27,931
Germany	413,291	68,354	63,096	–	65	3,386	893	64	850	41,540	16,902	24,638
France	88,740	852	77	7	–	548	132	3	85	1,280	644	636
Italy	27,362	1,535	1,178	1	–	180	11	82	83	350	139	211
Neth.	211,622	6,862	5,652	–	134	460	477	22	117	2,735	1,601	1,134
Belg.-Lux.	89,079	2,200	905	–	555	340	48	–	352	2,213	902	1,311
Japan	6,764	1,585	1,182	17	319	63	2	–	2	4	–	4
Australia	18,939	3,868	3,519	33	1	129	43	–	143	1,807	1,673	134
N.Z.	4,189	645	561	–	–	9	–	–	75	129	110	19

TABLE D-2

Other Light Manufactures, except Food, 1964

($ thousand)

Imports of	Total, All Sources	From Less Developed Countries								From Other Low-Wage Countries		
		Total	Hong Kong	India	Other Far East	Mexico	Other Western Hemi-sphere	Other Africa	Other LDC's	Total	Japan	So. Europe excl. Italy
Developed countries, total	17,816,439	414,065	242,224	34,458	43,858	21,960	38,967	20,753	11,845	1,264,304	1,123,675	140,629
U.S.	2,576,644	186,770	114,253	8,087	24,255	19,353	14,157	2,725	3,940	805,523	766,364	39,159
Canada	2,256,846	13,074	10,213	487	976	513	600	68	217	64,860	61,863	2,997
EFTA, total	4,392,233	120,703	79,787	13,739	7,941	401	11,068	3,499	4,268	147,988	114,972	33,016
U.K.	1,438,039	93,373	70,034	6,365	5,814	314	5,811	2,342	2,693	80,945	60,629	20,316
Sweden	862,498	5,295	3,623	256	479	14	535	133	255	22,712	19,215	3,497
Denmark	464,535	2,437	1,472	234	221	3	315	87	105	7,707	6,140	1,567
Norway	346,347	1,438	1,124	65	99	1	91	17	41	5,324	4,506	818
Switz.	810,684	17,065	2,846	6,634	1,317	42	4,215	860	1,151	26,818	21,879	4,939
Austria	405,367	958	581	82	104	2	47	35	107	4,169	2,420	1,749
EEC, total	6,864,127	67,976	21,715	10,518	6,579	458	11,239	14,086	3,381	187,504	123,369	64,135
Germany	1,553,396	24,803	9,257	4,239	2,721	172	5,281	2,060	1,073	89,776	57,375	32,401
France	1,640,887	26,774	2,682	4,974	2,235	49	4,265	10,999	1,570	33,266	18,854	14,412
Italy	1,068,891	6,672	4,037	587	789	51	787	171	250	23,000	15,337	7,663
Neth.	1,416,141	5,889	3,262	434	654	117	501	464	457	25,558	19,311	6,247
Belg.-Lux.	1,184,719	3,746	2,418	257	196	49	366	179	281	15,691	12,380	3,311
Japan	643,097	14,980	7,791	1,162	3,209	1,146	1,398	145	129	369	—	369
Australia	863,356	9,782	7,709	380	949	24	436	132	152	47,379	46,565	814
N.Z.	219,948	622	622	—	—	—	—	—	—	10,388	10,388	—

TABLE D-2

Other Light Manufactures, except Food, 1965
($ thousand)

Imports of	Total, All Sources	From Less Developed Countries								From Other Low-Wage Countries		
		Total	Hong Kong	India	Other Far East	Mexico	Other Western Hemisphere	Other Africa	Other LDC's	Total	Japan	So. Europe excl. Italy
Developed countries, total	20,127,458	520,443	298,370	41,015	70,165	24,841	46,651	25,066	14,335	1,636,043	1,464,962	171,081
U.S.	3,281,766	269,426	164,349	13,249	43,992	20,724	18,763	3,831	4,518	1,061,221	1,007,405	53,816
Canada	2,629,486	15,918	12,105	668	1,518	565	765	67	230	86,288	82,208	4,080
EFTA, total	4,844,564	115,818	72,083	13,291	7,880	945	11,842	5,287	4,490	159,597	127,995	31,602
U.K.	1,612,108	83,015	60,510	6,578	4,720	817	5,579	2,282	2,529	77,820	59,357	18,463
Sweden	1,002,952	7,401	4,436	298	927	41	1,138	183	378	29,083	25,478	3,605
Denmark	516,448	3,414	1,824	559	221	15	403	114	278	11,845	9,729	2,116
Norway	382,363	1,552	1,164	81	92	5	103	47	60	7,133	6,249	884
Switz.	854,536	18,603	2,890	5,617	1,836	54	4,427	2,625	1,154	28,463	24,056	4,407
Austria	476,157	1,823	1,256	158	84	9	191	34	91	5,250	3,124	2,126
EEC, total	7,562,981	83,769	27,720	11,701	9,575	886	13,356	15,618	4,913	245,717	166,369	79,348
Germany	2,024,390	32,792	13,657	4,456	3,970	219	6,978	2,113	1,399	130,881	89,269	41,612
France	1,767,808	31,456	3,281	5,607	3,336	122	4,370	12,246	2,494	43,075	25,290	17,785
Italy	888,197	7,009	3,968	594	1,024	25	767	412	219	20,894	13,193	7,701
Neth.	1,558,156	7,822	4,358	503	974	161	630	599	597	31,255	23,295	7,960
Belg.-Lux.	1,324,430	4,685	2,455	540	271	357	611	247	204	19,611	15,322	4,289
Japan	566,767	20,865	10,611	1,367	5,646	1,589	1,450	111	91	761	—	761
Australia	998,616	12,487	9,945	540	1,368	50	364	137	83	69,373	68,039	1,334
N.Z.	243,278	2,151	1,557	195	186	79	111	13	10	13,085	12,947	138

233

TABLE D-2a

Footwear and Other Leather, Rubber and Plastic Goods, 1964

(\$ thousand)

Imports of	Total, All Sources	From Less Developed Countries								From Other Low-Wage Countries		
		Total	Hong Kong	Phillippines	Other Far East	Western Hemi-sphere	Israel	Morocco, Algeria, Tunisia	Other LDC's	Total	Japan	So. Europe excl. Italy
Developed countries, total	1,110,215	81,199	54,682	6,337	9,991	4,981	2,181	2,387	640	156,902	129,827	27,075
U.S.	284,024	34,833	18,833	6,307	5,572	2,936	1,054	70	61	110,229	102,271	7,958
Canada	77,382	2,843	1,777	–	828	223	3	2	10	8,113	7,406	707
EFTA, total	332,459	30,310	25,705	3	2,048	1,152	872	284	246	16,496	7,669	8,827
U.K.	129,027	26,226	22,786	1	1,624	979	578	87	171	10,456	5,338	5,118
Sweden	64,471	2,236	1,752	2	267	60	112	13	30	2,815	1,251	1,564
Denmark	23,692	423	263	–	52	18	17	61	12	542	116	426
Norway	24,385	459	380	–	61	2	8	2	6	358	223	135
Switz.	71,355	719	358	–	22	77	137	82	43	1,722	573	1,149
Austria	19,509	229	151	–	20	–	9	32	17	568	151	417
EEC, total	378,283	10,513	6,258	–	1,184	584	190	2,002	295	18,403	9,076	9,327
Germany	148,694	5,790	3,283	–	728	361	72	1,143	203	12,187	5,082	7,105
France	64,034	1,720	773	–	137	139	86	570	15	2,301	1,474	827
Italy	23,102	1,164	925	–	141	32	1	43	22	978	493	485
Neth.	76,756	1,057	731	–	113	15	11	142	45	1,924	1,418	506
Belg.-Lux.	65,684	767	541	–	64	26	19	97	20	990	597	393
Japan	10,443	724	504	–	132	44	4	24	16	108	–	108
Australia	23,322	1,713	1,346	24	226	24	49	–	44	3,530	3,397	133
N.Z.	4,284	246	246	–	–	–	–	–	–	–	–	–

TABLE D-2a

Footwear and Other Leather, Rubber and Plastic Goods, 1965

($ thousand)

Imports of	Total, All Sources	From Less Developed Countries								From Other Low-Wage Countries		
		Total	Hong Kong	Phillippines	Other Far East	Western Hemi-sphere	Israel	Morocco, Algeria, Tunisia	Other LDC's	Total	Japan	So. Europe excl. Italy
Developed countries, total	1,250,896	97,763	61,084	7,869	16,899	6,738	2,248	1,975	950	173,211	145,372	27,839
U.S.	337,173	54,183	29,781	7,811	11,295	3,839	1,271	34	152	124,356	113,492	10,864
Canada	85,143	3,512	2,001	2	1,189	307	–	9	4	8,515	7,494	1,021
EFTA, total	330,127	25,450	20,336	6	2,267	1,584	596	257	404	15,000	9,112	5,888
U.K.	105,280	20,586	17,203	–	1,493	1,389	308	75	118	9,120	6,252	2,868
Sweden	72,551	2,689	1,747	4	611	34	82	23	188	2,789	1,515	1,274
Denmark	28,748	569	361	–	69	19	35	51	34	630	256	374
Norway	25,346	309	239	–	44	9	9	2	6	388	252	136
Switz.	73,127	720	357	–	35	66	144	78	40	1,439	638	801
Austria	25,072	561	426	–	15	61	14	27	18	629	196	433
EEC, total	456,833	11,727	6,890	1	1,583	915	347	1,655	336	20,740	11,073	9,667
Germany	194,936	6,906	4,029	1	817	699	180	949	231	14,553	6,986	7,567
France	72,646	1,747	864	–	314	128	93	338	10	2,293	1,539	754
Italy	22,319	886	624	–	163	26	2	51	20	984	459	525
Neth.	88,130	1,276	815	–	185	19	26	176	55	1,871	1,388	483
Belg.-Lux.	78,800	904	557	–	103	39	45	140	20	1,037	700	337
Japan	10,577	661	336	1	219	66	4	17	18	138	–	138
Australia	25,833	1,871	1,464	45	285	19	23	–	35	4,259	4,010	249
N.Z.	5,208	342	274	–	61	3	3	–	1	198	188	10

TABLE D-2b

Glassware, China and Pottery, 1964

($ thousand)

Imports of	Total, All Sources	From Less Developed Countries								From Other Low-Wage Countries		
		Total	Hong Kong	Taiwan	Other Far East	Mexico	Brazil	Jamaica	Other LDC's	Total	Japan	So. Europe excl. Italy
Developed countries, total	393,024	3,897	1,472	162	340	1,440	4	219	260	70,057	63,580	6,477
U.S.	102,729	2,228	529	154	110	1,262	2	84	87	45,996	44,436	1,560
Canada	45,396	728	351	3	122	77	–	128	47	3,501	3,320	181
EFTA, total	79,104	322	217	–	28	21	–	1	55	5,726	3,981	1,745
U.K.	25,596	209	140	–	18	8	–	–	43	3,175	1,718	1,457
Sweden	12,803	17	8	–	5	–	–	–	4	1,104	1,053	51
Denmark	11,637	37	32	–	1	–	–	–	4	421	331	90
Norway	4,939	10	10	–	–	–	–	–	–	333	305	28
Switz.	17,393	41	21	–	5	7	–	–	8	456	393	63
Austria	6,732	1	–	–	–	1	–	–	–	226	175	51
EEC, total	141,857	349	195	1	19	67	2	–	65	9,451	6,559	2,892
Germany	31,464	92	59	–	5	18	1	–	9	3,448	1,846	1,602
France	27,818	100	48	–	10	11	–	–	31	1,138	652	486
Italy	31,525	88	49	–	4	25	–	–	10	2,278	1,747	531
Neth.	31,263	17	10	–	1	–	–	–	7	1,314	1,209	105
Belg.-Lux.	19,784	48	26	–	1	11	–	–	10	1,267	1,101	166
Japan	3,041	106	68	–	30	6	–	–	2	8	–	8
Australia	16,582	159	108	1	35	3	–	5	7	4,665	4,579	86
N.Z.	4,310	–	–	–	–	–	–	–	–	701	701	–

TABLE D-2b

Glassware, China and Pottery, 1965
(\$ thousand)

Imports of	Total, All Sources	From Less Developed Countries								From Other Low-Wage Countries		
		Total	Hong Kong	Taiwan	Other Far East	Mexico	Brazil	Jamaica	Other LDC's	Total	Japan	So. Europe excl. Italy
Developed countries, total	436,312	5,135	1,896	188	499	1,776	253	208	315	78,523	71,388	7,135
U.S.	111,689	3,137	768	154	138	1,628	238	83	128	51,024	49,330	1,694
Canada	49,540	791	406	13	131	79	4	119	39	3,918	3,641	277
EFTA, total	86,331	392	270	–	26	19	–	3	74	5,739	4,033	1,706
U.K.	24,511	245	191	–	17	4	–	2	31	3,069	1,675	1,394
Sweden	15,786	22	11	–	1	–	–	–	10	1,092	1,038	54
Denmark	13,291	40	31	–	1	3	–	–	5	480	411	69
Norway	5,679	12	11	–	1	–	–	–	–	411	376	35
Switz.	18,747	64	23	–	5	8	–	–	28	435	355	80
Austria	8,315	4	–	–	1	3	–	–	–	246	175	71
EEC, total	161,098	367	229	1	23	42	9	–	63	10,977	7,627	3,350
Germany	43,291	106	71	1	3	20	7	–	4	5,200	3,028	2,172
France	28,871	119	69	–	12	18	2	–	18	1,422	837	585
Italy	30,819	61	38	–	5	–	–	–	18	1,427	1,062	365
Neth.	36,527	30	20	–	–	1	–	–	9	1,596	1,513	83
Belg.-Lux.	21,588	47	29	–	3	1	–	–	14	1,331	1,186	145
Japan	3,086	184	57	13	111	2	–	–	1	10	–	10
Australia	19,342	233	145	3	70	4	–	–	10	5,844	5,757	87
N.Z.	5,224	20	20	–	–	–	–	–	–	1,006	998	8

TABLE D-2c

Furniture, 1964

($ thousand)

Imports of	Total, All Sources	From Less Developed Countries								From Other Low-Wage Countries		
		Total	Hong Kong	Taiwan	Other Far East	Mexico	Other Western Hemisphere	Egypt	Other LDC's	Total	Japan	So. Europe excl. Italy
Developed countries, total	332,485	9,051	5,548	405	871	1,360	204	388	275	31,239	6,424	24,815
U.S.	46,529	5,317	2,903	314	593	1,279	151	32	45	13,066	4,846	8,220
Canada	19,533	389	301	16	11	53	–	5	3	930	501	429
EFTA, total	91,280	1,216	879	3	135	13	27	94	65	6,735	310	6,425
U.K.	23,315	820	637	–	86	–	21	42	34	5,030	176	4,854
Sweden	13,539	105	66	1	9	–	5	14	10	209	90	119
Denmark	8,854	69	38	–	19	–	–	2	10	79	12	67
Norway	4,580	40	33	–	4	–	–	–	3	21	9	12
Switz.	31,381	143	81	2	9	11	1	31	8	1,097	19	1,078
Austria	9,608	36	22	–	8	–	–	2	4	293	1	292
EEC, total	170,332	1,265	718	3	92	10	28	254	160	10,004	316	9,688
Germany	39,911	620	447	–	21	–	–	124	28	5,612	20	5,592
France	55,716	227	96	3	25	4	–	–	99	2,204	158	2,046
Italy	8,249	181	115	–	27	4	19	4	12	777	20	757
Neth.	39,715	161	38	–	4	1	2	100	16	914	34	880
Belg.-Lux.	26,739	74	21	–	14	1	4	24	10	495	83	412
Japan	1,472	148	102	20	21	1	–	2	2	3	–	3
Australia	3,100	713	643	46	22	1	–	–	1	494	448	46
N.Z.	236	–	–	–	–	–	–	–	–	–	–	–

TABLE D-2c

Furniture, 1965

($ thousand)

Imports of	Total, All Sources	From Less Developed Countries								From Other Low-Wage Countries		
		Total	Hong Kong	Taiwan	Other Far East	Mexico	Other Western Hemisphere	Egypt	Other LDC's	Total	Japan	So. Europe excl. Italy
Developed countries, total	397,974	10,968	6,304	948	939	1,558	314	465	440	36,143	8,733	27,410
U.S.	59,895	6,836	3,849	690	541	1,475	222	39	20	15,940	6,515	9,425
Canada	22,137	627	379	130	25	74	8	2	9	932	476	456
EFTA, total	104,753	1,054	738	1	125	4	31	78	77	5,883	407	5,476
U.K.	23,519	617	504	—	49	3	15	15	31	3,957	185	3,772
Sweden	18,596	143	78	—	30	—	14	13	8	272	156	116
Denmark	11,753	86	41	—	31	—	—	5	9	106	15	91
Norway	4,781	48	41	—	4	—	—	—	3	39	20	19
Switz.	33,452	130	58	1	7	—	1	42	21	1,078	26	1,052
Austria	12,650	22	14	—	2	—	—	1	5	426	3	423
EEC, total	205,426	1,586	655	11	206	2	51	336	325	12,500	499	12,001
Germany	53,827	680	377	5	79	—	7	170	42	6,974	101	6,873
France	62,403	256	81	—	34	1	1	2	137	2,919	209	2,710
Italy	7,518	299	114	—	59	—	37	1	88	814	25	789
Neth.	51,415	243	30	3	22	—	2	150	36	1,274	63	1,211
Belg.-Lux.	30,261	102	51	2	12	—	3	12	22	516	100	416
Japan	1,330	133	84	27	13	—	—	2	7	8	—	8
Australia	4,163	701	579	85	28	1	—	6	2	851	809	42
N.Z.	265	19	18	—	1	—	—	—	—	24	24	0

TABLE D-2d

Books and Other Printed Matter, 1964
($ thousand)

Imports of	Total, All Sources	From Less Developed Countries								From Other Low-Wage Countries		
		Total	Hong Kong	India	Mexico	Other Western Hemisphere	Middle East	Other Africa	Other LDC's	Total	Japan	So. Europe excl. Italy
Developed countries, total	421,743	5,711	967	576	1,455	696	1,237	546	234	7,304	4,824	2,480
U.S.	51,917	3,230	187	127	1,423	575	752	102	64	3,262	2,393	869
Canada	79,930	81	26	31	8	1	13	–	2	328	262	66
EFTA, total	114,785	1,602	593	348	4	74	351	149	83	1,732	1,201	531
U.K.	47,940	1,542	586	334	2	71	335	140	74	1,279	1,005	274
Sweden	13,261	15	1	4	–	1	4	3	2	87	60	27
Denmark	6,513	3	1	–	–	–	1	–	1	78	58	20
Norway	5,264	1	–	7	–	–	1	–	1	14	7	7
Switz.	27,903	26	2	–	–	1	6	5	5	255	65	190
Austria	13,901	12	2	–	–	–	3	–	7	15	4	11
EEC, total	131,226	520	25	25	16	37	111	294	12	1,346	369	977
Germany	30,904	51	7	14	–	2	26	1	1	386	128	258
France	47,312	377	3	4	6	21	54	284	5	614	118	496
Italy	11,059	25	7	1	2	10	2	1	2	102	33	69
Neth.	16,080	26	4	5	–	2	6	5	4	123	66	57
Belg.-Lux.	25,870	39	3	–	7	1	21	2	5	119	24	95
Japan	8,197	122	68	5	2	4	2	–	41	8	–	8
Australia	22,832	156	65	37	–	3	5	–	46	451	424	27
N.Z.	12,854	–	–	–	–	–	–	–	–	172	172	–

TABLE D-2d

Books and Other Printed Matter, 1965
($ thousand)

Imports of	Total, All Sources	From Less Developed Countries								From Other Low-Wage Countries		
		Total	Hong Kong	India	Mexico	Other Western Hemisphere	Middle East	Other Africa	Other LDC's	Total	Japan	So. Europe excl. Italy
Developed countries, total	495,271	6,980	1,158	566	2,166	1,237	1,080	424	349	8,867	5,807	3,060
U.S.	58,489	4,241	103	162	2,029	1,062	676	181	28	3,538	2,314	1,224
Canada	93,487	104	50	25	9	5	13	–	2	410	338	72
EFTA, total	128,643	1,697	710	271	101	103	260	154	98	1,776	1,243	533
U.K.	51,248	1,632	693	263	99	94	244	150	89	1,322	1,029	293
Sweden	16,143	21	4	3	–	4	6	1	3	78	57	21
Denmark	8,079	4	1	–	–	–	1	–	2	94	66	28
Norway	7,126	5	5	–	–	–	–	–	–	20	14	6
Switz.	30,576	21	5	3	–	4	5	1	3	232	71	161
Austria	15,469	3	1	–	–	–	1	–	1	26	4	22
EEC, total	149,765	332	28	23	24	34	115	87	21	1,772	616	1,156
Germany	36,798	50	6	2	8	3	29	1	1	571	283	288
France	53,268	159	8	4	10	20	43	69	5	806	186	620
Italy	10,639	31	1	9	–	6	10	–	5	120	37	83
Neth.	19,160	54	8	7	1	4	16	12	6	151	80	71
Belg.-Lux.	29,899	30	4	–	3	1	15	3	4	123	29	94
Japan	16,855	163	61	16	1	4	3	–	78	8	–	8
Australia	36,615	320	157	62	–	1	8	–	92	1,139	1,076	63
N.Z.	11,414	108	45	5	–	25	3	–	30	219	218	1

TABLE D-2e

Games, Toys, Sporting Goods and Musical Instruments, 1964

(\$ thousand)

Imports of	Total, All Sources	From Less Developed Countries								From Other Low-Wage Countries		
		Total	Hong Kong	Pakistan	Taiwan	Other Far East	Mexico	Other Western Hemisphere	Other LDC's	Total	Japan	So. Europe excl. Italy
Developed countries, total	841,883	51,913	44,261	3,266	729	793	1,267	1,192	405	204,448	197,365	7,083
U.S.	266,417	18,734	15,480	431	563	220	1,135	855	50	133,118	130,894	2,224
Canada	61,600	2,901	2,786	44	43	4	16	5	3	11,613	11,362	251
EFTA, total	231,322	22,293	19,765	1,639	21	374	66	306	122	32,617	31,186	1,431
U.K.	102,957	19,888	17,874	1,212	19	315	58	301	109	24,017	23,589	428
Sweden	37,717	996	811	150	–	26	1	–	8	3,620	3,332	288
Denmark	19,287	522	399	100	–	17	1	1	4	1,110	1,056	54
Norway	13,388	342	284	51	–	6	–	–	1	1,013	905	108
Switz.	41,453	305	216	68	1	11	2	2	5	2,175	1,741	434
Austria	16,502	230	173	55	–	2	–	–	–	660	551	109
EEC, total	226,099	5,318	3,957	930	42	110	27	14	238	19,799	16,714	3,085
Germany	60,565	2,178	1,539	543	19	52	11	4	10	7,814	6,699	1,115
France	48,387	437	163	29	–	27	4	3	211	3,771	2,535	1,236
Italy	24,075	953	744	189	16	8	1	4	7	2,973	2,800	173
Neth.	59,417	1,141	1,008	86	16	18	7	–	6	3,075	2,642	433
Belg.-Lux.	33,650	603	498	79	6	9	5	–	6	2,149	2,029	120
Japan	26,986	353	293	–	31	16	9	2	2	25	–	25
Australia	22,327	2,111	1,782	216	24	72	4	9	4	5,750	5,695	55
N.Z.	7,116	194	194	–	–	–	–	–	–	1,503	1,503	–

Games, Toys, Sporting Goods and Musical Instruments, 1965

($ thousand)

Imports of	Total, All Sources	From Less Developed Countries								From Other Low-Wage Countries		
		Total	Hong Kong	Pakistan	Taiwan	Other Far East	Mexico	Other Western Hemisphere	Other LDC's	Total	Japan	So. Europe excl. Italy
Developed countries, total	1,018,806	66,774	57,022	3,328	1,130	1,222	1,786	1,825	461	287,639	276,593	11,046
U.S.	368,487	25,848	21,532	500	696	573	1,445	1,056	46	203,373	198,933	4,440
Canada	72,422	3,680	3,498	54	59	9	29	20	11	18,174	17,885	289
EFTA, total	241,364	24,546	21,641	1,460	32	393	200	630	190	26,630	24,908	1,722
U.K.	90,998	20,685	18,528	993	9	352	150	486	167	13,606	13,192	414
Sweden	47,175	1,877	1,562	249	–	18	29	9	10	6,015	5,678	337
Denmark	23,652	929	700	62	15	12	6	129	5	2,073	1,827	246
Norway	14,987	447	393	42	–	4	1	5	2	1,552	1,499	53
Switz.	44,789	373	278	73	3	3	10	1	5	2,701	2,148	553
Austria	19,760	226	179	39	3	4	–	–	–	678	561	117
EEC, total	271,764	7,622	5,845	1,046	232	103	77	114	205	29,392	24,926	4,466
Germany	80,681	3,225	2,485	539	111	35	39	7	9	13,103	11,573	1,530
France	49,297	537	235	97	3	15	5	12	170	5,197	3,523	1,674
Italy	25,357	1,269	1,025	187	13	23	3	8	10	3,646	3,272	374
Neth.	77,153	1,681	1,417	139	80	13	25	–	7	4,520	3,820	700
Belg.-Lux.	39,275	902	681	83	23	17	4	85	9	2,923	2,737	186
Japan	27,700	691	616	–	9	48	15	2	1	33	–	33
Australia	29,666	3,908	3,529	190	98	75	10	2	4	8,234	8,144	90
N.Z.	7,401	463	358	74	–	21	6	–	4	1,797	1,794	3

TABLE D-2f

Jewelry and Silverware, 1964

($ thousand)

Imports of	Total, All Sources	From Less Developed Countries								From Other Low-Wage Countries		
		Total	India	Hong Kong	Other Far East	Brazil	Colombia	Other Africa	Other LDC's	Total	Japan	So. Europe excl. Italy
Developed countries, total	235,389	46,442	17,356	8,580	4,908	6,587	4,007	1,375	3,629	44,760	43,717	1,043
U.S.	46,069	11,547	3,953	2,351	1,662	1,553	1,501	28	499	20,862	20,561	301
Canada	7,723	307	29	187	43	25	-	-	23	1,002	966	42
EFTA, total	87,652	13,191	6,227	1,725	759	871	1,992	392	1,225	7,304	7,015	289
U.K.	8,598	1,440	41	183	173	556	-	142	345	149	88	61
Sweden	7,461	69	49	10	4	8	-	-	7	1,224	1,171	53
Denmark	2,879	191	21	10	16	25	-	-	119	301	267	34
Norway	3,176	4	1	-	-	-	-	-	3	209	182	27
Switz.	59,527	11,380	6,046	1,527	569	278	1,992	250	718	4,946	4,868	78
Austria	6,012	105	66	1	1	1	-	-	36	471	437	34
EEC, total	77,307	14,256	6,778	731	1,102	3,558	464	903	720	15,412	15,022	390
Germany	47,957	7,811	3,036	346	765	2,816	282	266	300	10,083	9,921	162
France	14,334	5,771	3,589	141	285	671	182	634	269	2,671	2,517	154
Italy	4,085	260	89	14	40	52	-	1	64	1,663	1,632	31
Neth.	1,993	67	5	27	11	13	-	-	11	180	170	10
Belg.-Lux.	8,939	344	60	201	2	5	-	-	76	812	780	32
Japan	14,865	7,085	367	3,550	1,330	577	48	49	1,164	16	-	16
Australia	1,358	55	1	34	15	-	-	-	5	156	152	4
N.Z.	414	-	-	-	-	-	-	-	-	-	-	-

TABLE D-2f

Jewelry and Silverware, 1965

($ thousand)

Imports of	Total, All Sources	From Less Developed Countries								From Other Low-Wage Countries		
		Total	India	Hong Kong	Other Far East	Brazil	Colombia	Other Africa	Other LDC's	Total	Japan	So. Europe excl. Italy
Developed countries, total	294,753	59,776	20,847	10,380	7,279	7,714	5,755	3,854	3,947	53,638	52,277	1,361
U.S.	61,784	17,552	7,061	2,342	2,406	1,955	2,755	372	661	23,323	22,911	412
Canada	6,993	312	36	185	44	5	9	–	33	1,031	978	53
EFTA, total	101,788	14,766	5,651	1,385	1,358	793	2,383	2,240	956	9,736	9,386	350
U.K.	8,766	1,110	38	210	211	3	–	145	503	1,592	1,531	61
Sweden	8,112	74	46	4	4	4	–	–	16	1,387	1,300	87
Denmark	3,621	378	268	8	17	21	–	–	64	527	486	41
Norway	2,981	22	10	–	–	–	–	–	12	233	196	37
Switz.	72,442	13,040	5,189	1,158	1,123	764	2,381	2,090	335	5,318	5,247	71
Austria	5,865	134	100	3	2	1	–	2	26	676	625	51
EEC, total	102,752	17,141	7,608	1,037	1,636	4,366	607	1,202	685	19,186	18,685	501
Germany	66,575	9,546	2,963	677	1,184	3,387	375	471	489	12,817	12,578	239
France	16,221	6,683	4,299	193	382	810	228	638	133	3,757	3,618	139
Italy	3,655	309	123	8	21	32	–	84	41	1,230	1,185	45
Neth.	4,541	258	9	72	43	128	–	–	6	210	189	21
Belg.-Lux.	11,760	340	212	85	6	8	4	9	16	1,171	1,115	56
Japan	19,135	9,900	475	5,392	1,806	592	1	35	1,599	28	–	28
Australia	1,629	72	1	35	23	–	–	–	12	216	201	15
N.Z.	672	24	11	4	6	–	–	2	1	117	117	–

245

TABLE D-2g

Miscellaneous Manufactures including Costume Jewelry, Stationery and Notions, 1964
($ thousand)

Imports of	Total, All Sources	From Less Developed Countries								From Other Low-Wage Countries		
		Total	Hong Kong	Taiwan	Other Far East	Mexico	Other Western Hemi-sphere	Other Africa	Other LDC's	Total	Japan	So. Europe excl. Italy
Developed countries, total	892,434	124,364	72,852	6,464	10,595	4,367	13,515	14,395	2,176	94,542	73,756	20,786
U.S.	209,293	69,630	51,426	2,301	3,427	4,180	5,574	2,441	281	53,048	46,299	6,749
Canada	62,203	3,401	2,965	14	77	65	237	6	37	4,424	4,273	151
EFTA, total	233,074	19,895	9,925	935	3,213	59	3,396	1,746	621	13,790	9,294	4,496
U.K.	90,099	15,160	9,063	516	2,367	35	1,846	1,076	257	6,299	3,992	2,307
Sweden	39,885	485	184	7	81	12	65	108	28	2,335	1,715	620
Denmark	27,122	454	311	–	63	2	30	24	24	1,084	724	360
Norway	14,840	207	165	–	15	–	7	14	6	561	445	116
Switz.	45,166	3,431	124	409	669	5	1,407	514	303	3,020	2,264	756
Austria	15,925	129	58	1	17	1	27	3	22	429	113	316
EEC, total	316,637	23,065	3,535	1,906	2,886	31	3,527	10,021	1,159	18,764	9,632	9,132
Germany	82,202	3,382	909	341	477	11	960	525	159	7,308	4,119	3,189
France	87,228	15,994	942	1,058	1,754	4	2,243	9,109	884	5,257	1,776	3,481
Italy	35,038	1,207	487	317	178	4	117	82	22	2,309	848	1,461
Neth.	59,871	1,609	490	182	414	2	180	266	75	2,247	1,731	516
Belg.-Lux.	52,277	853	693	7	66	4	22	29	32	1,610	1,143	467
Japan	36,775	5,428	2,708	1,220	844	11	519	69	57	76	–	76
Australia	29,888	2,909	2,262	76	161	8	270	100	32	4,280	4,123	157
N.Z.	4,523	–	–	–	–	–	–	–	–	107	107	–

TABLE D-2g

Miscellaneous Manufactures including Costume Jewelry, Stationery and Notions, 1965

($ thousand)

Imports of	Total, All Sources	From Less Developed Countries								From Other Low-Wage Countries		
		Total	Hong Kong	Taiwan	Other Far East	Mexico	Other Western Hemisphere	Other Africa	Other LDC's	Total	Japan	So. Europe excl. Italy
Developed countries, total	1,025,836	151,048	83,264	8,263	17,761	7,687	13,885	16,492	3,696	115,607	91,341	24,266
U.S.	242,621	90,288	61,838	3,852	8,066	7,309	6,012	2,882	329	61,065	51,986	9,079
Canada	65,521	3,542	3,101	32	79	94	194	17	25	4,620	4,419	201
EFTA, total	257,224	17,902	8,041	601	3,344	200	3,145	1,774	797	16,967	12,178	4,789
U.K.	91,193	13,502	7,204	296	2,505	173	1,992	1,119	213	7,957	5,362	2,595
Sweden	49,230	545	231	15	85	8	42	136	28	2,522	1,921	601
Denmark	30,793	416	215	—	86	4	48	48	15	1,941	1,427	514
Norway	16,112	258	155	1	31	2	4	44	21	644	503	141
Switz.	50,479	2,976	132	281	606	8	1,021	424	504	3,416	2,799	617
Austria	19,413	193	101	4	34	2	35	1	16	482	163	319
EEC, total	371,567	27,998	4,343	1,474	4,368	49	3,597	11,648	2,519	27,499	17,653	9,846
Germany	105,544	4,525	1,852	379	684	11	962	417	220	12,237	8,895	3,342
France	106,454	19,665	982	579	2,807	28	2,389	10,795	2,085	8,141	3,983	4,158
Italy	34,456	1,207	347	387	277	3	86	64	43	2,146	844	1,302
Neth.	66,219	1,858	612	120	508	4	139	339	136	2,997	2,351	646
Belg.-Lux.	58,892	741	549	8	94	2	19	32	37	1,974	1,578	396
Japan	47,486	7,689	3,260	1,984	1,728	15	638	54	10	71	—	71
Australia	32,631	3,245	2,397	314	166	19	226	109	14	4,810	4,539	271
N.Z.	8,784	375	281	4	12	—	70	6	2	571	565	6

TABLE D-2h

Optical Goods, Cameras, Watches and Instruments, 1964

($ thousand)

Imports of	Total, All Sources	From Less Developed Countries								From Other Low-Wage Countries		
		Total	Hong Kong	Pakistan	Other Far East	Western Hemisphere	Israel	Other Africa	Other LDC's	Total	Japan	So. Europe excl. Italy
Developed countries, total	741,046	6,111	4,525	613	352	304	27	178	112	81,365	80,473	892
U.S.	166,792	1,657	1,333	171	38	108	1	–	6	41,391	41,248	143
Canada	81,535	233	160	36	2	31	2	–	2	4,846	4,832	14
EFTA, total	198,160	2,679	1,945	206	285	53	11	93	86	15,982	15,690	292
U.K.	74,453	2,282	1,574	196	275	48	10	93	86	6,937	6,744	193
Sweden	38,413	99	95	–	3	1	–	–	1	3,991	3,976	15
Denmark	20,966	43	30	6	5	1	–	–	1	1,590	1,560	30
Norway	11,836	26	24	1	–	–	–	–	1	861	839	22
Switz.	35,574	188	184	–	–	–	–	–	4	2,164	2,158	6
Austria	16,893	27	27	–	–	–	–	–	–	413	394	19
EEC, total	236,979	877	570	89	8	97	10	81	22	14,024	13,633	391
Germany	69,168	351	190	69	3	18	9	52	10	6,192	5,966	226
France	64,694	90	14	2	1	49	–	23	1	2,143	2,088	55
Italy	45,464	190	179	3	–	1	1	–	6	2,045	1,992	53
Neth.	30,610	171	126	8	7	26	–	–	4	2,451	2,435	16
Belg.-Lux.	27,029	63	52	5	–	1	–	2	3	1,174	1,141	33
Japan	23,043	166	152	6	2	3	–	–	3	3	–	3
Australia	27,047	480	348	103	15	–	1	–	13	4,233	4,193	40
N.Z.	7,443	–	–	–	–	–	–	–	–	860	860	–

TABLE D-2h

Optical Goods, Cameras, Watches and Instruments, 1965

(\$ thousand)

Imports of	Total, All Sources	From Less Developed Countries								From Other Low-Wage Countries		
		Total	Hong Kong	Pakistan	Other Far East	Western Hemisphere	Israel	Other Africa	Other LDC's	Total	Japan	So. Europe excl. Italy
Developed countries, total	859,767	8,805	6,990	708	377	314	112	207	97	106,954	105,539	1,415
U.S.	200,909	3,019	2,633	207	72	92	10	2	3	52,059	51,676	383
Canada	99,189	504	470	16	7	9	2	–	–	6,774	6,725	49
EFTA, total	227,669	3,052	2,271	343	179	52	91	61	55	22,291	21,941	350
U.K.	85,547	2,344	1,613	318	163	51	90	57	52	10,110	9,926	184
Sweden	45,158	142	131	3	8	–	–	–	–	5,291	5,242	49
Denmark	24,766	109	89	12	6	–	–	1	1	2,165	2,126	39
Norway	13,660	49	42	6	1	–	–	–	–	1,147	1,117	30
Switz.	39,909	344	339	2	–	–	–	1	2	2,857	2,832	25
Austria	18,625	54	53	–	1	–	–	–	–	716	695	21
EEC, total	274,774	1,352	882	78	64	148	8	143	36	19,270	18,687	583
Germany	90,928	707	434	55	50	33	8	105	22	9,893	9,607	286
France	74,778	144	27	–	1	102	–	12	2	2,888	2,778	110
Italy	44,922	288	251	9	3	8	–	11	6	2,006	1,912	94
Neth.	32,859	142	116	7	3	1	–	11	4	2,708	2,677	31
Belg.-Lux.	31,285	70	53	6	7	–	–	2	2	1,772	1,712	60
Japan	18,653	148	127	–	11	9	–	–	1	14	–	14
Australia	29,954	603	516	48	38	–	–	–	1	5,319	5,289	30
N.Z.	8,617	111	90	13	6	1	–	–	1	1,222	1,220	2

TABLE D-2i

Cutlery, Tools, Hardware and Other Metal Products, 1964
(\$ thousand)

Imports of	Total, All Sources	From Less Developed Countries								From Other Low-Wage Countries			
		Total	Hong Kong	India	Other Far East	Mexico	Israel	Other Middle East	Other LDC's	Total	Japan	So. Europe excl. Italy	Italy
Developed countries, total	1,609,479	23,865	9,616	4,030	1,307	4,650	1,169	·893	2,200	156,551	142,158	14,393	—
U.S.	289,097	13,396	4,106	1,606	760	4,595	958	113	1,258	112,874	107,535	5,339	—
Canada	193,741	564	365	26	74	23	59	–	17	10,335	9,771	564	—
EFTA, total	385,671	6,426	3,738	1,574	307	8	76	331	392	9,341	7,985	1,356	—
U.K.	97,612	5,404	3,145	1,331	273	6	42	236	371	4,529	4,028	501	—
Sweden	72,898	415	291	65	4	–	–	39	16	2,513	2,241	272	—
Denmark	54,185	256	124	100	24	–	–	4	4	780	585	195	—
Norway	41,734	78	57	17	1	–	–	1	2	541	443	98	—
Switz.	80,601	236	104	48	8	1	31	36	8	781	644	137	—
Austria	38,621	28	6	5	4	–	–	11	2	166	30	136	—
EEC, total	642,372	2,770	997	764	111	19	67	446	366	18,145	11,062	7,083	—
Germany	127,116	919	288	212	76	3	10	262	68	7,265	4,663	2,602	—
France	163,901	578	244	121	13	3	9	6	182	2,678	1,540	1,138	—
Italy	89,547	557	132	234	13	8	18	84	68	2,558	1,484	1,074	—
Neth.	148,635	453	219	90	5	–	22	81	36	4,237	2,284	1,953	—
Belg.-Lux.	113,161	255	109	102	8	4	4	13	15	1,382	1,078	304	—
Japan	21,827	335	124	1	34	–	–	1	175	3	–	3	—
Australia	47,337	352	273	48	27	–	–	–	4	4,657	4,626	31	—
N.Z.	29,414	–	–	–	–	–	–	–	–	1,163	1,163	–	—

TABLE D-2i

Cutlery, Tools, Hardware and Other Metal Products, 1965

($ thousand)

Imports of	Total, All Sources	From Less Developed Countries								From Other Low-Wage Countries		
		Total	Hong Kong	India	Other Far East	Mexico	Israel	Other Middle East	Other LDC's	Total	Japan	So. Europe excl. Italy
Developed countries, total	1,806,654	26,187	11,522	5,346	2,401	2,885	1,379	808	1,846	199,242	182,345	16,897
U.S.	340,403	14,064	5,024	2,609	1,691	2,761	1,040	108	831	143,933	137,448	6,485
Canada	218,330	925	485	53	192	18	123	1	53	13,215	12,654	561
EFTA, total	435,119	6,677	3,914	1,526	248	16	152	353	468	10,476	8,703	1,773
U.K.	111,766	5,605	3,395	1,254	181	13	107	282	373	5,152	4,506	646
Sweden	84,935	303	116	74	17	—	3	18	75	2,463	2,186	277
Denmark	61,825	280	92	143	30	—	1	10	4	1,012	788	224
Norway	46,137	114	94	13	5	—	—	1	1	689	450	239
Switz.	84,652	315	200	29	10	2	39	26	9	863	716	147
Austria	45,802	51	15	11	5	—	—	14	6	293	56	237
EEC, total	703,684	3,641	1,552	1,042	187	13	56	346	445	22,822	14,839	7,983
Germany	162,547	1,372	421	411	77	4	19	257	183	11,008	7,231	3,777
France	164,249	846	550	169	12	1	6	11	97	3,391	2,338	1,053
Italy	75,182	402	76	143	69	1	2	17	94	2,004	817	1,187
Neth.	170,444	712	427	163	15	2	24	38	43	4,756	3,112	1,646
Belg.-Lux.	131,260	301	76	154	14	3	4	22	28	1,659	1,340	319
Japan	22,914	227	165	2	23	3	—	—	34	4	—	4
Australia	55,330	366	274	35	41	—	4	—	12	7,093	7,021	72
N.Z.	30,870	275	106	76	19	70	1	—	3	1,693	1,677	16

TABLE D-2j

Electrical Apparatus and Appliances, 1964[a]

($ thousand)

Imports of	Total, All Sources	From Less Developed Countries								From Other Low-Wage Countries		
		Total	Hong Kong	Taiwan	Other Far East	Mexico	Israel	Other Africa	Other LDC's	Total	Japan	So. Europe excl. Italy
Developed countries, total	3,803,017	48,606	38,588	1,173	5,647	850	431	450	1,467	363,581	347,979	15,602
U.S.	510,888	21,552	16,730	1,147	2,732	757	29	27	130	258,893	254,552	4,341
Canada	340,470	1,412	1,277	–	43	7	26	24	35	17,105	16,856	249
EFTA, total	961,653	18,803	15,089	6	2,187	63	311	354	793	30,588	27,060	3,528
U.K.	312,794	17,450	13,890	6	2,114	57	270	352	761	14,575	11,937	2,638
Sweden	210,803	429	386	–	38	–	–	–	5	3,854	3,742	112
Denmark	113,278	285	263	–	20	–	–	–	2	1,335	1,296	39
Norway	92,760	173	163	–	7	–	–	–	3	1,134	1,063	71
Switz.	146,478	299	226	–	9	3	37	–	24	8,858	8,435	423
Austria	85,506	144	140	–	1	–	–	–	3	779	551	228
EEC, total	1,697,827	5,670	4,465	11	586	12	59	38	499	41,877	34,531	7,346
Germany	322,035	2,651	2,102	10	420	4	7	3	105	21,083	17,476	3,607
France	304,208	373	235	–	12	1	27	17	81	4,838	4,015	823
Italy	302,879	1,522	1,369	–	39	1	4	–	109	3,467	2,434	1,033
Neth.	522,325	727	495	–	85	3	17	1	126	7,618	6,530	1,088
Belg.-Lux.	246,372	393	256	1	26	–	2	14	94	4,836	4,056	780
Japan	92,057	190	161	4	17	5	–	–	3	48	–	48
Australia	140,388	778	657	1	80	–	–	–	40	12,196	12,123	69
N.Z.	59,711	182	182	–	–	–	–	–	–	2,830	2,830	–

[a] Adjusted; see text of this appendix.

TABLE D-2j

Electrical Apparatus and Appliances, 1965ᵃ

($ thousand)

Imports of	Total, All Sources	From Less Developed Countries								From Other Low-Wage Countries		
		Total	Hong Kong	Taiwan	Other Far East	Mexico	Israel	Other Africa	Other LDC's	Total	Japan	So. Europe excl. Italy
Developed countries, total	4,303,544	73,355	57,167	4,944	7,322	1,697	652	404	1,169	488,908	467,731	21,177
U.S.	703,465	46,333	35,952	4,518	4,077	1,240	108	194	244	358,129	351,335	6,794
Canada	400,273	1,687	1,496	46	29	38	12	7	59	22,958	22,455	503
EFTA, total	1,060,578	15,937	12,453	29	2,365	65	441	160	424	34,494	30,254	4,240
U.K.	330,304	13,843	10,706	3	2,272	63	238	158	403	16,298	12,960	3,338
Sweden	243,669	587	543	4	33	—	4	—	3	5,226	5,065	161
Denmark	123,425	452	263	2	25	—	158	1	3	1,847	1,749	98
Norway	104,786	193	174	3	3	—	7	—	6	1,544	1,489	55
Switz.	160,023	384	315	12	21	1	31	—	4	8,836	8,479	357
Austria	98,369	469	449	3	11	—	1	—	5	736	509	227
EEC, total	1,832,002	7,875	6,000	256	725	350	89	45	410	53,389	44,104	9,285
Germany	423,750	4,085	3,242	207	495	5	16	—	120	29,503	25,667	3,836
France	321,402	349	230	—	35	3	20	27	34	5,420	4,257	1,163
Italy	265,845	1,687	1,466	44	41	—	29	7	100	4,012	2,704	1,308
Neth.	559,168	975	709	4	103	9	19	12	119	9,812	7,401	2,411
Belg.-Lux.	261,835	777	352	—	51	332	3	5	34	4,639	4,074	565
Japan	83,999	548	407	76	36	—	—	—	29	255	—	255
Australia	166,412	704	602	16	80	2	—	1	3	15,471	15,372	99
N.Z.	56,817	265	255	—	10	—	—	—	—	4,208	4,208	—

ᵃAdjusted; see text of this appendix.

253

TABLE D-2k

Nonelectrical Machinery and Equipment, 1964[a]

($ thousand)

Imports of	Total, All Sources	From Less Developed Countries								From Other Low-Wage Countries		
		Total	India	Hong Kong	Argentina	Brazil	Other Western Hemisphere	Israel	Other LDC's	Total	Japan	So. Europe excl. Italy	Italy
Developed countries, total	7,435,719	12,904	1,524	1,133	3,285	1,009	4,071	762	1,120	53,555	33,572	19,983
U.S.	602,889	4,646	59	375	141	485	3,265	239	82	12,784	11,329	1,455
Canada	1,287,333	215	10	18	20	37	91	24	15	2,657	2,314	343
EFTA, total	1,677,073	3,966	815	206	1,309	139	466	267	764	7,677	3,581	4,096
U.K.	590,204	2,952	730	156	515	111	457	239	744	4,499	2,014	2,485
Sweden	351,247	429	17	28	363	15	2	–	4	960	584	376
Denmark	176,122	154	–	1	136	–	–	4	13	387	135	252
Norway	129,445	98	–	8	75	–	6	–	9	279	85	194
Switz.	253,853	297	64	3	201	6	–	18	5	1,344	719	625
Austria	176,158	17	–	1	10	5	1	–	–	149	13	136
EEC, total	2,845,208	3,373	363	264	1,711	338	232	222	243	20,279	6,455	13,824
Germany	593,380	958	141	87	436	154	47	35	58	8,398	1,455	6,943
France	763,255	1,104	136	23	772	15	1	85	72	5,651	1,981	3,670
Italy	493,868	525	62	16	288	45	43	14	57	3,850	1,854	1,996
Neth.	429,476	460	24	114	112	7	110	41	52	1,475	792	683
Belg.-Lux.	565,214	307	–	18	101	117	17	38	16	857	348	509
Japan	404,391	323	240	61	9	–	–	–	13	71	–	71
Australia	529,175	356	26	191	84	–	12	–	43	6,971	6,805	166
N.Z.	89,643	–	–	–	–	–	–	–	–	3,052	3,052	–

aAdjusted; see text of this appendix.

TABLE D-2k

Nonelectrical Machinery and Equipment, 1965[a]

($ thousand)

Imports of	Total, All Sources	From Less Developed Countries								From Other Low-Wage Countries		
		Total	India	Hong Kong	Argentina	Brazil	Other Western Hemisphere	Israel	Other LDC's	Total	Japan	So. Europe excl. Italy
Developed countries, total	8,237,635	13,858	1,593	1,577	4,466	1,994	2,022	1,111	1,095	87,302	57,832	29,470
U.S.	796,847	3,917	78	521	1,214	681	941	452	30	24,472	21,462	3,010
Canada	1,516,446	226	9	30	114	14	32	20	7	5,731	5,138	593
EFTA, total	1,870,966	4,415	612	320	1,399	260	705	418	701	10,597	5,825	4,772
U.K.	688,972	2,841	536	259	185	128	682	365	686	5,628	2,735	2,893
Sweden	401,591	994	18	5	882	78	3	6	2	1,940	1,317	623
Denmark	186,489	147	–	18	117	4	1	3	4	960	573	387
Norway	140,763	91	3	6	60	6	12	–	4	455	327	128
Switz.	246,335	230	46	21	114	3	2	42	2	1,277	740	537
Austria	206,812	100	7	9	39	37	5	–	3	332	130	202
EEC, total	3,033,292	4,168	560	255	1,681	992	263	217	200	28,160	7,654	20,506
Germany	765,513	1,590	316	63	395	624	66	61	65	15,022	3,320	11,702
France	818,215	945	160	37	433	204	9	65	37	6,831	2,016	4,815
Italy	367,480	567	32	13	317	91	46	16	52	2,499	873	1,626
Neth.	452,533	589	39	126	140	71	121	63	29	1,348	696	652
Belg.-Lux.	629,569	467	11	14	394	–	21	10	17	2,457	748	1,709
Japan	315,028	516	214	102	–	–	75	–	125	186	–	186
Australia	597,036	459	89	242	45	46	6	3	28	16,126	15,817	311
N.Z.	108,002	145	27	104	10	–	–	–	4	2,021	1,933	88

[a]Adjusted; see text of this appendix.

TABLE D-3

Labor-Intensive Food Manufactures, 1964

($ thousand)

Imports of	Total, All Sources	From Less Developed Countries								From Other Low-Wage Countries		
		Total	Peru	Mexico	Other Western Hemisphere	Taiwan	Other Far East	Morocco Tunisia Algeria	Other LDC's	Total	Japan	So. Europe excl. Italy
Developed countries, total	1,855,945	469,663	157,873	22,438	71,294	36,847	69,153	48,014	64,044	381,523	193,864	187,659
U.S.	280,532	115,903	35,674	19,283	16,850	12,835	24,153	537	6,571	75,951	59,879	16,072
Canada	115,063	12,926	589	1,935	5,212	547	2,918	167	1,558	7,629	4,321	3,308
EFTA, total	692,506	80,511	21,996	218	18,597	2,309	13,184	2,121	22,086	154,921	83,063	71,858
U.K.	496,580	56,457	12,348	84	14,516	614	10,848	673	17,374	128,036	78,254	49,782
Sweden	63,216	5,404	2,464	11	244	560	579	354	1,192	4,821	1,221	3,600
Denmark	32,161	4,998	2,254	32	1,174	196	505	129	708	3,474	442	3,032
Norway	30,275	1,450	796	41	89	6	36	24	458	2,692	264	2,428
Switz.	47,272	7,046	2,306	20	1,018	849	1,178	386	1,289	9,464	2,429	7,035
Austria	22,978	5,132	1,820	—	1,566	78	32	547	1,089	6,407	440	5,967
EEC, total	674,191	226,821	88,366	715	28,824	15,734	15,944	45,119	32,119	134,093	39,341	94,752
Germany	305,276	93,046	39,593	551	10,935	14,107	12,266	3,944	11,650	64,310	20,663	43,647
France	129,631	68,220	7,691	14	7,339	32	465	37,308	15,371	23,981	6,403	17,578
Italy	52,516	17,566	9,951	58	3,041	56	105	2,524	1,831	15,445	567	14,878
Neth.	101,935	35,463	25,416	70	4,742	847	1,379	424	2,585	15,804	6,310	9,494
Belg.-Lux.	84,818	12,513	5,711	19	2,758	691	1,724	907	703	14,535	5,392	9,143
Japan	60,095	30,190	11,212	258	1,419	5,363	11,620	44	274	523	—	523
Australia	23,393	1,878	30	17	381	49	585	12	804	7,675	6,548	1,127
N.Z.	10,142	1,415	—	—	—	—	740	—	675	698	698	—

TABLE D-3

Labor-Intensive Food Manufactures, 1965

(\$ thousand)

Imports of	Total, All Sources	From Less Developed Countries								From Other Low-Wage Countries		
		Total	Peru	Mexico	Other Western Hemisphere	Taiwan	Other Far East	Morocco Tunisia Algeria	Other LDC's	Total	Japan	So. Europe excl. Italy
Developed countries, total	2,041,492	492,428	156,884	23,904	71,986	55,921	76,161	44,119	63,453	416,343	196,983	219,360
U.S.	268,276	112,434	24,184	19,378	17,915	17,831	26,497	557	6,072	72,032	54,744	17,288
Canada	120,488	11,023	377	2,585	2,698	639	3,039	52	1,633	9,584	5,035	4,549
EFTA, total	729,569	86,066	23,568	685	17,198	2,841	15,361	1,907	24,506	161,908	80,176	81,732
U.K.	510,666	59,841	11,072	499	13,966	625	13,086	584	20,009	132,180	74,804	57,376
Sweden	74,996	5,650	2,192	10	532	293	790	403	1,430	5,245	1,445	3,800
Denmark	39,386	5,085	2,799	5	858	281	347	111	684	3,596	578	3,018
Norway	23,596	1,809	1,031	20	91	18	22	27	600	3,062	227	2,835
Switz.	52,355	7,790	2,946	68	918	1,459	1,034	256	1,109	10,312	2,571	7,741
Austria	28,568	5,880	3,525	80	833	164	81	523	674	7,509	549	6,960
EEC, total	807,511	244,705	100,531	1,033	32,077	26,212	13,488	41,546	29,818	161,932	47,465	114,467
Germany	388,563	113,163	50,607	822	13,334	24,682	10,360	3,896	9,462	81,010	24,034	56,976
France	137,865	67,974	10,220	43	8,413	41	991	33,502	14,764	24,981	7,418	17,563
Italy	57,583	18,565	10,559	108	2,255	23	261	2,930	2,429	18,126	596	17,530
Neth.	126,407	33,813	23,610	32	4,956	880	1,374	468	2,493	21,517	9,679	11,838
Belg.-Lux.	97,091	11,183	5,533	26	3,119	585	501	749	670	16,295	5,736	10,559
Japan	74,259	35,098	8,222	209	1,566	8,250	16,117	28	706	249	—	249
Australia	30,197	1,860	—	10	476	136	716	25	497	9,808	8,817	991
N.Z.	11,188	1,230	—	1	56	9	943	—	221	824	743	81

TABLE D-3a

Canned and Preserved Seafood, Fish Meal and Fish Oils, 1964

(\$ thousand)

Imports of	Total, All Sources	From Less Developed Countries								From Other Low-Wage Countries		
		Total	Peru	Chile	Other Western Hemisphere	India	Morocco, Algeria Tunisia	Other Africa Excl. MoAlTu	Other LDC's	Total	Japan	So. Europe excl. Italy
Developed countries, total	766,061	237,491	157,752	18,588	18,456	2,260	20,916	12,285	7,234	213,544	156,258	57,286
U.S.	143,355	54,955	35,673	1,578	11,671	1,780	297	939	3,017	52,405	43,870	8,535
Canada	9,869	977	589	79	29	124	11	—	145	3,633	3,060	573
EFTA, total	291,118	29,789	21,919	3,812	1,170	216	685	759	1,228	84,612	69,812	14,800
U.K.	206,276	15,430	12,343	2,044	230	140	23	42	608	72,923	66,490	6,433
Sweden	25,514	2,814	2,463	86	26	7	73	—	159	1,191	513	678
Denmark	13,391	3,179	2,229	86	733	61	—	—	70	519	56	463
Norway	17,636	811	796	2	4	—	2	—	7	313	198	115
Switz.	16,706	3,243	2,262	306	9	5	185	98	378	6,214	2,135	4,079
Austria	11,586	4,304	1,820	1,285	169	—	400	619	11	3,447	417	3,030
EEC, total	277,364	138,689	88,324	13,066	4,332	30	19,919	10,544	2,474	65,325	32,399	32,926
Germany	104,643	51,903	39,560	4,709	855	2	3,136	2,930	711	27,979	15,203	12,776
France	61,012	30,785	7,691	1,226	686	3	14,013	6,307	859	12,956	6,365	6,591
Italy	31,911	16,483	9,945	376	2,631	22	2,006	849	654	8,978	552	8,426
Neth.	47,371	30,553	25,416	4,211	136	—	210	421	159	6,085	5,150	935
Belg.-Lux.	32,421	8,960	5,708	2,541	27	1	550	35	98	9,321	5,126	4,195
Japan	25,869	12,808	11,212	51	1,215	—	—	—	330	56	—	56
Australia	15,549	269	30	—	35	107	—	42	55	6,803	6,413	390
N.Z.	2,930	—	—	—	—	—	—	—	—	698	698	—

TABLE D-3a

Canned and Preserved Seafood, Fish Meal and Fish Oils, 1965

($ thousand)

Imports of	Total, All Sources	From Less Developed Countries								From Other Low-Wage Countries			
		Total	Peru	Chile	Other Western Hemisphere	India	Morocco, Algeria, Tunisia	Other Africa Excl. MoAlTu	Other LDC's	Total	Japan	So. Europe excl. Italy	Italy
Developed countries, total	829,926	238,066	156,623	16,305	19,891	3,433	20,924	10,979	9,911	220,168	155,304	64,864	
U.S.	124,414	44,617	24,175	992	12,674	2,109	377	1,068	3,222	45,160	37,103	8,057	
Canada	12,890	654	377	46	28	20	5	—	178	4,482	3,679	803	
EFTA, total	309,205	29,845	23,481	2,302	916	625	565	363	1,593	83,295	67,362	15,933	
U.K.	217,441	13,805	11,072	1,286	52	431	11	19	934	70,644	63,817	6,827	
Sweden	32,510	2,918	2,190	321	27	77	77	—	226	1,204	491	713	
Denmark	18,383	3,643	2,751	28	683	103	1	4	73	615	100	515	
Norway	7,978	1,050	1,031	1	9	—	3	—	6	395	137	258	
Switz.	19,422	3,618	2,910	180	3	12	101	66	346	6,574	2,293	4,281	
Austria	13,469	4,802	3,525	484	142	—	371	272	8	3,858	522	3,336	
EEC, total	325,211	150,258	100,367	12,931	4,799	527	19,964	9,363	2,307	77,271	37,896	39,375	
Germany	125,232	62,570	50,464	4,480	1,724	35	2,984	1,945	938	32,523	15,897	16,626	
France	67,787	33,118	10,220	901	1,169	437	13,999	5,705	687	13,446	7,369	6,077	
Italy	36,047	16,983	10,558	578	1,564	23	2,385	1,457	418	11,214	593	10,621	
Neth.	56,851	28,741	23,609	4,252	239	23	202	193	223	9,611	8,543	1,068	
Belg.-Lux.	39,292	8,839	5,514	2,719	103	7	392	63	41	10,474	5,493	4,981	
Japan	34,590	12,236	8,222	31	1,380	3	—	150	2,450	50	—	50	
Australia	20,728	443	—	—	93	147	11	35	157	9,177	8,552	625	
N.Z.	2,885	5	—	—	1	—	—	—	4	728	709	19	

259

TABLE D-3b

Preserved and Prepared Fruit and Vegetables, 1964

($ thousand)

Imports of	Total, All Sources	From Less Developed Countries								From Other Low-Wage Countries		
		Total	Taiwan	Philip- pines	Other Far East	Mexico	Israel	Morocco, Algeria, Tunisia	Other LDC's	Total	Japan	So. Europe excl. Italy
Developed countries, total	900,359	219,429	35,872	12,390	47,321	17,617	18,602	26,819	60,855	163,748	35,302	128,446
U.S.	107,624	57,992	12,748	7,686	11,782	14,684	91	218	10,783	20,343	14,266	6,077
Canada	83,841	10,939	540	152	2,130	1,907	649	154	5,407	3,861	1,157	2,704
EFTA, total	352,736	45,955	2,232	2,058	9,390	142	12,574	1,415	18,160	69,868	12,929	56,939
U.K.	269,929	37,028	579	1,122	8,309	39	10,136	640	16,203	54,974	11,704	43,270
Sweden	25,938	2,483	534	418	40	11	979	277	224	3,577	661	2,916
Denmark	12,607	1,737	183	160	250	32	337	129	646	2,747	178	2,569
Norway	9,446	607	6	7	17	41	161	22	353	2,369	66	2,303
Switz.	25,758	3,286	848	349	744	1	574	198	572	3,228	291	2,937
Austria	9,051	807	78	–	30	14	379	144	162	2,960	23	2,937
EEC, total	314,701	85,507	15,604	1,926	12,712	666	5,273	24,969	24,368	68,373	6,831	61,542
Germany	177,643	40,776	14,036	1,330	10,222	527	3,921	807	9,933	36,131	5,386	30,745
France	58,986	35,668	5	–	160	3	249	23,089	12,162	10,958	20	10,938
Italy	12,957	1,034	56	12	62	58	37	515	294	6,451	13	6,438
Neth.	36,113	4,663	819	339	853	70	780	213	1,589	9,694	1,150	8,544
Belg.-Lux.	28,997	3,363	687	244	1,412	6	284	340	390	5,132	260	4,872
Japan	30,418	16,353	4,699	565	10,387	213	–	44	445	467	–	467
Australia	4,149	1,260	43	–	180	–	8	12	1,017	820	115	705
N.Z.	6,881	1,415	–	–	740	–	–	–	675	–	–	–

TABLE D-3b

Preserved and Prepared Fruit and Vegetables, 1965

($ thousand)

Imports of	Total, All Sources	From Less Developed Countries								From Other Low-Wage Countries		
		Total	Taiwan	Philippines	Other Far East	Mexico	Israel	Morocco, Algeria, Tunisia	Other LDC's	Total	Japan	So. Europe excl. Italy
Developed countries, total	1,001,885	240,304	54,359	13,594	49,244	18,440	19,813	23,011	61,843	190,732	39,081	151,651
U.S.	117,396	65,282	17,456	8,366	13,407	14,299	98	168	11,488	23,013	15,667	7,346
Canada	84,743	9,397	625	257	2,184	2,552	513	47	3,219	4,960	1,274	3,686
EFTA, total	363,820	50,633	2,762	2,710	10,023	580	13,682	1,327	19,549	78,070	12,409	65,661
U.K.	269,199	41,441	609	1,739	9,137	415	11,003	573	17,965	61,424	10,955	50,469
Sweden	29,024	2,607	289	539	54	10	1,171	322	222	3,904	830	3,074
Denmark	13,811	1,230	222	32	187	3	348	109	329	2,780	281	2,499
Norway	11,750	707	18	–	9	20	331	23	306	2,614	50	2,564
Switz.	27,782	3,575	1,459	397	565	49	479	152	474	3,702	271	3,431
Austria	12,251	1,060	164	1	71	80	347	144	253	3,635	13	3,622
EEC, total	388,146	91,096	26,103	1,752	9,617	948	5,501	21,425	25,750	83,830	9,477	74,353
Germany	238,389	50,190	24,637	1,299	8,140	799	3,395	911	11,009	48,066	8,100	39,966
France	58,709	32,466	4	–	166	5	674	19,351	12,266	11,301	22	11,279
Italy	15,960	1,537	23	47	174	104	41	541	607	6,824	–	6,824
Neth.	43,976	4,783	859	255	815	32	1,138	265	1,419	11,858	1,114	10,744
Belg.-Lux.	31,111	2,111	580	150	321	5	251	355	449	5,778	239	5,539
Japan	35,204	21,604	7,296	505	12,916	59	–	28	800	198	–	198
Australia	4,807	1,096	104	–	189	–	16	14	773	559	218	341
N.Z.	7,766	1,182	9	–	908	–	1	–	264	95	34	61

TABLE D-3c

Miscellaneous Manufactured Food Products and Cigars, 1964

($ thousand)

Imports of	Total, All Sources	From Less Developed Countries								From Other Low-Wage Countries		
		Total	Hong Kong	Taiwan	Brazil	Jamaica	Israel	Other Africa	Other LDC's	Total	Japan	So. Europe excl. Italy
Developed countries, total	189,525	12,743	1,490	880	857	1,476	591	327	7,122	4,231	2,304	1,927
U.S.	29,553	2,956	604	35	87	383	205	22	1,620	3,203	1,743	1,460
Canada	21,353	1,010	366	7	17	24	83	4	509	135	104	31
EFTA, total	48,652	4,767	316	77	62	1,019	134	58	3,101	441	322	119
U.K.	20,375	3,999	279	35	–	1,005	76	45	2,559	139	60	79
Sweden	11,764	107	11	26	11	1	24	4	30	53	47	6
Denmark	6,163	82	11	13	12	2	–	–	44	208	208	–
Norway	3,193	32	4	–	3	1	–	–	24	10	–	10
Switz.	4,808	517	8	1	33	7	25	3	440	22	3	19
Austria	2,341	21	1	–	–	–	5	3	12	–	–	–
EEC, total	82,126	2,625	78	130	688	6	159	239	1,325	395	111	284
Germany	22,990	367	31	71	25	1	104	1	134	200	74	126
France	9,633	1,767	10	27	600	–	4	214	912	67	18	49
Italy	7,648	49	2	–	–	–	34	3	10	16	2	14
Neth.	18,451	247	31	28	10	4	8	1	165	25	10	15
Belg.-Lux.	23,400	190	2	4	52	1	7	17	107	82	6	76
Japan	3,808	1,029	11	621	–	–	–	–	397	–	–	–
Australia	3,695	349	110	6	–	40	4	–	189	48	20	28
N.Z.	331	–	–	–	–	–	–	–	–	–	–	–

TABLE D-3c

Miscellaneous Manufactured Food Products and Cigars, 1965

($ thousand)

Imports of	Total, All Sources	From Less Developed Countries								From Other Low-Wage Countries		
		Total	Hong Kong	Taiwan	Brazil	Jamaica	Israel	Other Africa	Other LDC's	Total	Japan	So. Europe excl. Italy
Developed countries, total	209,681	14,109	1,556	1,135	1,066	1,134	645	864	7,709	5,441	2,597	2,844
U.S.	26,465	2,535	516	31	91	406	132	10	1,349	3,856	1,973	1,883
Canada	22,855	971	398	13	4	46	33	–	477	140	81	59
EFTA, total	56,543	5,603	393	78	72	648	248	684	3,480	540	403	137
U.K.	24,025	4,593	348	15	–	636	110	669	2,815	111	31	80
Sweden	13,461	124	11	4	18	1	43	3	44	135	122	13
Denmark	7,191	212	13	58	8	5	53	–	75	199	196	3
Norway	3,867	50	6	–	5	–	4	–	35	51	39	12
Switz.	5,151	596	8	–	40	4	35	3	506	32	5	27
Austria	2,846	18	5	–	–	–	1	7	5	8	7	1
EEC, total	94,153	3,365	102	108	895	1	228	169	1,862	829	91	738
Germany	24,942	403	55	45	29	–	132	1	141	421	37	384
France	11,367	2,389	7	36	810	–	44	160	1,332	232	26	206
Italy	5,575	45	2	–	8	–	37	3	3	86	2	84
Neth.	25,580	289	35	21	8	–	8	2	215	44	20	24
Belg.-Lux.	26,687	233	1	5	47	1	6	2	171	42	4	38
Japan	4,464	1,257	17	871	–	–	–	–	369	–	–	–
Australia	4,662	320	100	31	–	20	1	–	168	70	46	24
N.Z.	536	41	27	–	–	10	–	–	4	–	–	–

TABLE D-4
Labor-Intensive Industrial Materials, 1964
($ thousand)

Imports of	Total, All Sources	From Less Developed Countries								From Other Low-Wage Countries		
		Total	India	Pakistan	Far East	Brazil	Other Western Hemisphere	Other Africa	Other LDC's	Total	Japan	So. Europe excl. Italy
Developed countries, total	4,488,007	696,846	281,640	35,012	165,615	37,859	88,370	78,221	10,168	296,654	156,833	139,821
U.S.	1,049,553	314,495	146,543	12,616	78,409	5,929	63,021	6,541	1,436	139,253	110,356	28,897
Canada	218,024	26,722	14,229	1,201	5,712	341	3,261	1,829	149	15,028	11,833	3,195
EFTA, total	1,409,198	167,503	52,844	5,774	39,349	17,920	4,968	40,613	6,035	56,445	18,655	37,790
U.K.	909,888	140,432	45,805	4,814	26,677	16,669	3,824	37,043	5,600	37,641	13,330	24,311
Sweden	119,327	7,465	998	489	4,742	152	350	546	188	5,226	1,906	3,320
Denmark	129,930	10,658	2,674	426	5,676	808	210	845	19	2,365	1,120	1,245
Norway	60,540	4,291	890	6	1,912	115	57	1,244	67	2,115	1,392	723
Switz.	138,426	3,536	1,794	35	284	138	425	703	157	6,567	604	5,963
Austria	51,075	1,091	673	–	58	33	97	226	4	2,508	294	2,214
EEC, total	1,612,963	123,486	38,445	4,776	24,143	12,731	12,850	28,005	2,536	78,850	9,960	68,890
Germany	552,564	46,078	15,466	1,083	6,316	8,252	8,071	6,230	660	27,145	5,022	22,123
France	280,898	32,534	7,233	1,596	6,792	510	1,649	14,487	267	12,145	604	11,538
Italy	260,276	11,552	4,900	961	1,033	224	1,834	1,313	1,287	23,762	711	23,051
Neth.	342,664	20,308	6,678	711	5,841	2,148	516	4,178	236	8,675	1,614	7,061
Belg.-Lux.	176,552	12,971	4,163	399	4,161	1,593	775	1,794	86	7,111	2,001	5,110
Japan	73,344	13,257	4,417	1,482	6,333	187	807	24	7	203	–	203
Australia	90,961	42,591	18,556	9,045	10,899	745	3,269	72	5	6,714	5,876	838
N.Z.	33,951	8,792	6,598	111	770	–	185	1,128	–	146	146	–

TABLE D-4

Labor-Intensive Industrial Materials, 1965

($ thousand)

Imports of	Total, All Sources	From Less Developed Countries								From Other Low-Wage Countries		
		Total	India	Pakistan	Far East	Brazil	Other Western Hemisphere	Other Africa	Other LDC's	Total	Japan	So. Europe excl. Italy
Developed countries, total	4,717,168	748,645	313,899	43,851	171,681	42,396	79,206	86,916	10,696	320,658	171,907	148,750
U.S.	1,093,593	341,666	168,019	16,220	84,305	8,755	55,435	7,635	1,297	142,527	114,014	28,513
Canada	230,686	27,607	17,047	629	5,378	623	2,124	1,694	112	17,419	13,803	3,616
EFTA, total	1,465,000	171,912	50,539	8,783	37,781	18,808	4,360	44,792	6,849	61,067	20,564	40,503
U.K.	921,815	142,726	42,797	6,893	26,952	15,527	3,225	41,048	6,284	37,615	13,165	24,450
Sweden	134,448	7,704	780	1,342	3,707	626	318	661	270	7,467	2,909	4,557
Denmark	154,584	12,220	3,465	476	5,062	2,223	224	737	33	3,914	1,881	2,033
Norway	66,413	4,335	1,075	27	1,701	243	42	1,197	50	2,088	1,264	823
Switz.	128,237	3,637	1,678	40	284	136	431	870	198	6,840	975	5,865
Austria	59,502	1,278	742	3	75	51	115	278	14	3,140	367	2,773
EEC, total	1,720,023	131,760	41,861	6,063	23,699	13,380	13,095	31,234	2,428	89,060	14,946	74,113
Germany	654,902	53,418	18,296	1,728	6,993	9,309	6,803	9,098	1,191	33,899	8,463	25,436
France	294,692	34,688	8,144	1,366	6,864	545	2,617	14,947	205	14,693	1,147	13,545
Italy	240,798	11,522	4,342	1,220	1,462	401	1,609	1,780	708	22,472	788	21,683
Neth.	351,095	18,533	6,087	967	4,694	2,092	667	3,872	154	10,966	2,409	8,557
Belg.-Lux.	178,536	13,591	4,991	780	3,686	1,032	1,396	1,536	170	7,028	2,137	4,891
Japan	68,544	13,182	3,547	1,631	6,980	75	924	19	6	328	–	328
Australia	105,662	52,554	25,379	10,309	12,935	752	3,019	159	1	9,056	8,104	951
N.Z.	33,656	9,949	7,505	213	603	–	245	1,380	3	1,197	474	723

TABLE D-4a

Products of Jute and Other Coarse Vegetable Fibres, 1964

($ thousand)

Imports of	Total, All Sources	From Less Developed Countries								From Other Low-Wage Countries		
		Total	India	Pakistan	Other Far East	Mexico	Other Western Hemisphere	Other Africa	Other LDC's	Total	Japan	So. Europe excl. Italy
Developed countries, total	430,683	290,198	226,605	25,990	5,655	23,554	6,227	2,034	133	25,687	5,514	20,173
U.S.	228,876	181,817	141,758	11,910	1,518	22,200	4,404	—	27	16,179	1,997	14,182
Canada	31,366	17,762	14,106	1,195	35	1,080	1,346	—	—	3,094	1,405	1,689
EFTA, total	50,218	28,817	23,500	2,684	2,543	1	15	64	10	2,493	728	1,765
U.K.	26,353	22,098	17,489	2,212	2,313	1	15	61	7	449	89	360
Sweden	5,453	1,009	802	74	133	—	—	—	—	811	219	592
Denmark	6,951	2,656	2,243	375	36	—	—	—	2	709	333	376
Norway	5,174	900	872	6	20	—	—	2	—	295	18	277
Switz.	5,287	1,767	1,709	16	41	—	—	1	—	224	66	158
Austria	999	383	383	—	—	—	—	—	—	—	—	—
EEC, total	80,774	26,699	22,189	1,054	666	272	453	1,969	96	2,750	216	2,534
Germany	21,047	9,070	8,479	226	191	168	5	—	1	451	28	423
France	17,872	4,565	2,127	35	131	4	334	1,843	91	1,667	22	1,645
Italy	3,680	2,083	1,729	36	109	99	98	10	2	481	28	453
Neth.	30,754	7,332	6,441	664	193	—	16	17	1	95	84	11
Belg.-Lux.	7,419	3,622	3,412	69	42	—	—	98	1	53	53	—
Japan	1,430	1,240	799	—	438	—	3	—	—	—	—	—
Australia	31,043	27,751	18,320	9,034	395	—	2	—	—	1,168	1,166	2
N.Z.	6,974	6,102	5,931	111	60	—	—	—	—	—	—	—

TABLE D-4a

Products of Jute and Other Coarse Vegetable Fibres, 1965
($ thousand)

Imports of	Total, All Sources	From Less Developed Countries								From Other Low-Wage Countries		
		Total	India	Pakistan	Other Far East	Mexico	Other Western Hemisphere	Other Africa	Other LDC's	Total	Japan	So. Europe excl. Italy
Developed countries, total	466,387	316,635	255,059	31,740	5,915	17,124	3,892	2,710	195	32,866	7,618	25,247
U.S.	238,158	194,619	158,505	15,023	1,674	16,231	3,115	68	3	15,785	2,573	13,212
Canada	32,757	19,153	16,912	621	3	814	324	465	14	4,076	1,688	2,387
EFTA, total	56,821	31,043	23,539	4,161	3,005	—	9	315	14	4,912	967	3,944
U.K.	28,285	23,618	16,800	3,766	2,752	—	4	293	3	913	91	822
Sweden	6,039	813	593	28	181	—	2	8	1	1,543	339	1,204
Denmark	8,545	3,377	3,049	308	20	—	—	—	—	1,456	436	1,019
Norway	7,706	1,141	1,062	27	26	—	2	14	10	472	45	427
Switz.	5,108	1,658	1,614	30	14	—	—	—	—	499	52	447
Austria	1,136	431	419	—	12	—	—	—	—	25	2	22
EEC, total	90,206	28,230	23,528	1,426	792	77	437	1,812	158	6,532	845	5,687
Germany	29,069	10,524	9,748	238	444	57	31	6	—	2,623	311	2,312
France	17,869	4,953	2,599	14	137	20	359	1,702	122	3,016	220	2,796
Italy	2,938	1,531	1,439	5	61	—	6	7	13	233	99	134
Neth.	30,546	6,692	5,569	886	116	—	38	64	19	420	188	232
Belg.-Lux.	9,782	4,523	4,172	281	34	—	2	30	4	238	25	212
Japan	797	636	511	—	122	—	—	—	3	—	—	—
Australia	39,406	35,724	25,080	10,303	290	—	1	48	2	1,502	1,486	16
N.Z.	8,239	7,215	6,981	204	29	—	—	—	1	57	57	—

267

TABLE D-4b

Leather and Tanned or Dressed Furs, 1964
($ thousand)

Imports of	Total, All Sources	From Less Developed Countries								From Other Low-Wage Countries		
		Total	India	Pakistan	Brazil	Argentina	Other Western Hemisphere	Other Africa	Other LDC's	Total	Japan	So. Europe excl. Italy
Developed countries, total	605,197	87,177	52,623	8,987	2,712	6,333	6,404	5,170	4,948	21,150	2,763	18,387
U.S.	62,630	12,336	3,867	691	1,973	2,761	2,764	76	204	4,898	1,123	3,775
Canada	30,871	502	71	6	11	45	1	–	368	187	46	141
EFTA, total	220,614	38,231	28,355	3,084	140	1,220	1,143	2,591	1,698	3,669	309	3,360
U.K.	91,752	35,610	27,560	2,597	78	884	634	2,485	1,372	697	68	629
Sweden	33,204	930	136	415	16	108	182	3	70	1,555	121	1,434
Denmark	20,993	516	291	51	–	–	111	8	55	184	1	183
Norway	11,991	6	1	–	–	–	2	–	3	171	98	73
Switz.	44,382	717	80	19	40	202	189	5	182	424	8	416
Austria	18,288	440	284	–	4	24	24	88	16	633	11	622
EEC, total	268,463	28,808	15,849	3,717	408	2,228	1,968	2,498	2,140	12,100	999	11,101
Germany	104,206	9,944	6,773	853	8	533	999	61	717	6,357	229	6,128
France	50,927	10,577	5,013	1,561	302	818	357	2,378	148	2,117	77	2,040
Italy	35,902	6,563	3,125	925	95	629	552	51	1,186	1,162	235	927
Neth.	39,239	364	199	47	–	90	12	5	11	1,298	405	893
Belg.-Lux.	38,187	1,353	738	329	1	157	48	2	78	1,164	52	1,112
Japan	10,558	6,366	3,594	1,480	178	74	527	3	510	4	–	4
Australia	7,981	237	218	7	–	2	1	–	9	289	285	4
N.Z.	4,076	686	667	–	–	–	–	–	19	4	–	4

TABLE D-4b

Leather and Tanned or Dressed Furs, 1965

($ thousand)

Imports of	Total, All Sources	From Less Developed Countries								From Other Low-Wage Countries		
		Total	India	Pakistan	Brazil	Argentina	Other Western Hemisphere	Other Africa	Other LDC's	Total	Japan	So. Europe excl. Italy
Developed countries, total	617,635	98,175	54,917	12,045	4,668	4,242	10,399	7,573	4,331	23,657	2,730	20,926
U.S.	78,659	20,478	7,531	1,183	3,979	2,570	4,948	239	28	5,787	985	4,802
Canada	33,501	464	77	8	5	11	1	–	362	130	70	60
EFTA, total	201,363	37,710	25,913	4,612	92	536	1,141	3,653	1,763	4,600	221	4,378
U.K.	81,424	33,947	25,075	3,122	32	296	507	3,526	1,389	1,039	41	998
Sweden	31,318	1,795	143	1,312	21	42	210	3	64	1,933	90	1,843
Denmark	21,728	674	333	165	–	9	105	15	47	207	9	197
Norway	9,947	12	1	–	–	–	3	–	8	155	18	136
Switz.	37,091	713	44	9	38	153	243	6	220	649	51	597
Austria	19,853	561	315	3	–	34	73	101	35	614	10	604
EEC, total	280,139	32,753	17,658	4,598	521	1,125	3,475	3,667	1,709	12,776	1,128	11,647
Germany	120,084	12,354	8,140	1,487	21	385	1,001	599	721	7,166	224	6,942
France	45,813	11,774	5,408	1,346	314	469	1,093	3,008	136	2,145	117	2,028
Italy	37,771	6,397	2,859	1,186	183	174	1,262	48	685	1,069	247	821
Neth.	40,262	666	450	80	2	8	108	8	10	1,350	481	868
Belg.-Lux.	36,208	1,555	799	498	–	88	11	2	157	1,045	57	987
Japan	11,129	5,930	2,976	1,630	69	–	832	4	419	8	–	8
Australia	8,902	250	237	3	–	–	–	–	10	311	283	28
N.Z.	3,940	578	522	8	–	–	–	8	40	41	41	–

TABLE D-4c

Lumber, Plywood, Veneers, Crates and Other Simple Wood Products, 1964

($ thousand)

Imports of	Total, All Sources	From Less Developed Countries								From Other Low-Wage Countries			
		Total	Philippines	Taiwan	Other Far East	Brazil	Other Western Hemisphere	Other Africa	Other LDC's	Total	Japan	So. Europe excl. Italy	Italy
Developed countries, total	2,559,373	305,828	39,179	30,783	86,449	34,127	38,496	70,540	6,254	188,491	102,727	85,764	
U.S.	628,293	109,272	37,191	21,775	16,911	2,989	23,574	6,465	367	80,233	73,776	6,457	
Canada	66,135	8,252	659	3,965	676	329	786	1,829	8	8,447	7,429	1,018	
EFTA, total	935,619	99,520	429	22	35,153	17,772	2,547	37,926	5,671	45,956	15,167	30,789	
U.K.	739,499	81,852	53	13	23,054	16,583	2,257	34,470	5,422	34,260	11,973	22,287	
Sweden	35,132	5,506	27	3	4,574	136	58	543	165	2,172	1,321	851	
Denmark	77,325	7,483	315	1	5,412	808	99	837	11	951	410	541	
Norway	23,285	3,378	24	—	1,877	115	54	1,242	66	1,565	1,201	364	
Switz.	50,106	1,031	8	3	190	98	30	697	5	5,497	203	5,294	
Austria	10,278	261	—	—	46	29	49	135	2	1,519	63	1,456	
EEC, total	847,155	66,597	170	31	22,862	12,282	7,951	23,095	206	51,376	4,893	46,483	
Germany	294,861	26,660	95	4	5,753	8,242	6,367	6,163	36	12,131	1,496	10,635	
France	124,501	16,781	2	12	6,545	184	159	9,853	26	6,841	328	6,513	
Italy	151,394	2,827	1	9	861	115	461	1,247	133	20,654	366	20,288	
Neth.	192,175	12,362	13	5	5,645	2,148	394	4,151	3	6,407	958	5,449	
Belg.-Lux.	84,230	7,967	58	—	4,058	1,592	570	1,682	7	5,348	1,747	3,601	
Japan	45,776	5,603	96	4,835	446	9	195	21	1	196	—	196	
Australia	25,386	14,580	631	157	9,710	745	3,264	72	1	2,293	1,469	824	
N.Z.	11,018	2,004	—	—	691	—	185	1,128	—	—	—	—	

TABLE D-4c

Lumber, Plywood, Veneers, Crates and Other Simple Wood Products, 1965

($ thousand)

Imports of	Total, All Sources	From Less Developed Countries								From Other Low-Wage Countries		
		Total	Philippines	Taiwan	Other Far East	Brazil	Other Western Hemisphere	Other Africa	Other LDC's	Total	Japan	So. Europe excl. Italy
Developed countries, total	2,668,724	320,222	35,378	31,597	94,607	36,799	38,381	76,420	7,040	195,799	108,658	87,141
U.S.	648,793	115,809	33,433	21,822	25,563	3,952	23,402	7,314	323	82,050	75,713	6,337
Canada	69,588	7,847	413	3,656	932	605	968	1,228	45	9,133	8,338	794
EFTA, total	978,576	102,061	463	64	32,903	18,711	2,638	40,796	6,486	46,488	16,103	30,384
U.K.	756,556	84,120	54	47	22,769	15,494	2,387	37,202	6,167	33,602	11,653	21,948
Sweden	42,971	5,070	33	–	3,474	605	63	649	246	3,081	2,179	902
Denmark	93,829	8,161	316	10	4,761	2,223	109	721	21	1,433	753	679
Norway	25,960	3,180	45	–	1,632	240	39	1,182	42	1,309	1,071	238
Switz.	46,275	1,234	8	–	229	97	30	863	7	5,086	379	4,707
Austria	12,982	280	4	3	38	49	7	176	3	1,975	66	1,908
EEC, total	886,516	69,253	235	74	22,387	12,775	8,019	25,584	179	53,729	6,046	47,683
Germany	334,505	29,608	197	32	6,271	9,273	5,336	8,475	24	12,720	1,693	11,027
France	129,270	17,666	2	11	6,620	170	728	10,132	3	7,523	586	6,936
Italy	142,202	3,508	8	2	1,299	213	153	1,697	136	19,800	389	19,410
Neth.	82,727	11,009	13	23	4,575	2,085	509	3,794	10	8,412	1,456	6,955
Belg.-Lux.	197,811	7,457	14	5	3,622	1,032	1,293	1,485	6	5,274	1,919	3,354
Japan	45,410	6,572	101	5,488	875	1	90	14	3	318	–	318
Australia	28,751	16,512	674	491	11,467	752	3,016	110	2	3,193	2,292	900
N.Z.	11,089	2,154	57	–	480	–	244	1,371	2	886	164	721

TABLE D-4d

Building Materials of Clay, Glass, Stone, etc., 1964

($ thousand)

Imports of	Total, All Sources	From Less Developed Countries								From Other Low-Wage Countries		
		Total	India	Hong Kong	Taiwan	Other Far East	Mexico	Israel	Other LDC's	Total	Japan	So. Europe excl. Italy
Developed countries, total	892,754	13,687	1,405	458	735	490	6,131	1,703	2,765	61,326	45,829	15,497
U.S.	129,754	11,070	544	199	731	454	6,099	842	2,201	37,943	33,460	4,483
Canada	89,652	206	51	12	—	—	2	134	7	3,300	2,953	347
EFTA, total	202,747	938	636	156	—	11	8	37	90	4,327	2,451	1,876
U.K.	52,284	872	630	143	—	8	1	11	79	2,235	1,200	1,035
Sweden	45,538	20	—	5	—	—	2	11	2	688	245	443
Denmark	24,661	3	3	—	—	—	—	—	—	521	376	145
Norway	20,090	7	—	5	—	—	—	—	2	84	75	9
Switz.	38,651	21	—	1	—	—	4	13	3	422	327	95
Austria	21,510	7	—	—	—	3	—	—	4	356	220	136
EEC, total	416,571	1,383	155	58	—	10	7	688	465	12,624	3,852	8,772
Germany	132,450	404	61	1	—	—	—	335	7	8,206	3,269	4,937
France	87,598	611	72	1	—	7	—	112	419	1,517	177	1,340
Italy	69,300	79	9	38	—	2	2	11	17	1,465	82	1,383
Neth.	80,496	250	11	9	—	—	4	218	8	875	167	708
Belg.-Lux.	46,716	29	—	6	—	1	—	10	12	546	149	397
Japan	15,580	48	4	17	4	13	8	—	2	3	—	3
Australia	26,551	23	11	10	—	2	—	—	—	2,964	2,956	8
N.Z.	11,883	—	—	—	—	—	—	—	—	146	146	—

TABLE D-4d

Building Materials of Clay, Glass, Stone, etc., 1965
($ thousand)

Imports of	Total, All Sources	From Less Developed Countries								From Other Low-Wage Countries		
		Total	India	Hong Kong	Taiwan	Other Far East	Mexico	Israel	Other LDC's	Total	Japan	So. Europe excl. Italy
Developed countries, total	964,420	13,669	2,740	1,218	1,077	262	5,879	2,014	479	68,334	52,899	15,435
U.S.	127,981	10,758	1,491	1,014	1,068	215	5,840	955	175	38,903	34,742	4,161
Canada	94,840	141	56	12	–	1	5	54	13	4,079	3,706	373
EFTA, total	228,238	1,114	829	116	–	10	5	72	82	5,067	3,270	1,796
U.K.	55,548	1,039	811	107	–	6	–	43	72	2,060	1,378	681
Sweden	54,118	24	8	2	–	–	–	13	1	908	301	607
Denmark	30,480	6	4	–	–	1	–	–	1	816	681	135
Norway	22,798	2	–	1	–	–	–	–	1	150	129	21
Switz.	39,761	31	3	3	–	2	4	15	4	605	492	113
Austria	25,530	4	–	–	–	1	–	–	3	525	287	237
EEC, total	463,162	1,534	296	56	–	18	25	931	208	16,021	6,926	9,094
Germany	171,244	932	161	11	–	–	2	732	26	11,390	6,235	5,155
France	101,739	293	118	3	–	7	4	43	118	2,007	222	1,784
Italy	57,886	84	5	21	–	6	14	4	34	1,369	51	1,317
Neth.	82,474	164	10	15	–	3	4	123	9	784	282	501
Belg.-Lux.	49,818	55	–	5	–	2	–	27	21	471	134	336
Japan	11,207	42	9	9	7	15	1	–	1	1	–	1
Australia	28,602	66	55	8	–	3	–	–	–	4,048	4,042	6
N.Z.	10,387	1	1	–	–	–	–	–	–	212	210	1

DERIVATION OF C.I.F./F.O.B. CONVERSION FACTORS

Table E-1 presents details of the computations made to derive the factors for adjusting imports where recorded c.i.f. to an f.o.b. basis (Tables 11 to 15).[1] These details come from estimates for 190 items made by the U.S. Tariff Commission on the basis of an examination of entry documents for some 13,000 import shipments in 1965 (only part of which relate to the import categories covered by the present analysis). The Tariff Commission's investigation was directed toward ascertaining the increases that would be needed to express U.S. import values on a c.i.f. basis comparable to the way most other countries' imports are recorded. One may therefore question the appropriateness of these factors for converting other countries' imports to an f.o.b. basis. The reasons for doing so are given in the first section of Chapter 4. It may be noted that the adjustment factors obtained are applied to the four main groups of products distinguished in Table E-1 and are not used at any finer level of detail.

[1] Table E-1 covers only the labor-intensive manufactures which are the main subject matter of this study. The same source (i.e., the Tariff Commission's report) has also been used to make a rough adjustment of other categories of trade given in Tables 10 and 17.

TABLE E-1

Derivation of Estimated Freight and Insurance Charges for Present Analysis from Tariff Commission Study

TSUS Schedule, Part and Subpart	Main Groups and Subgroups Used in Present Analysis (italicized) and Selected Items from Tariff Schedules of the United States	Recorded Value of U.S. Imports ($ million) (1)	Estimated Freight and Insurance as Per Cent of Recorded Value	
			T.C. Study (2)	Derived Average (3)
	Labor-intensive manufactures, total	1,010*		11.3
	1. Textiles, clothing and accessories	286*		7.0
	a. Yarn and thread	6*		n.a.
	(not reported separately from raw fibers in T.C. study)	n.a.	n.a.	
	b. Cotton fabrics, woven	62*		4.0
3/3/A	Woven fabrics, cotton	122	4	
	c. Other woven fabrics, excl. jute products	9*		6.5
3/3/C	Woven fabrics, wool	104	8	
3/3/D	Woven fabrics, silk	30	7	
3/3/E	Woven fabrics, man-made fibers	49	5	
3/3/F	Woven fabrics, other textile materials	2	6	
	d. Textile small wares and specialities	13*		10.0
3/4/A	Knit, pile, tufted, and narrow fabrics; braids and elastic fabrics	28	8	
3/4/B	Lace, netting, and ornamented fabrics	8	10	
3/4/C	Wadding, felts, and articles thereof; fish netting and nets; artists' canvas; coated or filled fabrics; hose; machine clothing; other special fabrics	35	14	
3/5/C	Tapestries, linens, and other furnishings	21	5	

(continued)

TABLE E-1 (continued)

TSUS Schedule, Part and Subpart	Main Groups and Subgroups Used in Present Analysis (italicized) and Selected Items from Tariff Schedules of the United States	Recorded Value of U.S. Imports ($ million) (1)	Estimated Freight and Insurance as Per Cent of Recorded Value	
			T.C. Study (2)	Derived Average (3)
	e. Carpets and other floor covering	16*		9.0
3/5/A	Textile floor coverings	44	9	
	f. Clothing and accessories, excluding goods of leather, rubber and plastic	181*		7.6
3/6/A	Handkerchiefs	14	3	
3/6/B	Mufflers, scarves, shawls, and veils; men's and boys' neckties	21	4	
3/6/C	Hosiery	5	n.a.	
3/6/D	Garters and suspenders; body-supporting garments; rainwear	18	5	
3/6/E	Underwear	2	3	
3/6/F	Other wearing apparel	403	8	
	2. Other light manufactures except food	269*		11.6
	a. Footwear and other leather, rubber and plastic goods	54*		10.5
7/1/A	Footwear	160	10	
7/1/C	Gloves	62	5	
7/1/D	Luggage: handbags; billfolds, card cases, coin purses, and similar flat goods	50	13	
7/12/C	Specified rubber and plastic products	88	10	
7/13/B	Articles of fur and leather	17	5	

(continued)

TABLE E-1 (continued)

TSUS Schedule, Part and Subpart	Main Groups and Subgroups Used in Present Analysis (italicized) and Selected Items from Tariff Schedules of the United States	Recorded Value of U.S. Imports ($ million) (1)	Estimated Freight and Insurance as Per Cent of Recorded Value	
			T.C. Study (2)	Derived Average (3)
	b. Glassware, china and pottery	3*		15.0
5/2/C	Table, kitchen, household, art and ornamental pottery	73	14	
5/3/C	Glassware and other glass products	35	17	
	c. Furniture	7*		18.0
7/4/A	Furniture, pillows, cushions, and mattresses	57	18	
	d. Books and other printed matter	4*		7.0
2/5	Books, pamphlets, and other printed matter	75	7	
	e. Games, toys, sport goods, and musical instruments	26*		12.0
7/3/A	Musical instruments	40	13	
7/3/B	Musical instrument parts and accessories	10	9	
7/5/D	Games and sporting goods	42	9	
7/5/E	Models; dolls, toys, tricks, party favors	76	14	
	f. Jewelry and silverware[a]	18*		10.0
7/6/A	Jewelry and related articles	27	17	
7/6/B	Cameos; natural, cultured, and imitation pearls; imitation gemstones; beads and articles of beads	34	5	

(continued)

277

TABLE E-1 (continued)

TSUS Schedule, Part and Subpart	Main Groups and Subgroups Used in Present Analysis (italicized) and Selected Items from Tariff Schedules of the United States	Recorded Value of U.S. Imports ($ million) (1)	Estimated Freight and Insurance as Per Cent of Recorded Value	
			T.C. Study (2)	Derived Average (3)
	g. Costume jewelry and notions	90*		16.0
7/7/A	Buttons, buckles, pins, hooks and eyes, and slide fasteners	11	5	
7/7/B	Artificial and preserved flowers and foliage; millinery ornaments; trimmings; feather products	45	24	
7/8/A	Combs, hair ornaments, brooms and brushes, paint rollers	11	15	
7/8/B	Umbrellas, walking sticks, whips, riding crops, and parts thereof	7	9	
7/9/B	Cigar and cigarette lighters and holders; tobacco pipes	12	7	
7/10	Pens, pencils, leads, crayons, and chalks	8	5	
	h. Optical goods, cameras, watches and instruments	3*		3.0
7/2/A	Optical elements, spectacles, microscopes, and telescopes; optical goods not elsewhere provided for	63	6	
7/2/B	Medical and surgical instruments and apparatus; x-ray apparatus	23	5	
7/2/E	Watches, clocks, and timing apparatus	101	1	
7/2/F	Photographic equipment and supplies	102	3	
	i. Cutlery, hardware, and other metal products	14*		9.0
6/3/D	Nails, screws, bolts, and other builders' hardware; furniture, luggage, and saddlery hardware	117	11	
6/3/E	Tools, cutlery, forks and spoons	80	2	
6/3/F	Miscellaneous metal products	106	12	
6/3/G	Metal products not specially provided for	33	9	

(continued)

TABLE E-1 (continued)

TSUS Schedule, Part and Subpart	Main Groups and Subgroups Used in Present Analysis (italicized) and Selected Items from Tariff Schedules of the United States	Recorded Value of U.S. Imports ($ million) (1)	Estimated Freight and Insurance as Per Cent of Recorded Value T.C. Study (2)	Derived Average (3)
	j. Electrical apparatus and supplies	46*		6.0
6/5	Electrical machinery and equipment	686	6	
	k. Nonelectrical machinery and equipment	4*		5.0
6/4/H	Other machines	70	8	
6/4/J	Parts of machines	65	2	
	3. Labor-intensive Food Manufactures	112*		9.2
	a. Fish and fish products	45*		6.7
1/3/B	Fish, dried, salted, pickled, smoked, or kippered	16	10	
1/3/C	Fish in airtight containers	43	5	
1/3/D	Other fish products	6	10	
	b. Fruit and vegetables	65*		11.0
1/8/B	Vegetables, dried, desiccated, or dehydrated	3	n.a.	
1/8/C	Preserved vegetables	23	13	
1/8/D	Mushrooms and truffles	9	6	
1/9/C	Fruit flours, pastes, pulps, jellies, jams, marmalades, and butters	6	11	
1/9/D	Glacé nuts, fruits, and other vegetable substances	2	5	
1/12/A	Fruit juices	10	12	
	c. Miscellaneous food and cigars	3*		8.0
1/10/C	Confectionery	23	8	
1/13	Tobacco and tobacco products	135	8	

(continued)

279

TABLE E-1 (continued)

TSUS Schedule, Part and Subpart	Main Groups and Subgroups Used in Present Analysis (italicized) and Selected Items from Tariff Schedules of the United States	Recorded Value of U.S. Imports ($ million) (1)	Estimated Freight and Insurance as Per Cent of Recorded Value	
			T.C. Study (2)	Derived Average (3)
	4. *Labor-intensive industrial materials*	342*		15.5
	a. Products of jute and other coarse fibers	195*		8.4
3/3/B	Woven fabrics, vegetable fibers (except cotton)	202	9	
3/2	Cordage	48	6	
	b. Leather and tanned or dressed furs	21*		5.0
1/5/A	Hides, skins, and leather	144	5	
	c. Lumber, plywood, etc.	116*		29.1
2/1/A	Rough and primary wood products; wood waste	74	8	
2/1/B	Lumber, flooring, and moldings	387	41	
2/1/C	Densified wood and articles thereof	1	3	
2/1/D	Wooden containers	7	12	
2/1/E	Miscellaneous products of wood	23	18	
2/1/F	Articles not specially provided for, wood	12	11	
2/2/A	Cork and cork products	9	3	
2/2/B	Bamboo, rattan, willow, and chip; basketwork, wickerwork, and related products of fibrous vegetable substances	17	12	
2/3	Wood veneers, plywood and other wood-veneer assemblies, and building boards	191	19	

(continued)

TABLE E-1 (concluded)

TSUS Schedule, Part and Subpart	Main Groups and Subgroups Used in Present Analysis (italicized) and Selected Items from Tariff Schedules of the United States	Recorded Value of U.S. Imports ($ million) (1)	Estimated Freight and Insurance as Per Cent of Recorded Value — T.C. Study (2)	Derived Average (3)
	d. Building materials of clay, stone, etc.	11*		17.6
5/1/C	Stone and stone products	22	22	
5/2/B	Ceramic construction articles	12	12	
5/3/B	Flat glass and products thereof	52	19	

Note: Figures in column 1, except those with asterisk, and all figures in column 2 are from tabulations by the U.S. Tariff Commission accompanying its release of February 7, 1967, entitled "C.I.F. Value of U.S. Imports." Items with asterisk in column 1 are from compilations prepared for present study on imports from less developed countries. The averages for subgroups in column 3 are weighted by total U.S. imports of component items in column 1. The averages for the four main groups and for all labor-intensive manufactures are then derived from the subgroup averages weighted by imports from less developed countries.

aSilverware is not given separately in Tariff Commission study.

AUTHOR INDEX

SUBJECT INDEX